Security and Sovereignty in the Former Soviet Union

Security and Sovereignty in the Former Soviet Union

Ruth Deyermond

LYNNE
RIENNER
PUBLISHERS

BOULDER
LONDON

Published in the United States of America in 2008 by
Lynne Rienner Publishers, Inc.
1800 30th Street, Boulder, Colorado 80301
www.rienner.com

and in the United Kingdom by
Lynne Rienner Publishers, Inc.
3 Henrietta Street, Covent Garden, London WC2E 8LU

Library of Congress Cataloging-in-Publication Data
Deyermond, Ruth, 1971–
   Security and sovereignty in the former Soviet Union / Ruth Deyermond.
     p. cm.
   Includes bibliographical references and index.
   ISBN 978-1-58826-576-0 (hardcover : alk. paper)
   1. Russia (Federation)—Foreign relations—Former Soviet republics.
2. Former Soviet republics—Foreign relations—Russia (Federation).
3. National security—Former Soviet republics. I. Title.
DK510.764.D49   2007
327.47—dc22   2007024798

British Cataloguing in Publication Data
A Cataloguing in Publication record for this book
is available from the British Library.

Printed and bound in the United States of America

The paper used in this publication meets the requirements
of the American National Standard for Permanence of
Paper for Printed Library Materials Z39.48-1992.

5 4 3 2 1

To my parents,
Ann and Alan

Contents

Acknowledgments

First and foremost, I would like to thank Neil Robinson for the guidance I received in the early stages of this project, and for his criticism and comments on drafts of the first two chapters of this book. I would also like to thank Sarah Birch, Han Dorussen, Margot Light, and Rachel Walker for their many helpful comments on early versions of the book. For the many and various ways in which they have helped, I would also like to thank Lesli Brooks Athanasoulis, Adam Ledgeway, Elisabetta Linton, Pontus Ekstedt, Luisa Ortiz Perez, Andrew Spicer, and Gulia Tagieva; my colleagues in the Department of War Studies at King's College London; the two anonymous but very helpful reviewers of the manuscript of this book; and, collectively, the students in my master's course "Security Issues in the Soviet Successor States" in the Department of War Studies. I am grateful to *Europe-Asia Studies* for permission to reproduce sections of my article "The State of the Union: Military Success, Economic and Political Failure in the Russia-Belarus Union" in Chapter 5. I am also extremely grateful to the Department of Government at the University of Essex for its support and financial assistance during my research, and to the Department of War Studies for the sabbatical leave to write this book. Finally, I owe a debt I can never repay to Ian James for his constant support and encouragement, for his invaluable practical advice, and for his questions and comments that encouraged me to think about some of the issues from a fresh perspective. This book could not have been written without him.

—*Ruth Deyermond*

1

Introduction

This book begins with a series of security puzzles. During the 1990s, following the collapse of the Soviet Union, a series of disputes developed between some of the Soviet successor states over the assets of the former Soviet armed forces. What made these disputes puzzling was both the nature of the assets being contested and the intensity of the disputes over them. It seemed curious, for example, that Russia and Ukraine should be arguing about the ownership of the nuclear weapons on Ukrainian territory given that the two states' governments were agreed that these weapons were to be removed and decommissioned, and given the commitment of Ukraine to nonnuclear status. It seemed equally puzzling that these two states should also be locked in a bitter dispute, which at points threatened to lead to something more serious, over the ownership of the Black Sea Fleet, which had lost its strategic value and which neither state could afford to maintain. Finally, the determination of Russia to retain the use of military facilities in now-independent Georgia, against the wishes of the Georgian government, was also superficially surprising given the need for cuts and restructuring in the Russian armed forces, and the fact that Russian troops were stationed in Georgia anyway, as peacekeepers. Adding to the puzzle was the fact that not all the states concerned with a stake in the issue of nuclear weapons ownership and the Russian use of military facilities viewed the problem in the same way; in both cases, Belarus, which appeared to have as much to lose or gain as Georgia or Ukraine, cooperated with Russia to dispose of the assets. Finally, the dispute over the Black Sea Fleet was resolved with the division of the fleet between Russia and Ukraine; although the fleet was also based in the territory of Georgia, it made no concerted attempt to acquire a part of the fleet and was effectively ignored by the other two states.

The answer to these puzzles, I argue in this book, lies in the intersection between security and sovereignty. The disputes over these security assets were not simply, or in some cases primarily, about the assets themselves; they were about what ownership and control of these assets meant for the security of these states and for their sovereignty in relation to one another. Critically, that sovereignty was not understood in the same way by all the actors involved in these disputes; different positions were informed by different understandings of what sovereignty meant for the states concerned. Emerging into independence, states such as Georgia and Ukraine appeared to constitute their political and legal structures on the basis of, and to found their political discourse in, a conception of sovereignty falling within the theoretical and legal tradition deriving from Western Europe and North America, which forms the legal basis of contemporary international relations. In contrast, political and especially military actors in Russia and (as the 1990s progressed) Belarus appeared to adopt a position on the sovereignty of these states that derived from the Soviet model of sovereignty.

This book, therefore, attempts to solve these security puzzles by examining the ways in which the disputes over nuclear weapons, the Black Sea Fleet, and military facilities turned around and reflected these competing conceptions of post-Soviet state sovereignty. I argue that only by understanding this contest over the meaning of sovereignty in this environment can we understand why these disputes developed in the way that they did, with long-term implications for relations between these states and for the security of each of them.

The Problem of the Post-Soviet Armed Forces

In the years immediately before the Soviet Union formally dissolved into fifteen independent states, the Soviet armed forces were the largest in the world, with 27,000 nuclear weapons, three fleets, and more than four million troops under arms. Not only did the armed forces dominate government spending, they occupied a prominent and highly symbolic position in Soviet political culture—as Richard Sakwa observes, the Soviet armed forces were "the cornerstone of national identity."[1] The mythology of the Great Fatherland War, the role of the armed forces as defenders of communism against a hostile and aggressive capitalist West, the annual parades of military hardware through Red Square on May Day—all of these factors had given the Soviet armed forces an enormously high symbolic and actual value within political culture not equaled by the status of most Western states' armed forces. William Odom, commenting on the collapse of the Soviet armed forces observes that "the army command was the embodiment of the [Soviet] regime's sovereignty and stability."[2] By the end of 1991, however, the armed forces had, for many people, become associated with an entirely different series of images—with the failures of the war in Afghanistan, with the violent suppression of independence movements in Tbilisi and Vilnius, and with the August Coup.[3] In some respects, both the positive and negative sets of images of the armed forces projected the same message about the nature of the military—that it was irreducibly Soviet, that it functioned as one of the most symbolically and actually powerful state structures of the Union of Soviet Socialist Republics (USSR).

With the disappearance of the Soviet Union, therefore, the armed forces were left without a clear identity or purpose. The state that they served had ceased to exist and the new security structures of the post-Soviet space were neither clearly defined nor agreed on by the new states. From the outset, it was clear that some of the former Soviet states, notably the Baltic states, would entirely reject any future linkage with the rest of the former USSR and that other states, particularly Ukraine, were extremely dubious about any long-term security or other arrangements that preserved any aspect of the former union structure. The armed forces thus found themselves in a structural and legal state of limbo and with no clear function.

Many analysts have understood the breakup of the Soviet Union as the breakup of an empire, comparable, therefore, to the end of other empires in the twentieth century and before.[4] This is, however, inaccurate in at least one critical way. The Soviet Union was a single state, and its armed forces were the property of that state—a political entity consisting of the fifteen republics, which, by the start of 1992, were formally independent from one another. They could not therefore simply revert to the core state from which they originated (as they would have done in a traditional movement of decolonization) because the core state had ceased to exist. As with other parts of the Soviet structure, therefore, the armed forces and, in particular, the fifteen former Soviet republics on whose territory they were located, were faced with the problems of determining their status and future, and deciding to whom the armed forces and their assets belonged.

Not surprisingly, the different parties involved held very different views of this question. Very broadly, three positions can be identified in relation to the future of the former Soviet armed forces at the start of the 1990s. First, the initial position of many of the senior military figures and members of the conservative ex-Soviet political elites (above all in Russia, but also evident in other states) was that the armed forces should remain unified—the collective property of all the member states of the Commonwealth of Independent States (CIS). Part of the broader moves to establish a range of CIS institutions, this was clearly an attempt to preserve both the armed forces and, more generally, some degree of suprastate structure within the post-Soviet area (in other words, to retain as much of the structure of the USSR as possible). By mid-1992, however, the idea of a Joint Armed Forces (JAF) had collapsed, and although the idea of a military collaboration between the states of the CIS persisted after the signing of the Collective Security Treaty in May 1992 and with later CIS military agreements, the idea of a single armed forces had been lost.[5]

With the failure of the Joint Armed Forces project, many of those who had supported the retention of Soviet-era military (and other) structures transferred their commitment to the idea of a Russian armed forces. If the armed forces could not be preserved as a single military structure for the whole post-Soviet (or—given the total disengagement by the Baltic states—CIS) space, then a single structure located across the same space but owned by one state, Russia, was clearly the next best option for the armed forces themselves.

The third position, taken by the nationalist political and military elites in the other CIS states, was a rejection of this view and a desire for independent military structures. During the period of the breakup of the USSR and immediately afterward, therefore, a number of states, such as Ukraine, established their own defense ministries and began to create independent armed forces. What this meant in terms of the former Soviet armed forces, however, was not immediately clear. The military assets and the former Soviet units stationed on their territories were not necessarily understood by all those concerned to be part of the armed forces being created in the newly independent states. Many of the military assets were clearly unsuited to the defense requirements of the new states, which were confronted with a range of internal and regional security threats, but which had inherited the military legacy of a Cold War superpower. The national, post-Soviet armed forces needed to be structured and equipped to address the range of emerging post-Soviet security challenges, challenges that were unlikely to require tank divisions and nuclear weapons. These assets were, in any case, far too costly for the new states to maintain given their extremely weak economic position and the multiple budgetary demands of state building. In addition, the troops themselves were not obviously candidates for inclusion in the new national forces, since they were not generally of the nationality of the states in which they were based.[6] They were also identified with the Soviet Union as an entity, and specifically, for a number of the new states, with attempts by the union center to suppress national independence movements.[7] However, neither were they clearly Russian—they were on non-Russian territory and had been maintained and funded by the Soviet republics as a whole. In addition, while the officer classes of the Soviet armed forces were disproportionately staffed by ethnic Russians, the armed forces as a whole were very far from being entirely Russian. There was, therefore, no clear case for ceding control to Russia.

The armed forces and their assets located in the non-Russian republics at the point of independence, then, clearly represented a problem for the former Soviet states. As an institution with a unique status in Soviet political life and one that was fundamentally associated—in both positive and negative ways—with the USSR, the armed forces were a high-profile, politically powerful and yet functionless residue of a state that had ceased to exist. The dual rationales for their creation and post–World War II development— the existence of the USSR and the Cold War—had disappeared, while they had remained. Because they represented a collective asset of the whole USSR, rather than the property of an imperial core that could determine their future without reference to a colonial periphery, their future (or, as was obvious after the collapse of the JAF, their division and disbandment) was an issue in which all the former Soviet republics were concerned.

This book considers the question of how some of the states of the former Soviet Union attempted to resolve this problem. It investigates the way in which these different positions on the fate of the former Soviet armed forces and their assets interacted and how the outcomes of negotiations over specific security issues were shaped by the relative success with which actors were able to impose these perspectives. It does this by examining three security problems arising from the breakup of the Soviet Union—the fate of the Soviet nuclear arsenal, the future of the Black Sea Fleet, and the use of military facilities outside the Russian Federation.

This problem of the fate of the former Soviet armed forces after 1991, and the competing perspectives of the different actors involved in attempting to resolve it, needs, I argue, to be understood in the context of the question of post-Soviet state sovereignty. There are four closely linked reasons for this. First, as mentioned above, the Soviet armed forces occupied a central position in the construction of Soviet identity and sovereignty. It is important, therefore, to understand what happened to this traditional interrelationship of sovereignty and the armed forces once the state it characterized had ceased to exist. Second, this focus on the military as guarantor and marker of sovereignty persisted into the post-Soviet period and both structured the way in which negotiations over military assets were conducted and helped to determine the competition for specific assets. This focus on military assets (particularly high-profile assets) as markers of sovereignty helps to explain disputes over assets for which one or more parties had no military use in the post–Cold War strategic environment (such as the Black Sea Fleet), were committed to relinquishing (as was the case with nuclear weapons), or could not afford to maintain. Third, I argue, the question of state sovereignty helped to shape the outcome of negotiations over these assets, both because actors' conceptions of sovereignty and what it entailed helped to drive them to pursue negotiations in particular ways, and also because such conceptions provided a substructure to the wider foreign and security policies which informed the interactions between these states on these questions. Finally, and importantly, the outcome of these disputes both depended on and affected the ability of Belarus, Georgia, and Ukraine to exercise sovereignty, above all in relation to Russia.

The States: Ukraine, Georgia, and Belarus

The position of Russia in the post-Soviet space has, from the start, been recognized as different from that of the other successor states by all actors. Russia, as the former imperial power; the politically, economically, and culturally dominant core of the USSR; and by far the largest and most powerful post-Soviet state has occupied a hegemonic position in relation to the region, even when it has been regarded as a regional hegemon in decline. The experience of former imperial dominance and the continued determination of Russian governments to assert their political, economic, and security agenda in the region have fundamentally shaped the politics of the former Soviet Union, particularly the bilateral relationships of other successor states with Russia and the attitudes of those states toward multilateral regional cooperation in the CIS. As discussed in the following chapters, Russia's distinct position in the post-Soviet space and the political and legal implications of its self-defined position as inheritor of the Soviet center in the immediate post-Soviet period, have shaped its approach to the legacy of the Soviet armed forces and to a sense of its authority in relation to aspects of other states' policymaking on foreign and security matters. Russia's security relations with Belarus, Georgia, and Ukraine, and the nature of negotiations over the Soviet military inheritance, cannot be understood outside this context.

Clearly, the relationships of Belarus, Georgia, and Ukraine toward Russia on security matters in general, and the division of assets in particular, do not provide an exhaustive survey of post-Soviet security relations. However, as I explore in later chapters, these three states demonstrate a range of relationships with Russia and a variety of attitudes toward, and ability to exercise, sovereignty in their security and other relations with Russia. This range indicates both the parameters of the debate over security assets and the contested understanding of the meaning of "sovereignty" as a principle in post-Soviet interstate relations.

The government of Ukraine, the largest of the other successor states, and the one widely regarded at independence as having the greatest potential economic and military capabilities, demonstrated a clear intention to distance the new state from Russia and to assert sovereignty in relation to it. Its comparative strength (relative to the other non-Russian successor states), the desire to lay claim to a share of the military legacy of the USSR, and a willingness to make political use of assets such as the location of nuclear weapons on its territory combined to enable Ukraine to achieve limited success in negotiations with CIS structures and with Russia.

The government and parliament of Georgia (though not the political elites in regions such as Abkhazia and South Ossetia) were likewise committed to asserting Georgia's sovereignty in relation to Russia. The first government of Georgia, led by nationalist president Zviad Gamsakhurdia, was more firmly opposed than Ukraine to even the temporary continuation of political and security links with Russia, refusing to join the CIS and demanding the immediate withdrawal of the former Soviet forces on Georgian territory. Unlike Ukraine, however, the catastrophic failure of Georgia's internal sovereignty and of its state-building process at the start of the independence period meant that Georgia was unable to assert any form of sovereignty in relation to Russia on matters of security. This failure extended to the fate of military assets on its territory, such as the Black Sea Fleet (to which it was unable to lay successful claim), and the military facilities on its territory, from which Russia had still not fully withdrawn by late 2007, more than fifteen years after the first demand that it do so.

The political elites of both Ukraine and Georgia demonstrated a clear commitment to the assertion of sovereignty in relation to Russia on security matters, even if the difference in capabilities led to dramatically different outcomes. In contrast, the government of the third state considered here, Belarus, never sought to establish sovereignty in relation to Russia on matters of security; indeed the military structures of the Belarusian state have never been entirely distinct from those of Russia. Since the mid-1990s, the presidency of Alyaksandr Lukashenka has moved Belarus still further away from independence in relation to Russia, with the commitment to the Russia-Belarus Union. Unlike the commitment to and partially successful assertion of sovereignty by Ukraine, and Georgia's unsuccessful attempt to assert sovereignty in relation to Russia, Belarus has, since the start of formal independence, demonstrated very little concern with establishing sovereignty over matters of security.

This is not a book about the politics or the state-building processes of Russia, Belarus, Georgia, and Ukraine—subjects on which a large literature already exists. Nevertheless, in order to make sense of the security challenges considered here, and their relationship to the problem of sovereignty, it is necessary to be aware of the main domestic and external challenges confronting these states in the post-Soviet period. The outlines of Russian domestic politics and foreign policy in the post-Soviet period are well known; less widely known, however, are the main challenges faced by the other three states at the start of the 1990s, and a brief summary of them is given below.[8]

Ukraine

Independent Ukraine has faced a series of domestic political crises, including the "Orange Revolution" in 2004 and most recently the constitutional deadlock between president and parliament in early 2007; contrary to the fears of some Western analysts, however, it has managed to avoid the type of separatist conflict that has characterized a number of other post-Soviet states.[9] In addition to the enormous tasks of state building and economic restructuring that confronted it, and the related problems of poor economic performance and corruption that emerged in the 1990s, Ukraine has had to contend with two interconnected problems that are the product of its long, shared history with Russia—the threat of separatism and the high priority that Ukraine has for Russian foreign and security policy.

As the disputed 2004 presidential elections clearly demonstrated, Ukraine is a nationally divided state. In very general terms, western Ukraine has a predominantly Ukrainian national orientation, is Ukrainian speaking, and is resistant to any policy orientation that suggests closer political or security ties with Russia, the former imperial center. In eastern Ukraine, however, a significant proportion of the population is Russian in national orientation, Russian speaking, and has, since independence, appeared to be more positive about the prospects for closer cooperation with Russia. The region of greatest potential instability since independence has been the Crimean peninsula, which was part of the Russian Soviet Socialist Republic until Nikita Khrushchev awarded it to the Ukrainian Soviet Socialist Republic in 1954, to mark the 300th anniversary of the union of Russia and Ukraine; clearly, at that point, there was no prospect that these two republics would ever become independent states. Once they did, however, it became apparent that the new Ukrainian state faced a grave problem on the peninsula. The population of Crimea is overwhelmingly Russian in national orientation and, from the start, appeared to be opposed to inclusion in an independent Ukraine. In 1992, the Ukrainian and Crimean governments and parliaments became locked in a dispute over the limits of Crimean autonomy and the relative authority of each structure, a dispute made far worse by a Crimean parliamentary resolution declaring Crimea independent, subject to a referendum. The threat of a serious escalation was averted when, faced with calls by the Ukrainian parliament for the government to take measures to restore its authority in Crimea, the Crimean parliament suspended its resolution and the referendum on it. Although this defused the immediate crisis, the potential for Crimean secession did not disappear. The election of the (Russian) nationalist Yuri Meshkov as Crimean president in early 1994, and the subsequent victory of his party in Crimean parliamentary elections, clearly indicated the continued strength of feeling among the Crimean electorate in favor of closer cooperation with, and possible reunification with, Russia. The actions of this new parliament, including the decision to readopt the Crimean constitution that had been suspended with the conclusion of the earlier crisis, reignited the dispute with Kiev. Although the crisis was defused once again, with subsequent laws passed by the Crimean and Ukrainian parliaments establishing an agreed framework for Crimea's continued existence within Ukraine, underlying tensions remain, as the mid-2006 public protests in Crimea over planned joint military exercises with North Atlantic Treaty Organization (NATO) states indicated.[10]

The dispute over the status of Crimea was made more serious by the role of Russian politicians. Russian nationalist politicians viewed Crimea as Russian territory and were clearly seen by Ukrainian politicians as agents provocateurs in the Crimean dispute. The 1992 resolution by the Russian parliament, at the height of the dispute, that the 1954 transfer of Crimea had been illegal caused particular concern in Ukraine. Another flashpoint in Russian-Ukrainian relations over Crimea came in 1993, with the Russian parliamentary resolution that because of the separate federal status of the city of Sevastopol (home base of the Black Sea Fleet) in the Soviet period, the city had not been transferred to Ukraine with the rest of Crimea and was consequently Russian. Although neither resolution was taken up by the Russian government, there was a perception that the Yeltsin administration was using Russian nationalist activism about Crimea to gain leverage in negotiations with Ukraine, particularly in the dispute over the Black Sea Fleet.

Georgia

Despite the problems of separatist conflict in the North Caucasus and the centrifugal forces apparently at work in Russia under Boris Yeltsin, and despite the threat of secession lingering over the Crimean-Kiev relationship, in the early 1990s it was Georgia that appeared to be the state most likely to lose regions through secession, or simply to "fail" entirely. Georgia, despite its small size and population, has a large number of self-identifying ethnic groups, several of whom have traditionally regarded the government of Tbilisi with suspicion or open hostility. This, combined with governmental instability, a disastrous economic position, corruption, and the consequences of its situation in a geopolitically sensitive region, led to the effective collapse of the Georgian state in 1993; the recovery during the rest of the 1990s was only partial, and Georgia remains a state divided by "frozen" conflicts and vulnerable to external intervention.[11]

Georgia's location has been both a source of insecurity and, more recently, an asset in its relationship with Western Europe and the United States. Positioned between Russia and Turkey, bordering the other Southern Caucasus states of Armenia and Azerbaijan, and with a long Black Sea littoral, it sits at the boundary between the post-Soviet space and NATO states and occupies a key position in relation to the transport of Caspian energy. Part of its northern border with Russia is a border with Chechnya; this area, particularly the Pankisi Gorge, has been the subject of Russian claims that Georgia is failing to prevent cross-border terrorist activity. Both this issue of terrorism and the development of energy pipelines transiting Georgia have been of increasing interest to states outside the region since the late 1990s, in particular the members of the European Union and the United States.

The security problems of Georgia in the 1990s cannot be separated from the state's fundamental problems of stability and governance. The nationalist politics of the president at independence, Gamsakhurdia, inflamed the tensions between the central government in Tbilisi and regions of the country identified with other national groups, in particular Abkhazia. Having lost the support of other senior military and political figures in the country, Gamsakhurdia was deposed in a coup, fleeing Tbilisi in early January 1992. The key figures in the coup, including Tengiz Kitovani, the head of the National Guard, and Jaba Ioseliani, the leader of the powerful Mkhedrioni militia, invited former Soviet foreign minister (and former first secretary of the Georgian Communist Party) Eduard Shevardnadze to head the interim government. Following elections, Shevardnadze became president of Georgia, a position he held until the "Rose Revolution" in November 2003.

The most serious of all Georgia's security problems have undoubtedly been the two separatist conflicts in South Ossetia and Abkhazia, which developed at independence and remain unresolved. Both South Ossetia, in the north of Georgia, and Abkhazia, which occupies approximately one-third of Georgia's coastline, border Russia; this has complicated the conflicts and reduced the possibility of a settlement acceptable to Georgia. In mid-1992, the dispute between Georgia and Abkhazia deteriorated into war, a war in which the Georgians—seemingly with good reason—accused the Russians of assisting the Abkhaz. In 1993, Georgian forces were driven out of Abkhazia, together with the ethnic Georgian population of the region, who numbered nearly 300,000 and who have been living as internally displaced people ever since. Following the ceasefire, Abkhazia became a de facto, unrecognized state, a status that has been consolidated by transport links with Russia, and by favorable Russian visa arrangements. Russian peacekeepers, acting on behalf of the CIS, were deployed in Abkhazia in 1994; they are viewed with profound suspicion by the Georgian government and parliament, which would like them to be replaced with extra-regional peacekeepers.

In addition to the two separatist conflicts, a number of other Georgian regions were under little or no central government control during the 1990s. The region of Adjaria, also on the Black Sea coast, existed in an uneasy relationship to Tbilisi and was, effectively, entirely autonomous, run by its powerful leader Aslan Abashidze. Other regions, such as the largely Armenian region of Javakheti and the western region of Megrelia, were also largely outside the control of the center. The relationship of Megrelia to the center has been made more difficult by its link to groups loyal to the deposed president Gamsakhurdia. In 1993, this dispute also led to conflict; in exchange for Russian assistance, Georgia became a member of the Russian-dominated CIS, an organization it had previously resisted joining. Thus, by the middle of the 1990s, Georgia lacked anything approaching territorial integrity and existed in a security relationship of profound dependence in relation to Russia; it was, as Dov Lynch notes, "a state that was hardly a state at all."[12]

Belarus

In contrast to Georgia and Ukraine, Belarus has faced no internal security threats and has maintained a strong relationship with Russia throughout the post-Soviet period.[13] Positioned between Russia to the east, Poland to the west, Ukraine to the south, and the Baltic states to the north, the geopolitical significance of landlocked Belarus disappeared with the end of the Cold War. Perhaps for this reason, Belarus attracted little international attention for most of the 1990s; arguably, most international interest in this period was directed toward the problem of Belarus's widespread contamination by the Chernobyl disaster. Yet, it is precisely the uneventful character of post-independence Belarus that is interesting. Unlike the other European Soviet republics, the transition from the USSR to independent statehood was not marked by widespread nationalist protests or by substantial changes in the composition of the political elite; large public demonstrations in the late Soviet period focused on the environmental catastrophe of Chernobyl and the suppressed history of mass killings under Stalin, but not on the anti-Moscow nationalism that characterized protest in the neighboring Baltic states. The much-noted absence of widespread, strong nationalist sentiment in Belarus was, from the start, reflected in the positive relationship with Russia.[14] Economic, security, and cultural ties to Russia remained strong and, despite Belarus's commitment to neutrality, security cooperation between Russia and Belarus has been continuous for effectively the entire post-Soviet period. From the start, then, Belarus has been an anomaly in the post-Soviet European picture,

Two significant, related issues have raised the profile of Belarus, however: the presidency of Lukashenka and the attempts to establish a Russia-Belarus union state. Since his election in 1994, Lukashenka has, in the Western view, moved Belarus decisively away from democracy to an authoritarian political structure. With the exception of a limited and heavily restricted nationalist opposition, this shift toward authoritarianism has not undermined public support for him—he remains broadly popular, in particular with older and rural voters. A central feature of his presidency has been his commitment to political, military, and economic union with Russia, although the project has stalled as the deadlines for taking concrete action on economic and political aspects of the union have approached. The union project has been weakened both by Russian concerns about the unpredictable activity of the Belarusian president and by the reluctance with which Vladimir Putin appears to view closer ties with this increasingly politically isolated state.

Constructing Sovereignty and Security

In considering the issue of sovereignty for the states of the former Soviet Union, I have made two assumptions that have a critical effect on the way in which sovereignty as a concept, and its relationship to security issues, is understood in this investigation. First, I have considered the concept (and practice) of sovereignty as historically contingent. Much analysis is predicated on "a blindness to the historicity of sovereignty"; I argue, that in order to attempt to understand the nature of relations between the post-Soviet states, it is essential to engage with the historically contingent meaning(s) of sovereignty.[15] The existence of a Soviet model of sovereignty, deriving from but distinct from the Western tradition of thinking about sovereignty, provides support for the theoretical assumption that the term needs to be understood as dependent on historical particularity for its meanings and for the nature of the practices surrounding it.

Second, and arising out of the assumption of historical contingency, I have considered sovereignty as a social construct.[16] Sovereignty, as a concept, in this view, is the product both of shared understandings, requiring some form of consensus about the meaning of the term, but also, for states (and for analysts) the subject of a contest to fix its meaning. As an investigation of the historically and culturally contingent nature of the idea of sovereignty, this book draws on and works within those approaches to the sovereignty problematic that found their inquiries in the assumption of sovereignty as a historical and social construct. In this respect, my research takes as a central assumption the position identified by Cynthia Weber that

> sovereignty marks not the location of the foundational entity of international relations theory but a site of political struggle. This struggle is the struggle to fix the meaning of sovereignty in such a way as to constitute a particular state—to write the state—with particular boundaries, competencies and legitimacies available to it. This is not a one time occurrence which fixes the meaning of sovereignty and statehood for all time and in all places; rather, this struggle is repeated in various forms at numerous spatial and temporal locales.[17]

This, I argue, is a struggle of particular importance and immediacy for the states of the former Soviet Union in the immediate post-Soviet period, when national identities and state priorities and capabilities were being constituted by these states in relation to one another and, necessarily, on the basis of their shared past. Despite the loosely constructivist approach taken here, however, this is not a constructivist book in the sense that it is not a book concerned with constructivist theory or with reading the post-Soviet security disputes that form its subject through the theory of Alexander Wendt, Nicholas Onuf, or postpositivist constructivist theorists.[18] Instead, my intention is to explore the ways in which a key, contested concept has been fundamental to the constitution of security relations within a group of states. As I argue, the disagreement about the nature of post-Soviet state sovereignty evident in the negotiations between the former Soviet states both reflect and inform profoundly different approaches to the interlinked problems of the post-Soviet armed forces, the nature of interstate relations within the post-Soviet space, the role of Russia, and the view of "the West."

The result of making these two claims about the nature of sovereignty is that primary emphasis is placed on text (reported speech and other texts) and on the detailed history of interactions between the key actors involved in the disputes over the military assets of the former Soviet Union. The methodological focus of the book is on two types of what might be broadly characterized as data. To begin with, I investigate the structure of the events that are the subject of my case studies—what happened and when. Thus, my analysis includes details of negotiations over the division of the Black Sea Fleet, for example, and outlines of the processes by which Russia leased military facilities from Belarus and Georgia. This is done for two reasons. First, and obviously, the aim is to give clarity to the discussion about what is taking place in respect to sovereignty in these cases—in order to consider the implications of what happened, it is first necessary to know what happened. Second, the structure of events can in itself indicate important issues in respect to the relationship between security and sovereignty. For example, the absence of Georgia from the main negotiations over the division of the Black Sea Fleet (despite the fact that its president had stated a Georgian claim to ownership of the portion of the fleet and its infrastructure on Georgian territory) suggests something about the weakness of Georgian sovereignty in relation to Russia. Similarly, the linkage of the Ukrainian and Russian dispute over the Black Sea Fleet bases in Sevastopol to the Russian Duma's statements about the status of Crimea indicates a view among sections of the Russian political elite about Ukrainian state sovereignty.

In addition to a consideration of the main events in relation to underlying disputes about sovereignty, this book focuses on the views of the key participants and the language of the central texts relating to both the three security issues investigated and to conceptions of sovereignty. Thus, the chapters on sovereignty, which approach the term as a concept with a particular set of Soviet and post-Soviet meanings, include analysis of the central texts relating to sovereignty in this context, including the 1977 USSR constitution and the CIS Charter. In considering the relationship between Russia and the other states as manifested in the issues investigated in the case studies, I consider the views expressed by the main participants (in particular the heads of government and state, and the senior military figures involved) about the negotiations and disputes over nuclear weapons, the Black Sea Fleet, and military bases; what they indicate about sets of understandings regarding sovereignty; and the impact of these understandings on the causes and conduct of these disputes. It should be noted that this is not intended to be a book about post-Soviet sovereignty theory; rather, it is concerned with the way in which the legacy of two critically different traditions of thinking about sovereignty informed the rhetoric and practices of actors involved in attempting to resolve the problems of the USSR's military legacy.

Outline of the Book

Chapter 2 considers the problematic nature of the idea of sovereignty (both for theorists and students of international relations, and for states), and the differences between Western and Soviet understandings of sovereignty. It argues that the Soviet conception of sovereignty and what may be termed the Western understanding of sovereignty are radically different from one another. Soviet usage of the term is not, I show, necessarily used to imply independence and, despite claims to the contrary, sovereignty in the Soviet context was understood to be limited when applied to actors other than the union center; critically, unlike traditional Western (broadly, Western European and North American) understandings of sovereignty, Soviet sovereignty implied relations between sovereign entities based on power inequalities. This, I argue, creates a tension between Western and Soviet meanings replicated in the post-Soviet environment and provides a structure of understanding that informs the conflicting approaches to questions of security and the division of military assets of states such as Georgia and Ukraine on the one hand, whose positions demonstrated a "Western" approach to sovereignty, and, on the other, the Russian (and Belarusian) political and military elites and the CIS Joint Armed Forces Command. The chapter therefore concludes with a discussion of the way that these different perceptions of sovereignty were evident in the documents and negotiations around the formation of the CIS and the abortive attempts to establish the JAF. All of this has important implications for Russia's disputes with other former Soviet states over the division and use of military assets, discussed in the following three chapters.

Chapter 3 compares the very different ways in which Belarus and Ukraine addressed the problem of how to dispose of the nuclear weapons stationed on their territory at the point of independence, and the ways in which this process was closely tied to wider debates and assumptions about post-Soviet state sovereignty. Both states were committed from the outset to achieving nonnuclear status, but the process of negotiating withdrawal and the nature of the bilateral relations with Russia on this issue were very different in the two cases. The first section of the chapter considers the issue of the weapons on Ukrainian territory and the ways in which the process of negotiating their removal was dominated by disputes over the question of ownership of and control over the weapons, and how this reflected wider struggles over the issues of sovereignty over foreign and security policy, and over Ukrainian territory. The second section considers the contrasting case of Belarus, focusing on the ways in which the approach to this issue (and the absence of the debates over ownership and control that had been present in the case of Ukraine) reflected a lack of concern within the government about the establishment and maintenance of Belarusian state sovereignty in relation to Russia, in particular after Lukashenka's election.

Chapter 4 explores the bitter, five-year dispute between Russia and Ukraine over the division and basing of the Black Sea Fleet, a dispute that threatened, at points, to escalate into military conflict, despite the facts that the fleet was of limited strategic value to either state in the post–Cold War environment, and that neither state could afford to maintain it. This peculiar situation can only be explained, I argue, by recognizing the extent to which the dispute turned around questions of state sovereignty, and the way that both the division of military assets and the understanding of sovereignty interacted with the states' relative capabilities—in other words, the relationship between the issue under dispute, understandings of sovereignty, and relative power. The interaction between these three factors also explains the failure of the other potential inheritor, Georgia, to establish claims either to a significant proportion of the fleet, or even to participation in the negotiation process. I argue that this failure is fundamentally linked to a failure of Georgian state sovereignty in the 1990s, not least in relation to Russia, with which it had to negotiate for part of the fleet.

Chapter 5 considers the issue of the Russian leasing of military facilities in other post-Soviet states—perhaps the single most contentious and persistent issue in post-Soviet security relations. Taking the contrasting cases of Georgia and Belarus, I investigate the ways in which the Russian acquisition of basing rights reflected and reinforced both the power relations between these states and the interplay of power with the understanding and exercise of state sovereignty. In the case of Belarus, I argue that the leasing agreements, taken together with the other agreements on military issues between Russia and Belarus, form part of a wider pattern of abdication of sovereignty on military and other issues on the part of the Belarusian government. In the case of Georgia, as in the case of the Black Sea Fleet, the Russian leasing of bases—most of which were located in autonomous or secessionist areas—demonstrates a failure of state sovereignty both externally, in relation to Russia, and internally, in relation to its own regions.

Chapter 6 considers the legacy of these problems of security in the twenty-first century. Having summarized the findings of the three case studies, the book concludes with a discussion of the problematic fact that although all three issues were officially resolved during the 1990s, they continue, in different ways, to pose serious political and security challenges for the states concerned, as well as raising questions for those Western states that have become increasingly engaged in Georgia and Ukraine and increasingly concerned about Belarus. It explores the ways in which the settlement of the disputes over the Black Sea Fleet and the Russian use of military facilities has been thrown into question by political changes in Georgia and Ukraine, and the relationship of these changes to the increasing regional involvement of extraregional states, particularly the United States.

Notes

1. Richard Sakwa, *Russian Politics and Society,* 2nd ed. (London and New York: Routledge, 1996), p. 300.

2. William E. Odom, *The Collapse of the Soviet Military* (New Haven and London: Yale University Press, 1998), p. 397.

3. For a discussion of the impact of the war in Afghanistan and the suppression of independence movements, see Odom, "The Army and Maintaining Domestic Order," *Collapse of the Soviet Military,* pp. 244–271.

4. See, for example, Pavel K. Baev, *The Russian Army in a Time of Troubles* (London: Sage, 1996), p. 3; Odom, *Collapse of the Soviet Military,* pp. 271, 272.

5. On the failure of the CIS Joint Armed Forces project, see Odom, *Collapse of the Soviet Military,* chapter 16.

6. This was, in large part, a result of the Soviet-era policy of basing troops outside the republics from which they originated. Two prominent individuals who experienced this policy were Kostiantyn Morozov, the first Ukrainian defense minister, who served as an officer in Turkmenistan, and Dzhokhar Dudayev, president of Chechnya, who commanded a bomber division in Estonia. For a discussion of this tactic, see, for example, Odom, *Collapse of the Soviet Military,* p. 45.

7. This was clearly a widely held view in, for example, the Baltic states and in Georgia. The impact of this perception on Georgian security questions, specifically basing arrangements, is discussed in Chapter 6.

8. The literature on Russian domestic politics and foreign policy is extensive. Examples include J. L. Black, *Vladimir Putin and the New World Order: Looking East, Looking West?* (Lanham, MD: Rowman and Littlefield, 2004); Karen Dawisha and Bruce Parrott, *Democratic Changes and Authoritarian Reactions in Russia, Ukraine, Belarus and Moldova,* Democratisation and Authoritarianism in Postcommunist Societies 3 (New York: Cambridge University Press, 1997); Neil Malcolm, Alex Pravda, Roy Allison, and Margot Light. *Internal Factors in Russian Foreign Policy* (Oxford: Oxford University Press, for The Royal Institute of International Affairs, 1996); and Richard Sakwa, *Russian Politics and Society,* 3rd ed. (London: Routledge, 2002). On Russia's military inheritance from the Soviet Union, and the post-Soviet Russian armed forces, see Baev, *The Russian Army;* Robert V. Barylski, *The Soldier in Russian Politics: Duty, Dictatorship and Democracy* (New Brunswick, NJ: Transaction, 1998); Christopher Bluth, *The Collapse of Soviet Military Power* (Aldershot, UK: Dartmouth, 1995); Odom, *Collapse of the Soviet Military;* and Brian D. Taylor, *Politics and the Russian Army, Civil-Military Relations, 1689–2000* (Cambridge: Cambridge University Press, 2003).

9. For a detailed discussion of Ukrainian security challenges in the post-Soviet period, see Sherman W. Garnett, *Keystone in the Arch: Ukraine in the Emerging Security Environment* (Washington, DC: Carnegie Endowment for International Peace, 1997); Taras Kuzio, *Ukrainian Security Policy* (Westport, CT: Praeger, 1995); Tor Bukkvoll, *Ukraine and European Security* (London: Royal Institute for International Affairs, 1997); Lubomyr A. Hajda, ed., *Ukraine in the World: Studies in the International Relations and Security Structure of a Newly Independent State* (Cambridge, MA: Harvard University Press for the Ukrainian Research Institute, Harvard University, 1998); Alexander J. Motyl, *Dilemmas of Independence: Ukraine After Totalitarianism* (New York: Council on Foreign Relations Press, 1993); Deborah Sanders, *Security Cooperation Between Russia and Ukraine in the Post-Soviet Era* (Basingstoke, UK: Palgrave, 2001); and Robert Legvold and Celeste A. Wallander, eds., *Swords and Sustenance: The Economics of Security in Belarus and Ukraine*, American Academy Studies in Global Security Series (Cambridge, MA: American Academy of Arts & Sciences, 2004). For a personal account of Ukrainian security politics during and after the collapse of the USSR, see Kostiantyn Morozov's autobiography, *Above and Beyond; From Soviet General to Ukrainian State Builder* (Cambridge, MA: Harvard University Press for the Ukrainian Research Institute, 2000). Light, Löwenhardt, and White's research project "The Outsiders: Russia, Ukraine, Belarus, Moldova, and the New Europe" provides a detailed analysis of a range of Ukrainian and Belarusian domestic and foreign policy issues. See, for example, John Löwenhardt, Ronald J. Hill, and Margot Light, "A Wider Europe: The View from Minsk and Chisinau," *International Affairs* 77, no. 3 (July 2001): 605–620.

10. For a discussion of this, see Chapters 4 and 6.

11. For analysis of Georgia's security threats and the problems of Georgian state building in the 1990s, see Shireen T. Hunter, *The Transcaucasus in Transition: Nation-Building and Conflict* (Washington, DC: Center for Strategic and International Studies, 1994); Jonathan Aves, *Georgia: From Chaos to Stability?* (London: Royal Institute of International Affairs, 1996); Svetlana Chervonnaya, *Conflict in the Caucasus: Georgia, Abkhazia and the Russian Shadow* (Glastonbury: Gothic Image, 1994); Roy Allison, ed., *Challenges for the Former Soviet South* (Washington, DC: The Brookings Institution for the Royal Institute of International Affairs, 1996); and Revaz Gachechiladze, *The New Georgia: Space, Society, Politics* (London: UCL Press, 1995). Dov Lynch considers the Abkhaz conflict in relation to Russian peacekeeping in *Russian Peacekeeping Strategies in the CIS: The Cases of Moldova, Georgia and Tajikistan* (Basingstoke, UK: Macmillan, 2000). For discussions of Georgia after the "Rose Revolution," see Jonathan Wheatley, *Georgia from National Awakening to Rose Revolution: Delayed Transition in the Former Soviet Union* (Aldershot, UK: Ashgate, 2005); Dov Lynch, *Why Georgia Matters*, Chaillot Paper 86 (Paris: The European Union Institute for Security Studies, February 2006); and Bruno Coppieters and Robert Legvold, eds., *Statehood and Security: Georgia After the Rose Revolution*, American Academy Studies in Global Security Series (Cambridge, MA: American Academy of Arts & Sciences, 2005).

12. Lynch, *Why Georgia Matters*, p. 17.

13. For a history of Belarus up to the immediate postindependence period, see Jan Zaprudnik, *Belarus: At a Crossroads in History* (Boulder, CO: Westview, 1993); literature on post-Soviet Belarus includes David Marples, *Belarus: From Soviet Rule to Nuclear Catastrophe* (Basingstoke, UK: Macmillan, 1996); David Marples, *Belarus: A Denationalized Nation* (Amsterdam: Harwood Academic Publishers, 1999); Sherman W. Garnett and Robert Legvold, eds., *Belarus at the Crossroads*

(Washington, DC: Carnegie Endowment for International Peace, 1999); Margarita M. Balmaceda, James I. Clem, and Lisbeth Tarlow, eds., *Independent Belarus: Domestic Determinants, Regional Dynamics, and Implications for the West* (Cambridge, MA: Ukrainian Research Institute and David Centre for Russian Studies, 2002); Dawisha and Parrott, *Democratic Changes;* and Legvold and Wallander, *Swords and Sustenance.*

14. On the related issues of the lack of a widespread Belarusian nationalism, Belarusian perceptions of Russia, and attitudes toward the Soviet past, see, for example, Steven M. Eke and Taras Kuzio, "Sultanism in Eastern Europe: The Socio-Political Roots of Authoritarian Populism in Belarus," *Europe-Asia Studies* 52, no. 3 (May 2000): 523–547; Marples, *Belarus: From Soviet Rule to Nuclear Catastrophe;* Timothy J. Colton, "Belarusian Popular Opinion and the Union with Russia," in Margarita M. Balmaceda, James I. Clem, and Lisbeth Tarlow, eds., *Independent Belarus: Domestic Determinants, Regional Dynamics, and Implications for the West* (Cambridge, MA: Ukrainian Research Institute and David Centre for Russian Studies, 2002), pp. 21–54; Marek J. Karp, "Escape from Freedom," *The Journal of Slavic Military Studies* 11, no. 4 (December 1998): 146–163; and David Marples, "Color Revolutions: The Belarus Case," *Communist and Post-Communist Studies* 39, no. 3 (September 2006): 351–364.

15. Cynthia Weber, *Simulating Sovereignty: Intervention, the State and Symbolic Exchange* (Cambridge: Cambridge University Press, 1995), p. 2.

16. The term used by Thomas J. Biersteker and Cynthia Weber in their edited volume on this topic, *State Sovereignty as Social Construct* (Cambridge: Cambridge University Press, 1996).

17. Biersteker and Weber, *State Sovereignty as Social Construct,* p. 3.

18. For an example of the ways in which security problems can usefully be read in relation to different constructivist approaches, see Maja Zehfuss, *Constructivism in International Relations: The Politics of Reality* (Cambridge: Cambridge University Press, 2002).

2

Competing Sovereignties in the Former Soviet Union

Sovereignty is one of the building blocks of legal and political theory about the state, providing a foundation for the authority of a state within its borders and for those international legal frameworks that are intended to delimit relations between states. Sovereignty, whatever the disagreements about certain aspects of its nature or its limits, is recognized as a precondition both for the exercise of power by a state within its own territory and for the possibility of international relations between states as actors equal under international law. Yet state sovereignty has proved to be both resistant to definitive definition as a concept and always compromised in practice. For these reasons, the problematization of sovereignty is common both to the study and the practice of politics; questions of sovereignty become a particular focus of debate, however, when a new state or group of states emerges—how new states constitute their domestic authority, legal identity, and status in relation to other states, and the impact of this process of constitution on the broader field of international politics are problems of, or relating to, state sovereignty.

The collapse of the Soviet Union and the creation of fifteen new states on its territory is an important case for the study of the constitution of state sovereignty through legal structures and political practice. The simultaneous creation of a number of new states is an unusual event, particularly when this creation entails the complete, formal dissolution of another state. These factors alone would make the post-Soviet case significant, but it is made still more so by the nature of these states' emergent relationships to one another and by the legacy of the prior, formal structures and theoretical understandings of sovereignty in the Soviet Union. The post-Soviet states moved from a relationship of structural equality as republics of a federal state to one of structural equality as sovereign states within international political and legal frameworks; however, the transition from one condition of formal equality to another was not reflected in the reality of relations between Russia and the other states, where Russia was widely understood to be appropriating the role of the defunct, Soviet federal center. Post-Soviet interstate relations, especially relations within the CIS, have been characterized by this tension between equality in sovereign statehood and the legacy of federal republic-center relations. That the issue of post-Soviet state sovereignty is complex and contradictory is not surprising given the particular nature of the Soviet legal and theoretical conceptualization of sovereignty; the highly differentiated, internally contradictory model of sovereignty developed in the USSR has, as this and later chapters argue, a clear echo in relations between the Soviet successor states.

As this implies, the Soviet model of sovereignty developed in ways that were distinct from the tradition of sovereignty theory that informed it and from which it emerged. Soviet understandings of sovereignty were set in opposition to Western, capitalist states' legal traditions and wider theoretical discourses of sovereignty. Thus, by the time of the Soviet collapse in 1991, two models of sovereignty were evident—a Soviet model and a much looser, but still identifiable, model arising from theory and legal practice in Europe and North America, and informing discourses of state sovereignty in international organizations and other interstate relations. This second model of state sovereignty, referred to here as the Western model, is the one to which the successor states of the USSR appeared to conform with independence. However, the rhetoric and practices of sovereignty within and between these states, particularly in relations between Russia and the other successor states, was also clearly informed by the legacy of the Soviet model, a model in which sovereignty did not connote equality or independence, and in which the interests of other political structures (the Soviet republics and the other socialist states) were understood to be most effectively secured by strengthening the power of the Soviet center. This interaction and tension between Western and Soviet sovereignties is a key problem both for the practice of post-Soviet relations and the conceptualization of state sovereignty. In particular, the Soviet model of sovereignty relations between the union republics and the union center, and between the USSR's socialist client states and the USSR itself, appears in key ways to have been replicated in the Russian political and military elites' approach to the sovereignty of the other post-Soviet states on matters of security.

The Western Model of Sovereignty

As is widely recognized in the literature, no fully agreed-on definition of *sovereignty* exists and, in fact, a number of contemporary analysts have rejected the idea that attempts to define it are useful.[1] Despite this, a set of commonly held assumptions about certain features of sovereignty are evident in both the field of (positivist) international relations theory developed in Western Europe and North America and in the frameworks of post–World War II international organizations. The first of these assumptions is that sovereignty is now primarily understood to be a property of the state, rather than other political entities. Theorists of sovereignty writing in the Western tradition from the early twentieth century onward overwhelmingly treat sovereignty as a condition of statehood; however problematic the exercise of sovereignty may be for states, the focus of analysis is on state sovereignty because it is the dominant form of sovereignty in contemporary politics.[2] Even this, however, is not a problem-free assumption—sovereignty is also sometimes described as a property of "nations" or a "people" as well as of states. This is linked in both theory and practice to the concept of the nation-state: Harry Gelber, for example argues that "the authority of the sovereign state rest[s] on . . . nationalism," that "the English, American, and French Revolutions irrevocably anchored the source of legitimate authority in the consent of 'the people,' and the definition of 'the people' was the nation."[3] Despite this basis of legitimacy for state sovereignty in the nation, the idea of nations possessing sovereignty is not reflected in the mainstream, positivist contemporary international relations literature on sovereignty or in the composition and practice of international institutions, such as the UN; it *is,* however, evident in some of the contemporary discourse of international politics—for example, in the frequently stated aim of the United States and UK to "return sovereignty to the Iraqi people" after the 2003 conflict.[4] (As discussed below, the concept of the sovereignty of nations was a critically important feature of the Soviet model.)

Another assumption about sovereignty generally evident in the Western literature is that it implies preeminence. For any political entity to be sovereign, no other political entity may be in a position to challenge its authority within its area of competence. For states, this means that political-legal relations within the territory of a state must be hierarchical—within the boundaries of the state, no other entity challenges the state's authority over its territory. It also means that, in theory, a system of international relations that assumes that sovereign states are its main components must also assume that no sovereign state has preeminence over any other sovereign state; that all states exist in a relationship of independence from, and sovereign equality in relation to, one another.[5] This view of the judicial equality of states as a—perhaps *the*—central component of sovereignty is one of the most widely held in Western writing on sovereignty.[6] One implication of these understandings of a state's sovereignty, in relation both to structures within its borders and to other states, is that sovereignty necessarily implies states' monopoly on the legitimate use of force within their territory. Whatever the political realities of relations between states, the theoretical assumptions underpinning international organizations and other formalized international regimes require states to be sovereign and sovereignty to be incompatible with state dependence or inequality.

As all this implies, a fundamental though problematic (and problematized) distinction exists in the literature between internal and external sovereignty. Although generally accepted as distinct, if not discrete, aspects of sovereignty, there is, again, no generally recognized definition of either term. Part of the reason for this lies in the fact that the boundary between the two terms is far from clear, and that the terms are highly interdependent. Broadly defined, internal sovereignty can be characterized as the legal and functional preeminence of a state over the territory it occupies. External sovereignty describes the legal and practical condition of independence and equality of a state in relation to other sovereign states. This means that a sovereign state is not permeable to another state, that intervention in the affairs of that state by another state is not possible. But this already starts to blur the boundaries between the two concepts because freedom from the possibility of intervention by another state (external sovereignty) is also a condition of internal sovereignty, since it pertains to the exercise of authority with the territory of a sovereign state. Thus Alan James has defined sovereignty as: "the presence, within a governed political community, of supreme legal authority—so that such a community can be said to possess sovereignty, or to be sovereign, if it does not look beyond its own borders for the ultimate source of its own legitimacy."[7] This merges the two concepts, stressing the dependence of internal sovereignty (the presence of supreme legal authority within a governed political community) on external sovereignty (the nonpermeability of its borders to an external authority providing legitimacy). Similarly, the definition of sovereignty as "a political entity's externally recognised right to exercise final authority over its affairs" stresses the dependence of internal sovereignty on external sovereignty since it depends on the granting of external recognition.[8] Conversely, external sovereignty is dependent on internal sovereignty as a prior condition of the state, since a state must exist as the preeminent authority over its territory in order to be regarded as an independent, functioning political entity, and thus a formally equal actor in interstate relations. As problematically for the theoretical literature, there is no consensus on whether external sovereignty is a formal, legal property of all states, and therefore conceptually separate from the issue of power inequalities in interstate relations, or whether it is a variable quality dependent—whatever the nominal condition of all states as formally sovereign—on a state's capability to exercise sovereignty in relation to others. For Stephen Krasner, the divergence between legal status and capability has created a condition in which the sovereignty principle in interstate relations is most appropriately characterized as an "organized hypocrisy."[9]

Closely linked to these issues is the idea that sovereignty implies illimitability, an idea that appears in the literature as early as Jean Bodin.[10] Both theory and practice recognize that sovereignty entails illimitability except in the case of voluntary restrictions placed on sovereignty by the state itself.[11] The view that sovereignty is, with this exception, illimitable is not, however, universal among theorists of sovereignty; Michael Ross Fowler and Julie Marie Bunck, for example, argue that sovereignty can be limited and that a state's sovereignty can increase or decrease over time.[12] Two significant obstacles exist to the illimitability of sovereignty—the relationship of sovereign states to one another and the possibility of placing limitations on internal sovereignty evident from the constitutional structures of federal states. The scope of external sovereignty has obvious limitations, not just in practice but also in theory. James's argument gives an indication of the difficulty in conceiving of unlimited external state sovereignty; for James, external sovereignty should be seen as

> connoting not supremacy but independence. Internally the state is supreme, and the external corollary of this internal condition is that all states are independent of each other. For if one state has ultimate control over its own internal affairs, no one else can exercise that control. Which, in turn, means that in principle the state can do what it likes not just within its borders but also in its external relations.[13]

Although a logical continuation of the sovereignty principle, this last statement leads, as James notes, into extremely problematic territory; if sovereignty means that any given state can truly do what it likes in its external relations then this must include actions that would undermine the principle of sovereignty as applied to all other states—unlimited intervention in the affairs of other states, for example. If sovereignty is defined in such a way as to necessarily undermine itself, then the concept of sovereignty is not achievable either in theory or in practice—thus, Öyvind Österud argues that "if external sovereignty is effective omnipotence, the very concept should be abandoned."[14]

Internally, political-legal practice, and particularly the existence of federal states in which sovereignty is shared between the center and the constituent units of the federal state, has ensured that modern conceptions of sovereignty incorporate the idea of divisibility as a possible feature of state sovereignty. This sharing of sovereignty, with center and constituent units each awarded competence in particular areas of state activity, necessarily also restricts sovereignty over those areas where others have competence. Thus, constituent units of a federal state do not have sovereignty over those areas of state activity that the constitutional structures of that state award to the center; they do, however, retain sovereignty in relation to the federal center over other areas—although the extent to which they have sovereignty over these other areas may be limited by the breadth of the federal center's competencies. Whatever the other powers of the federal center, they are likely to include authority on matters of defense and foreign policy; the German constitution, for example, is clear that "relations with foreign states shall be conducted by the Federation," although the länder have the authority to "conclude treaties with foreign states with the consent of the Federal Government" on matters within their constitutionally demarcated competence.[15] Under the US constitution, although the "powers not delegated to the United States by the Constitution, nor prohibited by it to the States, are reserved to the States respectively, or to the people," what this is understood to mean legally, and the extent of state sovereignty in practice, has varied considerably across the history of the United States; in all cases, however, the sovereignty of the constituent states has not been understood to extend to foreign or security policy.[16] Irrespective of the specific distribution of sovereignty within a federal state, constituent units of federal states do not have sovereignty as *international* actors; as James notes, even if they have some powers to participate individually in international relations, they do because of capacities awarded to them under the federal constitution, as members of that federation whose activities are restricted by federal law, not as independent actors.[17] As discussed below, both this constitutional sharing of sovereignty in federal systems and the issue of the international status of constituent federal units have had implications for the exercise and understanding of sovereignty within the USSR and its successor states, particularly because of the denial in Soviet theory that the USSR's structure entailed the limitation of republic sovereignty either domestically or internationally.

These, then, are some of the core aspects of the concept of sovereignty on which there is at least some consensus among analysts. It is clear, however, that even these issues on which there is some agreement become subjects of dispute when considered in any detail. One of the reasons for this is the fact that the term *sovereignty* is used to cover a wide field of meanings. The external-internal sovereignty issue is one example of this. Other examples of differentiation within the boundaries of the Western tradition of sovereignty theory focus on a differentiated conceptualization of the practice (although not the formal condition) of state sovereignty—for example, in Robert Jackson's work on "quasi-states" and Jorri Duursma's identification of "micro-states."[18] Both terms are used to identify discrete groups of states that, although internationally recognized as sovereign entities, do not have many of the core attributes that sovereign states are generally understood to possess.

All these aspects of the concept of sovereignty, and the interpretative differences that arise in relation to them, are part of the long tradition of legal and theoretical attempts to define sovereignty, to give it a clear, agreed meaning. The concept of sovereignty, however, is not confined to these fields, and it is important to note, briefly, that in political practice sovereignty is also important as a conceptual and rhetorical political tool, one that is used in negotiations between international actors and within states as part of a wider political discourse.[19] In the former field, the questions about sovereignty are about its meaning—historical origins, definition, and the possibilities and function of definition, and the relationship of that meaning to practice.[20] In the latter, sovereignty is a political instrument that rarely needs to be defined since it is used functionally, to establish political positions within a state or between states, and to assert or deny the right of territorially distinct political entities to be accepted as a formal equal by other sovereignty entities, with all the legal and political implications that acceptance or rejection entails.

Thus, the concept of sovereignty has several descriptive and performative functions. It is used to describe, in both legal and academic contexts, the boundaries of state authority and the nature of state independence through the development of the concepts of internal and external sovereignty. A conception of sovereignty, however unclear, thus permits the development of formal relations between states and the establishment of international institutions that have states as their members. In addition, it gives a framework to the way in which states represent themselves and to the ways groups within states can conceive of the nature of the state in which they exist and that state's place in relation to other states. Clearly this political, discursive function is dependent on assumptions about a shared understanding of the meaning and importance of sovereignty, deriving from the legal-theoretical attempts to define it and to establish its importance as a criterion for political identity and action. However, this use of the concept of sovereignty as a tool of political discourse within and between states is placed under strain when the actors concerned share different assumptions about what the content of "sovereignty" is. In this situation, a difference of interpretation in relation to the term *sovereignty* becomes a struggle over political meaning and, given the centrality of the concept of sovereignty to states in their dealings with one another, over relative power. Fortunately for the stability and coherence of interstate relations, sovereignty is not a concept that is widely contested in contemporary international politics—a consequence, I would argue, of the dominance of a single tradition of sovereignty in international politics: the Western tradition. However, not all states in the recent history of international politics have shared the Western approach to the concept of sovereignty; for most of the twentieth century, the Soviet Union operated with a very different model of sovereignty, and it is precisely that history of difference that constitutes the grounds for dispute over both the legal and political-rhetorical modes of sovereignty within and between the states of the former Soviet Union in the post-Soviet period. In order to understand how this has occurred and its implications for state security and interstate security relations, it is first necessary to understand the nature and extent of the difference between Western and Soviet approaches to sovereignty.

The Soviet Model of Sovereignty

Despite the absence of a widely accepted, single definition of sovereignty in the Western literature or in contemporary international practice, there are a set of broad understandings that have set conceptual boundaries for the Western model of sovereignty since at least the end of World War II. These understandings, however, did not dominate thinking about sovereignty in the USSR, and as a result, it is possible to identify a different tradition of writing about and practice of sovereignty—a Soviet model of sovereignty.

In some respects, the development of the Western and Soviet bodies of law and theory on sovereignty appear as mirror images of one another. The Western literature consists of multiple, competing definitions and interpretations of sovereignty and its functions, given by different analysts operating within various academic fields (law, international relations, domestic political analysis). Most of these different, competing analyses assume uniformity in the internal sovereignty relationship (in other words, that the character of state sovereignty over its territory and population is the same for all areas of that territory and population) and in the external relationship with other states (that all sovereign states share the same attributes of sovereignty; that, for the purposes of international relations, all states are formally, equally sovereign and sovereign in the same way, even if this formal equality is not reflected in the practice of international politics). Soviet theory, however, reversed this relationship of analytical multiplicity to uniformity of object. In contrast to the Western literature, a single analytical perspective was evident, with different analyses providing the same interpretations and definitions of sovereignty. However, the Soviet model of sovereignty was grounded in multiplicity in the *application* of the concepts of internal and external sovereignty. Rather than a single relationship of central, sovereign state to subject parts, the theories of sovereignty as applied to the USSR assumed a differentiated relationship of sovereignty between the center and union republics (Soviet Socialist Republics, SSRs), between the center and the autonomous republics (Autonomous Soviet Socialist Republics, ASSRs), and between the SSRs and the ASSRs. In addition to these differentiated relationships of internal sovereignty, the external sovereignty of states was viewed differently depending on the state's regime type and role—the sovereignty of the "vanguard" socialist state, the USSR, was different in character from that of other socialist states, and both were different from that of nonsocialist states. The Soviet tradition of sovereignty theory was thus grounded in a uniform understanding of a multiple, highly differentiated set of sovereignty relationships, in relation to all of which the Soviet federal government had preeminence.

At first glance it appears that Soviet and Western traditions of thought on sovereignty share many of the basic assumptions about the characteristics of state sovereignty. The idea of what constituted state sovereignty in relation to other states or internally is often described in Soviet-era analysis in ways consistent with the Western model. Thus, for one Soviet analyst: "State sovereignty is an integral comprehensive concept implying an internally organised aggregate of the intrinsic features of state power: paramountcy and independence."[21] What these principles meant for the USSR's relationship to other states was specified in Article 29 of the 1977 Soviet constitution:

> The USSR's relations with other states are built on the basis of the observance of the principles of sovereign equality and the mutual rejection of the use of force or the threat of force; the inviolability of borders; the territorial integrity of the state; the peaceful resolution of disputes; noninterference in internal affairs; respect for human rights and fundamental freedoms; the possession of equal rights and the right of peoples to control their own destiny; cooperation between states; the conscientious fulfilment of obligations resulting from universally recognized principles and norms of international law, [and] from the USSR's conclusion of international treaties.[22]

These statements are all consistent with, and reflect the language of, the Western model of sovereignty. However, although the basic theoretical principles of sovereignty appear to be shared, ideas about the nature of sovereignty begin to diverge when they are considered in particular contexts—within the USSR; in relation to the international status and powers of the union republics; in relations between the USSR and other socialist states; between socialist and nonsocialist states; or between two or more nonsocialist states.

The origins of this divergence into a distinctive Soviet model of sovereignty lie in the attempts by Soviet political and legal theorists to reconcile the basic principles of Marxist-Leninist thought—which appeared to be antithetical to state-centric politics and its attendant conceptions such as state sovereignty—with the pragmatic demands of twentieth-century international relations. Standard conceptions of the state and of sovereignty were rethought in a way that could be defended as compatible with Marxism-Leninism while providing a conceptual basis (or justification) for the USSR's engagement with the traditional business of international politics.[23] The different conception of the state and of international law, deriving from Marxist-Leninist theory, and the perception of a "deeply rooted fundamental difference of the legal and social order of capitalist society on one hand and socialist order on the other" meant that the Soviet thinking about international law involved a differentiated approach to international legal subjects, with different understandings of the obligations deriving from it in relation to socialist and nonsocialist states.[24] One consequence was the reformulation of sovereignty as an aspect and reflection of class conflict, so that the nature and status of sovereignty depended on the character of the specific state. One jurist writing in a US journal in the late 1940s noted that the sovereignty of capitalist states was not regarded as equivalent to social-ist state sovereignty because, as a Soviet theorist explained:

> The supremacy of the power of the state as the political organization of the ruling class is the essence of sovereignty. . . . In the bourgeois state the proclaimed form of "the sovereignty of the people" conceals class dicta-torship of the bourgeoisie. . . . Sovereignty is full power and independence of the state as the political organization of the class which possesses the tools and means of production and dominates economically. One cannot speak of sovereignty without these conditions.

Sovereignty, in this conception, is not only differentiated across differ-ent types of state, it is also formed by and subordinate to political impera-tives; in contrast to the Western model, it is a manifestation of conflict rather than equality, a conceptual tool for promoting revolution rather than order. This conception of sovereignty also contains a strong value content; this differentiation in the model between Soviet center, Soviet republic, socialist state, and capitalist state sovereignty identifies the sovereignty of the Soviet center, and the need to protect it, as the highest good, since the desired move toward a socialist mode of government elsewhere would depend on the strengthening of the authority of the Soviet center, its resist-ance to outside influence, and, in contrast, the permeability of other states to Soviet influence. Consequently,

> the principle of sovereignty is subordinated to the principle of democracy as a more general and universal principle of relations between states and within a state. A regime brought about by aggression and representing a constant threat of aggression, certainly cannot claim to be protected under the cover of the principle of sovereignty.[25]

Thus it becomes essential to protect the sovereignty of socialist states (and above of all the USSR, as the vanguard state) in relation to capitalist ones, not for reasons of legal or international relations theory concerned with the importance of sovereign equality as a cornerstone of the international sys-tem, but because:

> Sovereignty, as conceived by Soviets, is a weapon in the struggle of the progressive-democratic forces against the reactionary-imperialistic ones. Under contemporary conditions sovereignty is destined to act as a legal barrier protecting against the imperialistic encroachment and securing the existence of the most advanced social and state forms.[26]

In this way, Mintauts Chakste argues, the Soviet conception of sovereignty "establishes the right of the Soviet state to independence, including the right to reject any outside interference. In relations with . . . the West, this concept, however, lacks reciprocity, as it does not grant these states the protection of sovereignty."[27]

As all this implies, the Soviet adoption and adaptation of the concept of sovereignty involved not just some variation in interpretation within an existing theoretical tradition, but a fundamental difference of understanding about the nature of sovereignty as a consequence of an entirely different ontology of politics. In consequence, Chakste observed that: "The term 'sovereignty' will be retained but the subject-matter of this term will be different. The Soviet federal law has already developed a new notion of sovereignty which no longer means internal and external independence of the state to carry out its functions."[28]

Sovereignty Within the USSR

The Soviet model of internal sovereignty as set out in the 1977 Soviet constitution and in Soviet academic expositions attempted to combine a federal structure with nationalism informed by Marxist-Leninist theory.[29] The federal structure of the USSR was characterized by a complex hierarchy of relationships between (in descending order) the union center, the SSRs, the ASSRs, and the Autonomous Areas, each of which was linked to a particular national grouping, the "titular nationality."[30] Adding to this complexity was the problematic attempt to combine the principles of the sovereignty of the union center, union republic state sovereignty, and autonomous republic national sovereignty, while maintaining that national and state sovereignty was indivisible and illimitable.

Chapter 9 of the 1977 USSR constitution addresses the question of union republic sovereignty within the structure of the USSR:

> Article 76: A union republic is a sovereign, soviet socialist state, which has united with other Soviet republics in the Union of Soviet Socialist Republics. Outside the limits stated in Article 73 of the USSR constitution, a union republic independently realizes state power on its own territory. A union republic possesses its own constitution, conforming with the constitution of the USSR and taking into account the particular features of the republic. . . .
>
> Article 78: The territory of a union republic cannot be altered without its consent. The borders between union republics may be changed by mutual consent of the relevant republics, subject to confirmation by the union SSR.
>
> Article 79: A union republic determines its own division into territories, provinces, regions, and districts, and decides questions of administrative-territorial organization.
>
> Article 80: A union republic possesses the right to enter into relations with foreign states, to conclude agreements with them, and to exchange diplomatic and consular representation, [and] to participate in the activities of international organizations.

Article 81: The sovereign rights of the union republics are protected by the union SSR.[31]

These articles appear to provide for a very high degree of authority on the part of the constituent republics. In particular, Article 80 appears to have given republics a far greater international role than would normally be the case for the constituent units of a federal state—indeed, it suggests that the SSRs had an independence of action implying at least limited external sovereignty as independent international actors.[32] The most visible evidence of this was the UN membership of the Belarusian and Ukrainian SSRs, but the extent of the foreign policy capacities of all the union republics also represented, at least in theory, a significant difference from the standard federal model. The international capacities of the Soviet republics were regarded by Soviet commentators as an important feature of the Soviet system and as further evidence of the sovereignty of the republics. A Soviet commentator claimed that

The Soviet Union as a whole and every union republic in particular are autonomous subjects of international law with all the rights and obligations towards other states which derive from this status. . . . Union republics, as well as the Soviet Union as a whole, are truly sovereign states.[33]

However, although Article 76 begins with the assertion that a union republic was a sovereign state (a term that is not defined in the constitution), and despite the impressive list of its powers, other sections of the constitution clearly indicate that it was not sovereign in any sense understood within the Western tradition. Republic sovereignty, in the Western sense, was rendered impossible by the statement that the SSRs independently exercise state power in areas not covered by Article 73, since Article 73 sets out the areas of competence of the USSR, covering all the functions that would be traditionally associated with a sovereign state:

(1) Admission of new republics into the structures of the USSR; ratification of the formation of new autonomous republics and autonomous oblasts within the structures of the union republics; (2) determination of the state border of the USSR and ratification of the alteration of borders between union republics; (3) the establishment of a common basis for the organizations and activities of the republic and local organs of state power and administration; (4) ensuring the unity of legislative changes throughout the whole territory of the USSR, establishing a basis of legislation of the union SSR and the union republics; (5) conducting united social-economic policy; the direction of the country's economy; the determination of the fundamental direction of scientific-technical progress; . . . (8) questions of peace and war, defense of sovereignty, the protection of state borders and territories of the USSR, the organization of defense, direction of the armed forces of the USSR; (9) ensuring state security; (10) representation of the USSR in international relations; links between the USSR

and international organizations; establishment of the procedure for, and coordination of, union republic relations with foreign states and international organizations.

In addition to the areas normally falling under the authority of a federal center, such as matters of war and peace, areas cited as falling under the competence of the SSRs in Article 76 were still conditional on the agreement of, or initiated by, the USSR. These included matters of political organization and administrative structure internal to the SSRs—in other words, precisely those areas of policy over which constituent units could be expected to have sovereignty in a federal system. So, although "the territory of a union republic may not be altered without its consent . . . [and] a union republic resolves . . . questions of administrative-territorial organization," Article 73 gave the USSR the power of confirming the formation of new autonomous republics and provinces within the union republics; the center also had authority to establish "a common basis for the organizations and activities of the republic and local organs of state power and administration." More vaguely, Article 73 also stipulates that the USSR had authority over all matters of "all-union importance."[34] As A. Shtromas notes, this last provision gave the union center final authority over any matter it chose to define as having "all-union importance," undermining the principle that the constituent republics had final authority in some matters, and thus destroying the possibility of the shared sovereignty that characterizes federal states.[35]

The heart of this constitutional overlap between the sovereignty rights of the republics and those of the USSR is found in the disparity between, on the one hand, Articles 75 and 73, which state, respectively, that "the sovereignty of the USSR extends throughout its entire territory" and that the center has authority over all matters of all-union importance and, on the other, Article 76, which states that "a union republic is a sovereign Soviet socialist state."[36] This relationship was different from that of other federal states in two crucial ways. First, whereas federal states such as the United States operate a system of shared sovereignty, with some aspects of state activity falling within the competence of the center and others within the competence of constituent units, the provisions of the Soviet constitution make it clear that sovereignty, in the Western sense, lay with the center, that sovereignty was not in fact shared, and that the center and republics existed in a hierarchical relationship.

The second distinctive feature of this arrangement was the assertion that the sovereignty of neither the center nor the union republics was in any way limited by it. Soviet analysis returns repeatedly to this problem of sovereignty held simultaneously by the USSR and by its constituent union republics, and attempts to provide clarification of how they can coexist. Thus one commentary on the 1977 constitution states that:

> In the Soviet Union, sovereignty is possessed both by the Union of Soviet Socialist Republics as a whole and the union republics which comprise it. The sovereignty of the Union as a whole and the sovereignty of the union republics do not negate each other but, rather, are harmoniously combined within constitutionally established limits.[37]

Another analyst claims that "in the Soviet Union state, territorial supremacy belongs to the USSR as regards the union state's entire territory and to every union republic as regards its own territory," while another argues that the union of the republics acts, in itself, as a protection of republic sovereignty.[38] That the extensive competencies granted to the center under the constitution might in some respect limit the sovereignty of the union republics was denied:

> As concerns Article 76 of the USSR Constitution, which states that a union republic exercises independent authority on its territory outside the spheres listed in Article 73, it has to do here with dividing terms of reference between the USSR and the union republics. It also follows that [what is] limited is merely the extent of the terms of reference, not the sovereignty of the union republics.[39]

This claim that the powers of the center did not limit the sovereignty of republics in any way was not a new feature of commentaries on the 1977 constitution, but was a long-standing principle of Soviet constitutional theory; one analysis from the 1940s cites a contemporary Soviet claim that "the sovereignty of [the USSR] not only does not exclude, but presupposes the sovereignty of the republics which compose the Union."[40]

The basis for this seeming contradiction appeared to be twofold. First, as a particular kind of state, a socialist state, the relationship between the center and constituent parts and between political structures and the people was held to be fundamentally different from that characterizing nonsocialist states. In this conception, the dictatorship of the proletariat, manifested in the guiding role of the Communist Party, provided the best guarantee of rights, for constituent republics as for the population. The strengthening of the powers of the center thus necessarily strengthened all those within the USSR whose interests were represented by the center—according to this logic, the sovereignty of the republics was not limited by the extensive powers of the center if the strength of the center was itself the best guarantee of republic sovereignty. The argument that it *did* weaken republic sovereignty was thus entirely incorrect because it was based on a flawed understanding of the function of socialist political structures and their relationship to one another. One Western analyst summarized the Soviet position as that

> the sovereignty [of] the federation and of its members are in organic unity; that the federation is sovereign not because of any delegation of sovereignty

to it by member republics but because at its inception in 1922 the attributes of sovereignty attached to the federation from the start. The republics lost no sovereignty by entering the federation but retained their full sovereign rights. This retention did not exclude the complete sovereignty of the federation.[41]

A Soviet account of the position was as follows:

> The union of the republics in the USSR took place on the basis of a treaty and it is well known that the voluntary conclusion of an equal and mutually advantageous treaty, far from limiting, strengthens sovereignty, being a striking expression of it. . . . The formation of the USSR by the Soviet republics is a supreme manifestation of their sovereignty, and not a renunciation of it. This is a form of preserving it by delegating definite rights to the USSR. . . . The USSR possesses sovereignty because it is an expression of the sovereignty of the union republics.[42]

Second, the extensive powers of the union center did not limit republic sovereignty because of the supposedly voluntary nature of the decision to join the USSR and the constitutional provision for SSR secession. This was a widely cited argument in favor of the unlimited character of republic sovereignty made in relation to both the 1977 and 1936 constitutions.[43] V. S. Shevtsov, for example, asserts that "the union republics voluntarily transferred some of their rights to the Union when they joined it but this does not mean that they limited their sovereignty."[44] Therefore, whatever the restrictions apparently placed on republic sovereignty by the provisions of the constitution, the right of secession theoretically guaranteed them a baseline of inalienable sovereignty.

Thus, Soviet sovereignty theory assumes that two claims to sovereignty can be supported in relation to the same territory without any form of division of sovereignty between them or without either limiting the other when the political structures in which these sovereignties are vested exist in a hierarchical relationship to one another. Certainly, in the context of Western understandings of sovereignty, this would appear to be a logically untenable position, since two authorities would not be able to exercise *unlimited* sovereignty over the same space, nor would sovereignty, as it is usually conceived, be able to be exercised by both bodies in a hierarchical relationship. Shevtsov attempts to explain the constitutional position on the sovereignty of the union republics in relation to the center:

> As a complex politico-legal attribute of the state, implying the supremacy of state authority, sovereignty may not be divided, transferred or circumscribed. Therefore, the sovereignty of union republics, too, is full and *indivisible* [emphasis added]. It is, nevertheless, an essential distinguishing feature of a union republic that it is a sovereign state and simultaneously one of the subjects of the Soviet federation, the USSR. Having become

> members of the USSR, the union republics have voluntarily transferred some of their rights to the federation, but that does not mean at all that they have circumscribed their sovereignty. It means merely that the union republics, in full conformity with the constitution of the USSR and their own constitutions, exercise their state authority within the limits of the powers reserved to them.[45]

It is this paradox of an unlimited and indivisible sovereignty held by two bodies—the union center and the republics—in relation to the same space that distinguishes Soviet conceptions of internal sovereignty from those of other states in which sovereignty is divided between the federal center and constituent units of the federal state. The fact that this fundamental contradiction of sovereignty as illimitable and yet radically limited forms the basis of the relationship between the union federal center and the constituent union republics has, as discussed below, important implications for the constitution of post-Soviet relations among the successor states.

Sovereignty, as framed by Soviet analysts, was a key concept underpinning the constitutional structure of the USSR and also, from a Western perspective, a theoretical and legal paradox undermining it. In theory, the union republics retained full sovereignty even while constituent states of the also-sovereign USSR, the sovereignty of which extended over all areas of state activity at all levels. As Soviet analysts themselves were quick to point out, this was an extremely unusual constitutional relationship which, at a theoretical level, gave the republics complete sovereignty and, despite voluntarily ceding the functions of an independent state to the union center, supposedly retained their sovereign condition.[46] Whatever the nature of republic sovereignty in practice, the absolute sovereign status of the republics was a key theoretical basis for the USSR. The Soviet Union itself was legitimated by the idea that the constituent republics had voluntarily entered into a federation and voluntarily remained in it. In order for both these propositions to be true, the republics had to be conceived of as sovereign both before and after joining the Soviet Union, thus giving them the necessary authority over their own territory and state structures to enable them to freely enter into federation with the other republics, and to withdraw from the USSR without the need for consent. In the international arena, this republic sovereignty was demonstrated by the United Nations membership of Belarus and Ukraine and the constitutionally enshrined right of the individual union republics to establish bilateral foreign relations with other states. At the same time, however, the structure of a centralized state demanded the location of sovereignty with the center, particularly in relation to certain key areas such as defense and foreign policy but also in a range of other key areas of state activity. This model of internal Soviet sovereignty was thus one in which the union republics existed in a condition of dependent, or nonsovereign, sovereignty in relation to the union center—a structural paradox that continued to inform relations between the republics after independence.

The Brezhnev Doctrine:
Interstate Relations and Limited Sovereignty

The constitutional relationship between the federal center and constituent republics of the USSR was not the only aspect of sovereignty theory that emphasized the preeminence of the Soviet center over other supposedly sovereign entities. Unlike the theory regarding the character of the USSR's internal sovereignty, which emphasized the unlimited character of republic sovereignty, the view of external sovereignty within the socialist bloc emphasized the limited character of sovereignty for states other than the USSR. This approach to relations between a powerful state and its weaker allies, exemplified by the Brezhnev Doctrine, is another aspect of Soviet sovereignty theory with implications for the relationship between Russia and its weaker post-Soviet neighbors after independence.

As noted earlier, the USSR's commitment to the principle of sovereignty as a basis for interstate relations as well as within its borders was notable because of its seeming incompatibility with central aspects of Soviet ideology, in particular the commitment to internationalism, in which the legitimacy of and requirements for political action were defined by the boundaries of class not state.[47] Given that state sovereignty was inextricably associated with the development of the capitalist state and the structuring of relations between capitalist states, it appears surprising that it formed a key basis for the USSR's relations with other socialist states. Nevertheless, emphasis was placed on sovereignty as a central principle of relations between the Soviet Union and European allies. Indeed, Robert Jones notes that in the period after World War II the sovereignty principle was asserted to be a "fundamental aspect of the Marxist theory of the state."[48] Margot Light notes, however, that despite the denial that the principle of internationalism characterizing the Brezhnev Doctrine was incompatible with the principle of state sovereignty, Soviet theory provided no resolution of the apparently contradictory commitment to both.[49] Once again, Soviet theory departed significantly from Western theory, notably in its concept of "limited sovereignty," which formed the basis of the Brezhnev Doctrine.

The Brezhnev Doctrine—the principle that, in cases where socialist regimes were threatened by internal or other attempts to undermine them, the Soviet Union, as the vanguard socialist state, had not only the right but the obligation to intervene to protect the socialist character of the state—represented a fundamental challenge to sovereignty as understood in the Western tradition. The USSR's right of intervention denied the external sovereignty of these states in relation to the USSR; it also, therefore, effectively denied their internal sovereignty, since it gave the USSR ultimate power of decision over the direction of domestic policy and the character of internal political structures. This view was not, however, reflected in Soviet analysis, which maintained that far from undermining the sovereignty of other socialist states, the leading role of the Soviet Union protected it—a position grounded in the distinctive conception, mentioned earlier, of sovereignty as linked to and dependent on a state's socialist or capitalist character. As Bhagirath Prasad notes, "If a state whose sovereignty was defined by its membership of the socialist system was threatened by counter revolution, then action in its defence did not deny its sovereignty, did not interfere in it, quite the contrary, it upheld it."[50]

This position closely reflected the assertion that the leading role of the Soviet center acted to reinforce rather than undermine union republic sovereignty.[51] It also acted to reduce the distinction between domestic and international political relations in the Soviet center's dealings with client structures. One Western analyst noted a convergence in Soviet theories concerned with the sovereignty relationship between the USSR and the other socialist states, and the union center and the republics, speculating that further convergence in the two sets of relationships might make objections by external actors to Soviet intervention in other socialist states no more necessary than they would be in the case of Moscow's intervention in Ukraine.[52] The legacy of policies and of constitutional and ideological structures that blurred the distinction between "internal" and "abroad" by awarding Moscow primacy in relation to both can be seen in the relationship between Russia and the other former Soviet republics—Russia's "near abroad"—in the post-Soviet period.

Thus, in both the USSR's relations with other allied, socialist states and with its own constituent republics, the same theoretical principles and problems emerged. In both cases sovereignty was held not only to be possible but fundamental for all the political entities concerned; it was, however, a restricted form of sovereignty over which the USSR had various forms of preeminence. These restrictions, in as far as they were acknowledged, were held to enhance rather than undermine the essential sovereignty of the entities concerned. Despite Mikhail Gorbachev's renunciation of the Brezhnev Doctrine, this set of understandings, which restricted other actors' sovereignty in key aspects and awarded control over these aspects to the Soviet center while asserting that such restrictions enhanced rather than reduced sovereignty, continued to be reflected in many of the disputes over security and over post-Soviet structures after 1991.

Sovereignty and the Post-Soviet Environment

With the collapse of the Soviet Union, the concept of shared sovereignty and the primacy of a legal interrelationship between the former Soviet states also disappeared. However, the conceptions of sovereignty that had underpinned the Soviet Union's constitutional structure appear to have been an important influence—positive or negative—on the way in which the former republics were constituted as independent states and, in particular, on the way in which they conceived of this new status in relation to one another. This influence would be likely to have been strongest in the immediate post-Soviet environment, when Soviet theories provided the point of departure for the formulation of sovereignty by the emergent states. At least in some cases, the assumptions about the nature of state sovereignty that underpinned the exit strategies of the former republics appear to draw on the Soviet theories of republic and union sovereignty. In particular, the degree to which prior constitutional structures and conceptions of sovereignty influenced the political rhetoric surrounding the breakup of the Soviet Union can be seen by examining some of the official documents of the SSRs and CIS that emerged in the periods immediately before and after it. These documents and some of the views articulated by political and military elites suggest that both the Soviet and the Western models of sovereignty appear to provide the conceptual framework for the constitution of sovereignty in post-Soviet interstate relations. In particular, they suggest fundamental differences in the way in which sovereignty is understood by different actors, that the CIS was conceived by some as an institution intended to substantially replicate the centralization and sovereignty model of the USSR, and that these actors also saw the central CIS structures as interchangeable with the structures of the Russian Federation (a perception seemingly shared by those actors who regarded the CIS with suspicion). Thus, the Soviet conception of sovereignty appears to survive into the post-Soviet period to characterize relations between Russia (which regarded itself as the Soviet successor state) and the other former republics, as well as between these republics and the Russian-dominated structures of the CIS.

Declarations of Sovereignty

Emergent differences in the usage of the term *sovereignty* are evident even before the final breakup of the USSR—they can be seen in the contrast between declarations of state sovereignty adopted by the different union republics in 1990, where both Soviet and Western understandings of sovereignty are evident. The "Declaration of Belarusian State Sovereignty," which was adopted by the Supreme Council of the Belarusian Soviet Socialist Republic (BSSR) on 27 July 1990 stated that:

> All questions concerning the borders [of the BSSR] shall be decided only on the basis of mutual consent of the BSSR and the adjacent sovereign states through concluding corresponding agreements subject to the ratification of the Supreme Council of the BSSR [Article 6].

Within the territory of the BSSR the constitution of the BSSR and the laws of the BSSR shall be supreme [Article 7]. . . .

The BSSR proposes to immediately commence the elaboration of an agreement on a union of sovereign socialist states [Article 11].[53]

This declaration had been preceded by the "Appeal of the Initiating Group of the Confederation of Belarusan Associations to Belarusan Youth," which provided a different view of sovereignty in its statement that:

It ensues from the constitutions of the BSSR and the USSR that the Belarusian SSR is a sovereign state. In practice, however, this sovereignty does not exist. We believe that only factual sovereignty would guarantee a harmony of interests of the BSSR and other republics constituting the USSR.[54]

This implies an understanding of sovereignty at variance with Soviet theory, one that entails, again by implication, independence. The Declaration of Belarusian State Sovereignty, in contrast, appears to reflect the Soviet conception of sovereignty, not least in its commitment to Belarusian sovereignty within a continued union state. Although the BSSR Supreme Council's act of adopting this declaration suggests that it is stating something that was not already the case, the declaration actually stays extremely close to the wording of the existing Soviet constitution, which the appeal cited above had already declared to be an ineffective instrument for ensuring Belarusian sovereignty. Indeed, it appears to raise questions about any commitment to change in the relationship between Belarus and the USSR, and thus to the delivery of functioning state sovereignty for Belarus; concern over this precipitated a walkout of the Democratic Opposition parliamentary bloc, but this failed to prevent the article being passed.[55]

This declaration of sovereignty, seemingly grounded in Soviet understandings of the concept, is notably different from the Declaration of Ukrainian State Sovereignty, also adopted in July 1990. This declares that:

Article 3: The Ukrainian SSR is independent in determining any issue of its state affairs. The Ukrainian SSR guarantees the supremacy of the constitution and laws of the republic on its territory. . . .

Article 5: The Ukrainian SSR has supremacy over all of its territory. The territory of the Ukrainian SSR within its existing boundaries is inviolable and cannot be changed or used without its consent. The Ukrainian SSR is independent in determining the administrative and territorial system of the republic and the procedures for establishing national and administrative units. . . .

Article 9: The Ukrainian SSR has the right to its own armed forces. The Ukrainian SSR has its own internal armies and bodies of state security subordinated to the Verkhovna Rada of the Ukrainian SSR. . . . The Ukrainian SSR solemnly declares its intention of becoming a permanently neutral state that does not participate in military blocs and adheres to three nuclear-free principles: to accept, to produce, and to purchase no nuclear weapons.[56]

Although some aspects of the declaration echo the Soviet constitutional formulation, the statements in Articles 3, 5, and 9 indicate a clear movement away from the Soviet model of "nonsovereign" sovereignty and toward the Western model. This movement toward a model of sovereignty implying independence is also suggested by the fact that although the declaration also makes reference to relations with other union republics, it does so in the article on "International Relations."

Sovereignty and the Early CIS Agreements

All possibilities for this projected "union of sovereign socialist states" disappeared with the dissolution of the USSR, brought about, in part, and signaled by the assertions of (Western-style) sovereignty by the union republics, beginning with the Baltic states. Clearly, however, the practical and cultural legacy of a shared state system was felt by key actors in many (although not all) of the republics to require the continuation of some shared structures during the process of transition of the Soviet republics to independence. This shared structure took the form of the Commonwealth of Independent States. As was clear from the start, perceptions of the role of the CIS varied widely among its founding members.[57] Contrary to the perceptions of both the Russian and Belarusian governments, the government of Ukraine stated from the outset that the CIS was no more than a mechanism to smooth the process of separation. Other states, including Russia and some of the Central Asian states, appeared to see it as a mechanism for preserving as many of the characteristics of the USSR as possible. These divergent interpretations of the role proposed for the CIS hinged, among other things, on differing conceptions of the newly independent states' sovereignty. For Ukraine, as members of its government repeatedly made clear from the outset, any supranational functions assumed by the CIS would pose a threat to the sovereignty of the member states and was therefore to be resisted. In contrast, other states appeared to regard the CIS as a mechanism for retaining joint exercise of powers in certain policy areas indefinitely; in as far as sovereignty was a consideration, it appeared to be one that could be addressed by a statement of member sovereignty, even though practice, or other sections of the same document, appeared to undermine it. The documents of the CIS provide a starting point for thinking about the way in which its member states describe their own sovereignty in the context of the post-Soviet space. Although, as I will argue, it is clear that these documents do not reflect either unanimity (with the exception of the founding documents, CIS agreements do not require the signature of all members) or a direct reflection of either the intentions of member states or their behavior in respect to one another, in setting a framework for the CIS as an organization, they provide the only available description of a shared conception of sovereignty within the former Soviet space. Any attempt to investigate the relationship between sovereignty and security in relations between states of the former Soviet Union must therefore take these collective statements about the nature of sovereignty as a starting point.

The CIS founding agreement. The first document of the CIS to address the issue of sovereignty is its founding document—the Agreement on the Creation of a Commonwealth of Independent States signed by Belarus, Russia, and Ukraine in December 1991. Echoes of the Soviet approach to sovereignty are evident in the agreement, despite the opening commitment to "develop our relations on the basis of mutual recognition of and respect for state sovereignty, the inalienable right to self-determination, the principles of equality and non-interference in internal affairs, repudiation of the use of force and economic and any other methods of coercion."[58] Despite this commitment to noninterference in one another's internal affairs, later articles raise the question of how far this is envisaged in practice. Article 4 commits the members of the CIS to developing "cooperation of peoples and states in the spheres of politics, the economy, culture, education, public health, protection of the environment, science and trade and in humanitarian and other fields."[59] Although very general, this nevertheless indicates cooperation across a wide range of domestic policy issues, at precisely the moment when the signatory states were supposedly also assuming their independence from one another. The breadth of the field of intended cooperation calls into question the possibility of noninterference in one another's internal affairs, to which the opening preamble commits members. This is raised again by Articles 6 and 7, which commit member states to cooperation in the security and foreign policy spheres:

> Article 6: The member-states of the commonwealth will cooperate in safeguarding international peace and security and in implementing effective measures for reducing armaments and military spending. . . . The member-states of the commonwealth will preserve and maintain under united command a common military-strategic space, including unified control over nuclear weapons. . . . They also jointly guarantee the necessary conditions for the stationing and functioning, of the strategic armed forces and for their material and social provision. . . .
> Article 7: The high contracting parties recognize that within the sphere of their activities the following will be implemented on an equal basis through the common coordinating institutions of the commonwealth: cooperation in the sphere of foreign-policy; cooperation in forming and developing the united economic area and the common European and Eurasian markets, and in the area of customs policy.[60]

The extent of cooperation envisaged in these articles, covering social, economic, foreign, and military policy, raises questions about the degree to which full independence and thus state sovereignty as understood in the Western theoretical tradition is actually envisaged by the agreement. There appears to be little scope for decisionmaking on an autonomous basis by member states in any of the central areas of state activity. In particular, the commitment to cooperation on security and foreign policy issues raises questions about the degree to which member states can formulate independent policy in these areas; indeed, it implies that membership of the commonwealth involves a pooling of external sovereignty. This recalls the framework set out in Chapter 9 of the 1977 Soviet constitution in which foreign and security policies were determined by the center rather than by the union republics, who were nevertheless described as sovereign entities. From its inception, the CIS appeared to be committed to developing structures and policies that rendered assertions of commitment to member-state sovereignty (in the Western sense) questionable. While some interstate coordination would not, in itself, be remarkable, two aspects of this agreement raise questions. First, the scope of the cooperation it envisages is very broad, covering all key areas of policymaking and apparently involving a high degree of centralized coordination on foreign and security policy questions. Second, as noted above, these states were also in the act of establishing their independence from one another. Rather than marking out their independence from one another, however, this document appears to tie the signatories together through a level of cooperation above that usually found between independent states—for example, the retention of united structures securing a single strategic space, and a coordinated foreign policy.

Indeed, the degree to which the structures of military cooperation are specified in a document intended to set out the general principles of the foundation of the commonwealth is striking.[61] While the formulation of spheres of economic and social cooperation is wide ranging but relatively generalized, the areas of security cooperation are set out in a surprisingly high level of detail in Article 6. This focus on the question of security within the CIS was to be reflected in the intensive activity over the issue of joint armed forces, and control of strategic forces in particular, which characterized the early period of the CIS.[62] It also reflects the degree to which CIS cooperation in this period was driven by the unsuccessful attempts of the former Soviet military elite to retain unified armed forces. It is therefore not surprising that the structures of the CIS envisaged in its founding agreement and in later documents reflect both a focus on military questions and a desire to replicate those structures that weakened member sovereignty in favor of a strong, unified center.

This focus on foreign policy and security cooperation and its implications proved problematic. In the process of ratifying the agreement, the

Ukrainian Supreme Soviet made twelve amendments to the text. In Article 7, dealing with foreign policy, the amendment substituted the concept of consultations on foreign policy for the agreement on CIS foreign policy cooperation. In Article 6, detailing the retention of a united armed forces command and a common military-strategic space, the Supreme Soviet added the statement: "The member-states of the Commonwealth will reform the groupings of the Armed Forces of the former USSR stationed on their territory and, creating their own armed forces on the basis of these groupings, will cooperate in ensuring international peace and security."[63]

This emphasis on moving further away from a replication of the union center's control over policy is reflected in the (slightly) greater emphasis placed on member-state sovereignty in the Alma-Ata declaration. This states that signatories

> seeking to build democratic law-governed states, the relations between which will develop on the basis of mutual recognition and respect for state sovereignty and sovereign equality; the inalienable right to self-determination, principles of equality and non-interference in internal affairs, the rejection of the use of force and economic and any other means of pressure . . . recognising and respecting each other's territorial integrity and the inviolability of existing borders . . . are making the following statement: Cooperation between members of the Commonwealth will be carried out in accordance with the principle of equality through coordinating institutions formed on a parity basis and operating in the way established by the agreements between members of the Commonwealth, which is neither a state, nor a super-state structure.[64]

From the inception of the CIS, then, it is possible to see the way in which the question of member-state sovereignty is problematized in two ways—first by the very broad scope of cooperation envisaged for member states, which recalled aspects of the Soviet model, and second by the disagreement between actors apparently endorsing a framework based on this approach and others, notably Ukraine, seeking to establish a CIS framework based on a Western model of sovereignty.[65]

The Collective Security Treaty. Signed in May 1992 by Russia, Armenia, Tajikistan, Kazakhstan, and Uzbekistan, the Collective Security Treaty (CST) was envisaged as the key structure defining security policy within the CIS, following the failure of the attempt to preserve a single post-Soviet armed forces.[66] The development of the treaty as a mechanism for preserving as much of the idea of unified defense structures as possible in itself raises problems in relation to the sovereignty and independence of member states. Nevertheless, as with other CIS documents, it opens with a statement of commitment to the idea of member-state sovereignty, asserting that the treaty signatories have been "guided by the independent states' declaration

of sovereignty."[67] The relationship between the treaty and a traditional conception of sovereignty is, however, as elsewhere, a complex one. Most
problematic are the key commitments made in the CST by its signatories
that undermine this opening assertion that state sovereignty is the basis of
the treaty, in particular Article 1, which prevents members from participating in any alliances or actions directed against another member, and Article
2, which commits members to consultation and coordination "on all important questions of international security affecting their interests."[68] Commitments to security policy coordination and the attempt to restrain member
states from membership of any grouping or organization perceived to be
hostile to other member states necessarily presents a significant challenge
to both external sovereignty (in that it constrains a signatory's ability to act
freely in the international arena) and internal sovereignty (in that it requires
signatories to involve other signatories in their state policymaking processes in critical areas of security policy). Yet, paradoxically, and in an
echo of similar sovereignty paradoxes in the Soviet model of sovereignty,
the challenge to the internal and external sovereignty of the signatory states
posed by this treaty is represented in it as a mechanism for preserving
member sovereignty. Article 2 states that:

> In the event of the emergence of a threat to the security, territorial integrity,
> and sovereignty of one or several participating states . . . the participating
> states will immediately activate the mechanism of joint consultations for
> the purpose of coordinating their positions and taking measures to elimi-
> nate the threat that has emerged.[69]

One of the problems presented by the document is that it fails to define the
concepts of security, territorial integrity, or sovereignty, or what would constitute a threat to them—or, in the absence of such a definition, who would
identify them. This allows for an extremely broad interpretation of these
terms, which given the requirements for military and other action imposed
on signatories in the event of such a threat raises questions about the ability of signatories to control their security commitments.[70] This was clearly
a concern of Ukraine, whose representatives at the meeting where the treaty
was signed cited the document's failure to specify the nature of the external
threat envisaged as one of the reasons for refusing to sign it.[71]

The CIS Charter. The CIS Charter, signed by seven member states (of
which Ukraine was not one) in 1993, provides a still clearer picture of the
problematic approach to sovereignty underpinning the CIS as an organization. The charter demonstrates a simultaneous commitment to upholding
those rights and competencies that are traditionally characterized as the
main features of state sovereignty, and to creating organizational structures
that would found relations between CIS member states on a reinstituted

Soviet model. As with the founding agreement, what is important here is not simply the fact that a commitment to the principles of sovereignty run directly counter to the structures and practices envisaged for this organization, but rather the fact that this contradiction is embedded in the organization's central conceptual document. The CIS Charter, as with any organization's charter, aims to set out the principles of theory and practice to which the CIS is committed. The fact that it is precisely in this theoretical framework that the contradiction between intended theory and intended practice is most clearly demonstrated suggests that this contradiction forms, in itself, a theoretical framework for the CIS.

Article 1 of the charter states that "the Commonwealth is based on the principles of the sovereign equality of all its members. Member-states are independent and equal subjects of international law."[72] It goes on to state that "the commonwealth is not a state and does not enjoy supranational powers." Despite this declaration of member-state autonomy, however, Article 2 envisages the aims of the CIS as including "the realization of cooperation in the political, economic, ecological, humanitarian, cultural, and other spheres; . . . cooperation between member states in ensuring international peace and security." The simultaneous commitment to member-state autonomy and to the development of structures that would radically undermine such autonomy is evident, in greater detail, in the later articles of the charter which address areas of CIS organizational competence. Article 3 sets out what the outline commitment to sovereignty and autonomy of Article 1 means:

> In order to achieve the commonwealth's aims, member states, proceeding from the generally recognized norms of international law and the Helsinki Final Act, build their relations in accordance with the following inter-linked and equivalent principles:
>
> - respect for the sovereignty of member states, for the inalienable right of peoples to self-determination, and for the right to decide their fate without outside interference;
> - the inviolability of state frontiers, recognition of existing frontiers . . . ;
> - the territorial integrity of states and rejection of any actions aimed at dismembering another's territory;
> - the non-use of force or the threat of force against the political independence of a member state; . . .
> - noninterference in each other's domestic and foreign affairs.[73]

The charter thus appears to commit member states to a mutual recognition of external sovereignty consistent with Western-model understandings. This commitment is, however, brought into question by the content of the subsequent articles. Article 4 states that:

The following belong to the spheres of joint activity of member states realized on an equitable basis through common coordinating institutions: . . . the coordination of foreign policy activity; cooperation in the formation and development of a common economic space, . . . cooperation in the development of systems of transport and communications; health and environmental protection; . . . cooperation in the sphere of defense policy and the guarding of external borders.[74]

Commitment to member-state cooperation in these areas undermines the possibility of noninterference in one another's domestic and foreign affairs, since cooperation and coordination in areas such as foreign policy, defense, and the guarding of "external" borders (in other words, what had been the Soviet borders) obviously necessitates a high level of interdependence. It implies mutual vulnerability to intervention in those areas of state activity that have an impact on other members' domestic or foreign policies—which, given the comprehensive nature of cooperation envisaged under the charter, would actually mean all areas.

The reference to coordinating institutions also raises the issue of supranationality as an aspect of CIS organization, despite the opening assertion that the commonwealth does not have supranational powers. This recalls those aspects of the 1977 constitution that deal with the relationship between the republics and the union center. Articles 11–15 dealing with "Collective Security and Military-Political Cooperation," Article 19 dealing with economic and social policy cooperation, and Article 20 dealing with legal cooperation set out in greater detail the extent to which many of the key functions of the member states are expected to be coordinated through the medium of the CIS. These lists of CIS responsibilities echo many of the items in the list of areas falling within the jurisdiction of the USSR, as set out in Article 73 of the 1977 constitution. The statement in Article 20 of the charter, for example, that "member states practice cooperation in the sphere of law . . . and promote the harmonization of national legislation" echoes Clause 4 of Article 73 that one of the functions of the USSR is "ensuring the unity of legislative changes throughout the whole territory of the USSR, establishing a basis of legislation of the union SSR and the union republics."[75] The charter's Article 19, which includes commitments to "the formation of a common economic space," "the coordination of social policy," and "the realization of joint projects in the sphere of science and technology," recalls the 1977 constitution's Article 73, which also groups these issues together in Clause 5, which opens with a statement of the USSR's responsibility for "a unified social-economic policy; the direction of the country's economy; [and] the determination of the fundamental direction of scientific-technical progress."[76]

The CIS Charter, then, sets out a clear commitment to the idea of sovereign statehood as a condition of its member states, together with a general explanation of what that might mean in practice—one that falls clearly within the boundaries of the Western model of sovereignty. Yet side by side with this formal recognition is an elaboration of the ways in which these member states are, or should be, permeable to external actors—specifically, the CIS and its members. The areas covered by the charter—social policy, law, relations with other states, the economy, customs, defense strategy (including joint armed forces), and defense of state borders—cover much of the political territory usually regarded by states as fundamental to the exercise of sovereignty as understood in the Western tradition. Taken together, these commitments to coordinate policy present a serious challenge to the commitment to noninterference in the internal affairs of member states given elsewhere in the charter and directly challenge the charter's assertion in Article 1 that "the Commonwealth is not a state and does not enjoy supranational powers." That these two contradictory commitments coexist in a founding document, without any indication that they are thought to be in any form of opposition to one another, recalls the similarly contradictory approach to sovereignty that characterized the Soviet model.

Taken together, these three CIS agreements provide a contradictory picture of the conception of sovereignty within the institutional context of the CIS. On the one hand, the framework agreements make it clear that the CIS is not intended to present a challenge to the state sovereignty or independence of its member states. Not only this, but, as outlined in the opening sections of the framework document and the CIS Charter, the understanding of the meaning of the term *state sovereignty* is consistent with Western understandings of this term. Thus, these documents reinforce their commitment to sovereignty with outlines of the CIS's commitment to members' independence from one another; noninterference in internal affairs; and the renunciation of the use of force or the threat of the use of force against one another. However, this conception of state sovereignty is not the only one implied by either the agreements or the structures of the CIS. Indeed, the fact that the commitments outlined above are made in addition to, rather than as part of, a commitment to state sovereignty suggests the possibility for alternative understandings of this concept to exist as part of the conceptual framework of these documents and structures.

Such an alternative interpretation of the concept of sovereignty is indeed present in the textual and institutional frameworks of the CIS. While claiming to endorse a traditional approach to the idea of state sovereignty, these frameworks appear, from the founding agreement onward, to have inherited a conception of sovereignty from the constitutional theory of the Soviet Union, and to thus run directly counter to the commitments to independence, noninterference, and renunciation of the use or threat of force in dealings between member states that they also endorse. Thus, despite these claims, the

CIS Charter also asserts the intention of member-state signatories to engage in a system of relationships on virtually all domestic and foreign policy matters, which precludes either independence or mutual noninterference.

If it is helpful to think of the CIS's conceptualization of member states' sovereignty in relation to the theoretical legacy of the Soviet Union, it is also important to think of it as a (re)active formulation rather than a purely passive one, dependent on historical circumstance. The construction of the idea of state sovereignty within the CIS needs to be seen equally as a product of the emergent relationship between Russia and the other CIS states. Several contributory factors can be identified in this context: the desire on the part of Russia—above all, the Russian military establishment—to retain central (initially CIS, now Russian) control of key assets of the Soviet Union after its dissolution, in particular, control of the armed forces and above all the former Soviet nuclear arsenal; and the resistance of other states to this attempt to undermine their independence on domestic and security policy issues. For these other states, it appears that asserting sovereignty as formulated in the Western model required them to conceive of themselves not simply as emergent states in an international arena populated by other sovereign states, but specifically as states sovereign in relation to the old Soviet center and the new influence of Russian regional hegemony.

Perceptions of Sovereignty Among CIS Actors

The conception of sovereignty evident in the early CIS documents is important for understanding the basis on which relations between member states were constituted at the start of the post-Soviet period, since it provides an indication of the mutually agreed understandings of the condition of sovereignty that formed the basis for members' interaction as independent states. It is, thus, a key aspect of the conceptual basis underpinning post-Soviet interstate relations, and one that demonstrates the extent to which these relations were constituted by the legacy of Soviet views of sovereignty and of the power of the center. At least as important for understanding the views of, and the differences between, CIS member states on questions of mutual independence and continued unity are the ways in which member states have conceived of the status of and possibility for member-state sovereignty within the CIS as an institution. The scope and strength of disagreement in this period among CIS members and institutional actors about the relationship between member states and the CIS as an organization, a disagreement reflecting the differences between Soviet and Western models of sovereignty, can be seen in the divergent attitudes toward the idea of sovereignty within the CIS of Ukraine on the one hand and Russia and the former Soviet military elite on the other.

Ukraine. The relationship between the CIS and Ukraine was one of the most prominent factors in the debates around sovereignty and the CIS in the early and mid-1990s, both because of Ukraine's vocal opposition to perceived attempts to accord the CIS supranational functions, and because of the importance that Russia, in particular, attached to the continued CIS membership of Ukraine. Indeed, the history of the CIS is often characterized as driven by the split between those members, led by Russia, who viewed it as a mechanism either for full reintegration or at least for retaining key features of the union, and those members, most prominently Ukraine, who saw it as a mechanism for civilized divorce.[77]

Clearly, as in other states, perceptions of the CIS varied considerably across the Ukrainian political spectrum. Not surprisingly, Ukrainian nationalists expressed suspicions about the function of the CIS; the perception that the CIS posed a direct threat to the independence and sovereignty of Ukraine was voiced, for example, in a statement in July 1994 made by a group of Ukrainian political parties and movements, including the nationalist Rukh, which talked about "Russia's plans for turning the CIS into a new superpower" and stated that "the Eurasian expanse where the President sees Ukraine playing a leading role is nothing other than the space that is economically and politically subordinate to Russia."[78] Although successive governments have, in contrast, been prepared to engage with the CIS, remaining within the organization and signing agreements on a range of issues, it was clear from the start that the Ukrainian government also viewed the CIS with suspicion and of use primarily as a divorce mechanism. Consequently, in the early post-Soviet period, the Ukrainian government rejected those agreements that involved signatories in substantial policy coordination or appeared to award suprastate powers to the CIS as an organization, including the CIS Charter. Nevertheless, if the Ukrainian government has regarded the CIS as primarily a divorce mechanism, it appears to have envisaged a relatively slow divorce process, requiring Ukraine to remain within the commonwealth beyond the period immediately following the breakup of the USSR.

Despite Ukraine's continued membership, the ambiguity of the CIS on the question of sovereignty and concerns about the extent to which it represented an attempt on the part of Russia to undermine member-state sovereignty in key areas led to the adoption of a firm Ukrainian position on two central aspects of the CIS—the issue of joint armed forces and security policy, and the issue of commonwealth suprastate authority. Both were addressed by the Ukrainian president Leonid Kravchuk in an interview in January 1992, in which he made clear not only the position of the Ukrainian government in relation to these issues but also his view that the Ukrainian position derived from the founding documents of the CIS:

Ukraine's position is a consistent and principled one: compliance with the accords adopted in Alma-Ata and Minsk. If in Alma-Ata we said that the Commonwealth of Independent States is not a state, and is not even a state entity, then we construct our policy on the basis of this principle. That is, the domestic and foreign policy of each state is determined by the people and the government structures of that state. The representatives of other states—I do not want to specify them here—forget this truth and are attempting again to create something that would resemble a state. For instance, the idea of a single army is based on the principle of a single state, because there cannot be 11 states and a single army.[79]

The issue of CIS supranationality was a long-standing concern among sections of the Ukrainian political elite; as early as December 1991, the Ukrainian Supreme Soviet raised questions about the possible supranational character of the CIS. It declared in a resolution of that month that "Ukraine is against turning the Commonwealth of Independent States into a single state with its own bodies of state authority and government . . . it is against making the Commonwealth a subject of international law. The Commonwealth's international bodies should not have a commanding character" and noted that the resolution was the result of concerns prompted by ambiguous interpretations of the founding agreement.[80]

For Ukraine, the question of the CIS being invested with suprastate functions presented a double problem—first, that this would in itself pose a challenge to member-state sovereignty, since it would necessarily involve the assumption of powers to determine policy and actions on the part of member states by the CIS, thus encroaching on internal sovereignty; and second that Russian domination of the structures of the CIS would enable Russia to assert control over member states, thus undermining sovereignty.[81] This concern was voiced, for example, in an interview with Kravchuk in January 1992, in which he stated that

It is Ukraine's objective to live as an independent state, because the commonwealth itself does not constitute a state structure. All our members are independent states. . . . There is no first among equals, no "tacit" leader. If one of the states were to try to assume a role to which it is not entitled, then the commonwealth would not survive much longer. We will never tolerate Ukraine being subordinated.

In answer to the question "Do you think Yeltsin has understood that?" Kravchuk replied, "I think he will have to understand."[82] These concerns led to moves such as Ukrainian opposition in March 1994 to the request for the CIS to be given observer status at the UN, when its representative objected both to the recognition of the CIS as a subject of international law and as an organization able to conduct peacekeeping operations (in practice, involving the deployment of Russian troops on the territory of other member states).[83]

In the immediate post-Soviet period, Ukrainian reluctance to participate in CIS structures was particularly strong in the area of security policy. It was one of the few member states not to sign to the CST in May 1992, and its commitment to establishing its own armed forces both provoked much of the activity in the security sphere of the CIS and made such activity ultimately ineffective, since unified armed forces were not considered possible or desirable without the participation of Ukraine. (This already appeared to be the view of Joint Armed Forces Commander Evgenii Shaposhnikov by the time of the signing of the CST, when he stated that he believed that Ukraine's activities with regard to the strategic forces called the existence of the commonwealth strategic forces into question.[84]) The Ukrainian government made its position on the idea of a post-Soviet united armed forces clear from the outset, with Kravchuk stating in early 1992 that "the option of maintaining unified CIS armed forces does not exist. . . . You can only have unified armed forces in a unified state."[85] On the same day, Ukrainian defense minister Kostiantyn Morozov, echoing earlier comments made by Kravchuk, stated that "there are no commonwealth armed forces. One can only speak of armed forces of independent states."[86] For the Ukrainian government in the early 1990s, unified armed forces—and indeed any significant degree of security coordination within the CIS that concerned more than the division of assets—was fundamentally incompatible with Ukraine's (non-Soviet) sovereign statehood.

Russia. In contrast, Russian politicians and commentators tended to present the CIS as a positive factor in securing state sovereignty, although the sovereignty in question appeared, at points, to be Russian rather than a property shared equally by all CIS member states. In these interpretations of the term, Russian sovereignty frequently appeared to extend beyond the borders of the Russian Federation and to include the ability of Russia to do whatever it believed to be necessary to defend its interests within the wider territory of the commonwealth—a maximalist interpretation of Russian external sovereignty in respect to the CIS. Indeed, the widespread use of concepts such as the "near abroad" and the "external borders" of the CIS suggested that the demarcation between Russia and the other CIS states was not acknowledged as the boundary between sovereign states. Given the leading role of Russia, this blurred the issue of sovereignty within the CIS, since what appeared to be regarded by Russia as the exercise of its rights as a sovereign state (securing or opening its borders, protecting its territorial integrity through its security policy, and defending the rights of Russian nationals living in other CIS states, for example) often resulted in fundamental challenges to the internal and external sovereignty of other member states. This was evident, for example, when the perception that instability in other states threatened Russian territorial integrity led to Russian intervention in the internal affairs of these states or to the presence of Russian troops within these states; or when concerns about borders led to the deployment of Russian border troops on the "external" borders of CIS states. In this context, the CIS was widely viewed by Western analysts and by politicians in other CIS states as a mechanism for legitimating Russian interventions at the expense of other states' sovereignty—perceptions of CIS-sanctioned Russian peacekeeping has been one obvious example of this.[87]

This Russian perception of the CIS and its member states as subordinate to the interests of Russian external sovereignty did not emerge in all political quarters immediately. Interviewed in mid-December 1991, for example, Russian president Boris Yeltsin—whose political success was built on his support for (Russian) republic sovereignty in opposition to the federal center—stated that the drafts of the proposed new union treaty "proceeded from a mistaken basis" because they incorporated a strong center that was "repelling to all the republics." He stated that "in the CIS such a center, which could command every step of ours, does not exist and will not, and that is why this appeals to all the republics."[88] A complicating factor in the assessment of Russia's role in and intentions toward the CIS in the early independence period was the fact that Russia, the dominant state of the CIS and the state most instrumental in attempting to develop a commonwealth framework, particularly in the area of security, was also widely perceived by commentators in 1991–1992 as neglecting the CIS in favor of securing closer ties with Western states. Subsequently, however, with the much-discussed shift in Russian foreign policy away from Atlanticism and toward an emphasis on Russia's continued "great power" status (before, but especially after the 1993 election of a strongly nationalist parliament), a consensus that "the entire geopolitical space of the former Soviet Union is a sphere of Russia's vital interests"[89] began to be visible in statements made by members of the Russian executive and Russian commentators. In this view:

> In geographic terms our main priorities lie in the CIS. Promoting integration, developing the Commonwealth into a workable regional organisation, maintaining stability on CIS territory and ensuring reliable protection of its external borders; settling local conflicts; and safeguarding the rights of our compatriots—these are the major goals directly determining Russia's security.[90]

In 1993, a speech by Yeltsin provoked a strong response from the Ukrainian government and others because it contained the claim that "the time has come for the appropriate international organizations to grant Russia special powers as the guarantor of peace and stability on the territory of the former union."[91] Similarly, comments by Andrei Kozyrev as foreign minister in 1994 provoked concern over the Russian government's approach to security questions in the former Soviet space:

> The CIS and the Baltic states constitute the area in which Russia's principal vital interests are concentrated . . . [and] from which the main threats to its interests emanate. . . . Raising the question about complete withdrawal and removal of any Russian military presence in the near abroad is just as extreme, if not extremist, as the idea of sending tanks to all republics to establish some form of imperial order.[92]

As with the CIS documents discussed above, however, this discourse of Russian rights and interests in the CIS was often described as coincident with, rather than undermining, the sovereignty of the other commonwealth members. Thus Yeltsin could state that:

> We should really strive to set up an effective security system within the CIS. . . . Likewise, Russia favours closer interaction in external policy, and coordination of positions taken by Commonwealth member-states on very important questions of international affairs. We favour further cooperation between our diplomatic services, and a firm defence of the common interests of CIS member-states. . . . I believe that we posses all the opportunities to turn the Commonwealth into an effective association of sovereign partners with equal rights, based on a commonality of interests and voluntary participation in various forms of cooperation.[93]

As in the CIS documents, the external sovereignty of member states is not seen to be undermined by the proposed coordination of foreign and security policy.

Integration within the CIS as a key objective for Russia was the subject of a 1994 discussion between politicians and analysts, in which Kozyrev argued that the CIS "rests on two principles which may be paradoxical but exist as realities of life: the republics want to be independent but at the same time there is an objective need for a commonwealth. . . . We want a more closely-knit commonwealth, one advancing to integration." He also asserted—in a claim that echoed the Soviet perspective on the role of the USSR in relation to other socialist states—that "the stronger Russia becomes economically and politically, the better this will be for other independent states and for integration because . . . Russia is the motor of reform and progress in the commonwealth." Another participant, reflecting the paradox at the heart of integrationist perspectives on the CIS, viewed "integration at this particular stage as a mild form of confederation whose every member remains an independent state and part of the international community, with all the ensuing consequences."[94]

In the more formal context of policy documents, the summary of the Russian Foreign Policy Concept published by *International Affairs* in January 1993 states that "Russia is to exercise its responsibility as a great power for the maintenance of global and regional stability," a regional management role that recalls the management role assumed by the USSR in relation to other socialist states.[95] Similarly, the "Basic Provisions of the Russian Federation's Military Doctrine" of 1993 states Russia's commitment to "respect for the sovereignty and territorial integrity of states, non-interference in their internal affairs, the inviolability of state borders, and other generally recognized principles of international law."[96] It nevertheless also defines its security threats as:

> existing and potential areas of local wars and armed conflicts, above all those in direct proximity to Russia's borders; . . . the suppression of the rights, liberties and legitimate interests of Russian Federation citizens in foreign states; attacks on military installations of the Russian Federation Armed Forces located on the territory of foreign states; the expansion of military blocs and alliances to the detriment of the interests of the Russian Federation's military security.[97]

Clearly any Russian intervention on any of these points would pose a fundamental challenge to the sovereignty of the states concerned. The document does not acknowledge any potential incompatibility between the acceptance of the sovereignty of other states and the implied requirement to intervene in them when Russian security interests are perceived to be under threat in this way. This contradiction, embedded in core policy documents, and other Russian views of the function of the CIS and Russia's place in it recall the sovereignty paradox underpinning both the relationship between the center and republics formulated in the Soviet constitution and the relationship between the Soviet Union and other socialist states.

The CIS military elite. Three interconnected views can be identified in the statements made by those members of the former Soviet armed forces working within the framework of the CIS in the early 1990s: (1) the need to retain unified forces and security policy across the CIS, if possible; (2) the need for these to be driven from the center, in the form of the CIS organization; and (3) the identification of CIS security priorities with those of Russia. Taken together they do not allow space either for any distinction to be drawn between Russian and CIS priorities or, therefore, for any conception of member-state sovereignty (other than Russia's) in the security sphere. Statements made by CIS military personnel indicate a complete disregard for the independent security priorities of CIS states—Nikolai Stolyarov, chairman of the CIS Armed Forces Main Command Committee, claimed, for example, that "it can scarcely be said that any of the countries that make up the CIS has its own distinctive strategic-military interests."[98]

Not surprisingly, opinions expressed by personnel and commentators within the armed forces in the period immediately following the breakup of the USSR indicated a view that the institutional needs of the armed forces took precedence over questions of member-state sovereignty. Impatience with the politicians engaged in negotiating the new structures of the CIS was evident in an article published in the armed forces' newspaper, *Krasnaia Zvezda,* in late December 1991, which asserted that the CIS's security problems could easily be resolved if politicians left such matters to the armed forces rather than intervening in negotiations.[99]

Another *Krasnaia Zvezda* article, published in January 1992, demonstrated both a preoccupation with the need to preserve unified armed forces and the perception that this should be done through a subordination of individual member-state decisionmaking in the area of security to a central CIS concept:

> While acknowledging in principle the rightfulness of the existence of a national guard in each sovereign state, we suggest at the same time that its name be changed to "republican guard" or "territorial people's army," which would make it possible for not only people of indigenous nationality but also any citizen of the state to serve in it. . . . We consider it essential to stop right now all talk about the armed forces and all attempts to divide them and to administer republican oaths of loyalty to the troops. We must urgently elaborate single political views of the CIS and political doctrines for each component state and determine military doctrines in accordance with them.[100]

This desire to limit state sovereignty in the security arena to parameters set by the military personnel within the CIS was reflected shortly afterward by Lieutenant General Leonid Ivashov, then chief of the CIS Armed Forces Administration of Affairs, who commented that "today there is an obvious need to coordinate the activity of the legislative structures of the Commonwealth participant states as regards defence problems with a view to implementing to a certain extent the uniform regulation of legal relations in the military sphere."[101]

CIS military elite attitudes to the commonwealth and to the relationships between its member states were complicated during this period by the fact that the demarcation between senior CIS military personnel and the Russian executive was far from clear.[102] Suspicions about this relationship were exacerbated by factors such as the apparently interchangeable character of posts within the two structures suggested by the move of Konstantin Kobets from his post as Russian presidential defense adviser to the CIS High Command in March 1992, and the move of Shaposhnikov from the CIS Joint Armed Forces to chair of the Russian Security Council in 1993. This perception was exacerbated by the fact that Shaposhnikov tended to travel in Yeltsin's entourage on foreign visits, and by the appearance of CIS and Russian personnel in the same delegation to negotiations with other

CIS states (discussed in the context of the dispute over the Black Sea Fleet in Chapter 4). Another factor reinforcing the perception that the CIS military structures treated the CIS and Russia as interchangeable concepts were comments such as that made by Shaposhnikov in early 1993 that "sometimes, speaking with ministers of defence or foreign affairs I forget my role and say 'my president' and 'your president.' . . . All the CIS presidents are 'my presidents' of course. But at the same time I'm a citizen of Russia . . . whom do I serve if not Russia?"[103]

Conclusion

The former Soviet republics, emerging into independence during 1991, were faced with two particular challenges in their attempts to establish sovereign statehood—one conceptual, one practical. The first of these concerned the problem of sovereignty itself: what it meant to the states individually and how they collectively negotiated the development of their relations to one another. This was a difficult matter for the new states, since they emerged from a prior political structure that had encoded a very specific understanding of sovereignty in its legal structures and its foreign relations, one that differed in fundamental respects from the Western set of understandings about sovereignty. The Soviet model of sovereignty—the starting point for the post-Soviet states—asserted the illimitability of union republic sovereignty while awarding all the key properties of sovereign statehood to the union center, a center that, Soviet theory asserted, enhanced the sovereignty of the republics by assuming these powers. This paradox was paralleled in the relationship between the USSR and the other socialist states, where the USSR's right to intervene in the internal affairs of its allies was held to ensure, not undermine, their sovereignty. In both cases, the approach assumed a hierarchy of relationships—sovereignty, in this model, was always subordinated to the powers of the Soviet center without, in theory, limiting the sovereignty of the less powerful republics or states. It was from this starting point—a state that encoded, in law and practice, a set of political relations where the sovereignty of other entities was nominal, with all the powers of sovereign statehood residing with the center; where this structure was held to enhance the sovereignty of all parties; and where theoretical contradictions and conceptual impossibilities were dealt with by denying their existence—that the new states of the former Soviet Union had to constitute their relations to one another and to the rest of the world.

It was clear from the start that the views among the political elites and other actors differed about what sovereignty was going to mean in relation to the new states, both in theory and in practice. The comments by political leaders and documents such as declarations of state sovereignty clearly showed that states such as Ukraine viewed their sovereignty in Western terms; others, in particular senior officers of the former Soviet armed forces and members of the Russian government and parliament, appeared to view the sovereignty of those states other than Russia as conforming to the Soviet model of "nonsovereign" sovereignty, where "the center" would reserve key powers, in particular over security policy. The conflation of the structures of the CIS with those of the Russian government on the part of both members of the Russian political elite and military officials within the CIS further reinforced the view that the Moscow-as-center/republics-as-periphery model of sovereignty continued beyond the breakup of the Soviet Union to inform the structures of the CIS and the relations between member states.

It was in the context of this tension between different understandings of sovereignty, and thus different understandings of the status of both the CIS and Russia in relation to the other post-Soviet states, that the states were confronted with the second problem specific to the post-Soviet environment—the division of the assets of what had been the USSR. Unlike traditional processes of decolonization by empires, with which the Soviet Union was frequently compared in Western analysis, the collapse of the USSR was total, meaning that no metropolitan center remained to claim the residual assets. The question of what belonged to whom was thus entirely open—no universally recognized, single successor state to the USSR existed in the immediate post-Soviet period, and as a result, all the states were able to claim individual or shared ownership of what the USSR had left behind. Not surprisingly, the former Soviet armed forces were the most obvious and the most sensitive aspect of the Soviet Union's legacy. Their critical place in the political mythology of the USSR, the size of the forces (in terms of both personnel and assets), and the exceptionally high proportion of Soviet expenditure they represented, all meant that the former Soviet armed forces occupied the central place in negotiations over the USSR's residual assets, once the project to retain unified armed forces had failed. At stake in these negotiations—or disputes as they became in several cases—was not just the assets themselves, but the idea of entitlement, an idea that was critically dependent on the understanding of the rights of the states concerned. The contested understandings of what state sovereignty actually meant for the former Soviet republics, and in particular the Soviet-era idea that state sovereignty did not preclude (was, in fact, enhanced by) a hierarchical structure in which the center reserved key powers—that, to adapt the Orwellian aphorism, particularly on matters of security "all states are sovereign, but some states are more sovereign than others"—informed the negotiations over the future of the Soviet military legacy, compounding both the severity of the disputes and the difficulty in resolving them. It is with this problem that the rest of the book is concerned, beginning with most sensitive inheritance of all—the Soviet nuclear arsenal.

Notes

1. See Jens Bartelson, *A Genealogy of Sovereignty* (Cambridge: Cambridge University Press, 1995) and Thomas J. Biersteker and Cynthia Weber, "The Social Construction of State Sovereignty," in Biersteker and Weber, eds., *State Sovereignty as Social Construct* (Cambridge: Cambridge University Press, 1996). Bartelson— and Biersteker and Weber, drawing on Bartelson's analysis—argues that attempts to fix a definition of *sovereignty* contribute to beliefs that the term is ahistorical and therefore undercuts the possibilities for recognizing sovereignty as a changing, historically contingent idea. While not adopting a constructivist or postpositivist approach to the investigation of sovereignty, Hideaki Shinoda also focuses on "the struggles that took place over evaluating notions of sovereignty," rather than on providing a definition (*Re-examining Sovereignty: From Classical Theory to the Global Age* [Basingstoke, UK: Macmillan; London and New York: St. Martin's, 2000], p. 7).

2. Examples include F. H. Hinsley, *Sovereignty* (London: C. A. Watts, 1966); Sohail H. Hashmi, ed., *State Sovereignty: Change and Persistence in International Law* (University Park, PA: Pennsylvania State University Press, 1997); Alan James, *Sovereign Statehood: The Basis of International Society* (London: Allen and Unwin, 1986); and Stephen D. Krasner, *Sovereignty, Organized Hypocrisy* (Princeton, NJ: Princeton University Press, 1999).

3. Harry G. Gelber, *Sovereignty Through Interdependence* (London: Kluwer Law International, 1997), p. 99.

4. For example: Tony Blair's comment that "our aim from the outset has been to transfer power and sovereignty to the Iraqi people as soon as possible" ("PM Welcomes Iraqi Governing Council Announcement," available from www.number-10 .gov.uk/print/page4842.asp); and George W. Bush's assertion that "one central commitment is the transfer of sovereignty back to the Iraqi people," cited in Marc Grossman, "Testimony Before the House Armed Services Committee," 21 April 2004, available from www.state.gov/p/31719.htm.

5. Gelber, *Sovereignty*, p. 74.

6. See, for example, the work of James, *Sovereign Statehood;* Joseph A. Camilleri, "Rethinking Sovereignty in a Shrinking, Fragmented World," in R. B. J. Walker and Saul H. Mendlovitz, eds., *Contending Sovereignties: Redefining Political Community* (Boulder, CO: Lynne Rienner, 1990), p. 22; and Gelber, *Sovereignty*, p. 74.

7. James, *Sovereign Statehood*, p. 3. This definition rather confusingly blurs the distinction between the state and the political community it governs by apparently locating sovereignty with both.

8. Biersteker and Weber, "The Social Construction of State Sovereignty," p. 2.

9. Krasner, *Sovereignty, Organized Hypocrisy.*

10. Jean Bodin, *On Sovereignty, Four Chapters from the Six Books of the Commonwealth,* ed. and trans. by Julian H. Franklin (Cambridge: Cambridge University Press, 1992), p. 3.

11. Discussion of this point in relation to particular theorists can be found in James, *Sovereign Statehood*, p. 20.

12. Michael Ross Fowler and Julie Marie Bunck, *Law, Power, and the Sovereign State: The Evolution and Application of the Concept of Sovereignty* (University Park, PA: Pennsylvania State University Press, 1995), p. 70.

13. James, *Sovereign Statehood,* p. 5.

14. Öyvind Österud, "The Narrow Gate: Entry to the Club of Sovereign States," *Review of International Studies* 23, no. 2 (April 1997): 170.

15. The Basic Law of the Federal Republic of Germany, Article 32, available from www.bundestag.de/htdocs_e/ parliament/function/legal/germanbasiclaw.pdf.

16. The Constitution of the United States, Article 1, Section 10. For a discussion of US federalism, see David McKay, "Federalism: Why the States Still Matter," Chapter 4 in David McKay, *American Politics and Society,* 6th ed. (Oxford: Blackwell, 2005), pp. 59–78.

17. Alan James, "The Equality of States: Contemporary Manifestations of an Ancient Doctrine," *Review of International Studies* 18, no. 4 (1992): 380.

18. Robert H. Jackson, *Quasi-States: Sovereignty, International Relations, and the Third World,* Cambridge Studies in International Relations 12 (Cambridge: Cambridge University Press, 1990); Jorri Duursma, *Fragmentation and the International Relations of Micro-States: Self-determination and Statehood* (Cambridge: Cambridge University Press, 1996).

19. A point made in Fowler and Bunck, *Law, Power, and the Sovereign State,* pp. 21–24.

20. James (*Sovereign Statehood,* p. 17) notes this failure of the UN—an organization based, according to Article 1 of its charter, on "the principle of the sovereign equality of all its members" (The Charter of the United Nations, available from www.un.org/aboutun/charter/chapter1.htm).

21. V. S. Shevtsov, *National Sovereignty and the Soviet State* (Moscow: Progress Publishers, 1974), p. 71.

22. Article 29, Konstitutsiia (Osnovnoĭ Zakon) Soiuza Sovetskikh Sotsialisticheskikh Respublik (Moscow: Izdatel'stvo Politicheskoĭ Literatury, 1977).

23. On Soviet thought in this field, see Margot Light, *The Soviet Theory of International Relations* (Brighton, UK: Wheatsheaf, 1988). On the development of Soviet sovereignty theory, see Chapter 2 from Robert A. Jones, *The Soviet Concept of "Limited Sovereignty" from Lenin to Gorbachev: The Brezhnev Doctrine* (Basingstoke, UK: Macmillan, 1990).

24. E. A. Korovin, *Sovremennoye Mezhdunarodnoye Publichnoye Pravo* (1926), p. 8, cited in Mintauts Chakste, "Soviet Concepts of the State, International Law and Sovereignty," *The American Journal of International Law* 43, no. 1 (January 1949): 26.

25. I. D. Levin, *Printsip Suvereniteta v Sovetskom i Mezhdunarodnom Pravo* (Moscow, 1947), pp. 6–8, 24, cited in Chakste, "Soviet Concepts," p. 32. For a discussion of the Soviet distinction between socialist and capitalist state sovereignty, see also Shinoda, *Re-examining Sovereignty.*

26. Taken from a 1947 lecture by Korovin, cited in Chakste, "Soviet Concepts," p. 31.

27. Chakste, "Soviet Concepts," p. 34.

28. Ibid., p. 35.

29. See, for example, R. G. Abdulatipov, *Konstitutsiia SSSR i Natsional'nye Otnosheniia na Soveremennom Etape* (Moscow: Mysl', 1978).

30. On the federal structure of the USSR, its relationship to nationalism, the theory that informed it, and its role in the collapse of the USSR, see Gail Lapidus, Viktor Zaslavsky, and Philip Goldman, eds., *From Union to Commonwealth: Nationalism and Separatism in the Soviet Republics* (Cambridge: Cambridge University Press, 1992); Graham Smith, ed., *The Nationalities Question in the Soviet Union* (London:

Longman, 1990); and Ian Bremmer and Ray Taras, eds., *Nations and Politics in the Soviet Successor States* (Cambridge: Cambridge University Press, 1993).

31. Konstitutsiia SSSR.

32. For a contemporary exegesis of this point, see V. Vadimov, *Mezhdunarodnoe Znachenie Konstitutsii SSSR* (Moscow: Mezhdunarodnye Otnosheniia, 1977).

33. V. V. Yevgenyev, "Subjects of International Law, Sovereignty and Non Interference in International Law," *Sovetskoye Gosudarstvo i Pravo* 2 (March 1955): 76–77, quoted in Vernon V. Aspaturian, "The Union Republics and Soviet Diplomacy: Concepts, Institutions, and Practices," *The American Political Science Review* 53, no. 2 (June 1959): 387. For Western commentators, the constitutional and practical aspects of this issue were an anomaly in international politics that had arisen as a result of the Soviet desire to extend its influence internationally, above all in the UN, and these aspects did not in themselves act as markers of SSR sovereignty (on this point see, for example, Alan James, "Sovereignty: Ground Rule or Gibberish?" *Review of International Studies* 10, no. 1 [January 1984]: 1–18). The constitutionally specified capacities of the SSRs to make foreign policy were treated with skepticism. Writing in the late 1950s, Aspaturian noted that the authority of the SSRs over foreign relations was undermined by the fact that the union center had the authority to overturn a republic action of which it disapproved "in the unlikely event of a disagreement between the republics and central government"; he also observed the restriction in practice that was indicated by the fact that none of the republics had ever exchanged diplomatic or consular representation with another state (Aspaturian, "The Union Republics and Soviet Diplomacy," pp. 405, 408).

34. Konstitutsiia SSSR.

35. A. Shtromas, "The Legal Position of Soviet Nationalities and Their Territorial Units According to the 1977 Constitution of the USSR." *Russian Review* 37, no. 3 (July 1978): 270.

36. Konstitutsiia SSSR.

37. *The Soviet Constitution: A Dictionary* (Moscow: Progress Publishers, 1986), p. 246.

38. Shevtsov, *National Sovereignty,* pp. 84–85; Vadimov, *Mezhdunarodnoe Znachenie,* p. 85.

39. Shevtsov, *National Sovereignty,* p. 121.

40. Mark Vishniak, "Sovereignty in Soviet Law," *Russian Review* 8, no. 1 (January 1949): 39.

41. John N. Hazard, "Renewed Emphasis upon a Socialist International Law," *The American Journal of International Law* 65, no. 1 (January 1971): 146.

42. P. Y. Nedbailo and V. A. Vassilenko, *Soviet Yearbook of International Law,* Soviet Association of International Law (Moscow: Nauka, 1963), cited in Ivan Bernier, *International Legal Aspects of Federalism* (London: Longman, 1973), p. 23.

43. On the argument that republic sovereignty was preserved by the provision for secession see, for example, Aspaturian, "The Union Republics and Soviet Diplomacy," pp. 386–387; Hazard, "Renewed Emphasis," p. 146; and Shtromas, "Legal Position of Soviet Nationalities," p. 269. Vishniak, writing in the late 1940s, cites a contemporary Soviet text that asserts that the sovereignty of the republics was not undermined by membership of the USSR because the republics entered voluntarily ("Sovereignty in Soviet Law," p. 39).

44. Shevtsov, *National Sovereignty,* p. 95.

45. V. S. Shevtsov, *The State and Nations in the USSR* (Moscow: Progress Publishers, 1982), p. 121.

46. "The Soviet federation is a federation of an absolutely new, socialist type, harmoniously combining the advantages of a democratically centralised state with

broad independence and initiative of each nation within the framework of its national statehood." Shevtsov, *The State and Nations in the USSR,* p. 112.

47. For a more detailed discussion of this contradiction, see Bhagirath Prasad, "Rules of the Game: Communist Concept of Sovereignty," in *The Post-Communist Dilemma: Sovereignty as Fulcrum of Change in Eastern Europe* (New Delhi: Har-Anand, 1997).

48. Jones, *The Soviet Concept of "Limited Sovereignty,"* p. 11.

49. Light, *Soviet Theory,* p. 199.

50. Prasad, *The Post-Communist Dilemma,* p. 27.

51. On the arguments that the Soviet role strengthened the sovereignty of other socialist states, see Jones, *The Soviet Concept of "Limited Sovereignty,"* Chapter 1.

52. Hazard, "Renewed Emphasis," p. 146.

53. Jan Zaprudnik, *Belarus: At a Crossroads in History* (Boulder, CO: Westview, 1993), pp. 152–153.

54. Ibid., pp. 146–147.

55. Ibid., p. 153.

56. Declaration of State Sovereignty of Ukraine, available from http://gska2 .rada.gov.ua:7777/site/postanova_eng/Declaration_of_State_Sovereignty_of_Ukraine _rev1.htm.

57. See the discussion of the CIS and actors' perceptions in Chapter 3.

58. TASS (Telegraph Agency of the Soviet Union) International Service, 9 December 1991, *FBIS-SOV-91-237,* p. 56.

59. Ibid.

60. Ibid., pp. 56–57.

61. Also a feature of Russian-Belarusian integration and union agreements, as noted in Chapter 6.

62. One example of the priority given to military issues in the early period of the CIS was the fact that at the CIS heads of state meeting in Moscow in January 1992, eight out of ten items on the agenda addressed military issues (although in the event most of these were postponed to a later meeting).

63. *Rossiiskaia Gazeta,* 14 December 1991, in *The Current Digest of the Post-Soviet Press* (CDPSP) 43, no. 50 (1991), p. 13.

64. TASS, 21 December 1991, *FBIS-SOV-91-246,* pp. 29–30.

65. Richard Sakwa and Mark Webber argue that:

> The sensitivity to sovereignty among the CIS member states has had a major impact on the manner of the organisation's political development. It has affected its working practices and also the nature of political cooperation. The latter has tended to be effective where it has reaffirmed sovereignty and weak where it has implied supranationality and thus a compromise of state prerogatives. ("The Commonwealth of Independent States, 1991–1998: Stagnation and Survival," *Europe-Asia Studies* 51, no. 3 [May 1999]: 390)

66. For a discussion of the failed attempts to develop CIS security structures in the early 1990s, see William E. Odom, *The Collapse of the Soviet Military* (New Haven, CT: Yale University Press, 1998); Ronald M. Bonesteel, "The CIS Security System: Stagnating, in Transition or on the Way Out?" *European Security* 2, no. 1 (Spring 1993): 115–138.

67. CIS Treaty on Collective Security, *Rossiiskaia Gazeta,* 23 May 1992, *FBIS-SOV-92-101,* pp. 8–9.

68. Ibid.

69. Ibid.

70. "Article 4: If any one of the participating states is subjected to aggression by any state or group of states, this will be perceived as aggression against all participating states to this treaty. In the event of an act of aggression being committed against any of the participating states, all the other participating states will give it the necessary assistance, including military assistance."

71. ITAR-TASS (Information Telegraph Agency of Russia), 15 May 1992, *FBIS-SOV-92-099*, p. 19.

72. Ustav Sodruzhestva Nezavisimykh Gosudarstv, available from www.cis .minsk.by/main.aspx?uid=180.

73. Ibid.

74. Ibid.

75. Konstitutsiia SSSR.

76. Ibid.

77. See for example, Alexander Goncharenko, "Ukraine: National Interests Between the CIS and the West," in Roy Allison and Christopher Bluth, eds., *Security Dilemmas in Russia and Eurasia* (London: Royal Institute of International Affairs, 1998), pp. 121–133; Bobo Lo, "The CIS—Fact and Fiction," in *Russian Foreign Policy in the Post-Soviet Era: Reality, Illusion and Mythmaking* (Basingstoke, UK: Palgrave Macmillan, 2002), pp. 72–86; and Roman Solchanyk, "Ukraine, Russia and the CIS," in Lubomyr A. Hajda, ed., *Ukraine in the World: Studies in the International Relations and Security Structure of a Newly Independent State* (Cambridge, MA: Harvard University Press for the Ukrainian Research Institute, Harvard University, 1998), pp. 19–43.

78. *Segodnia*, 27 July 1994, in *The Current Digest of the Post-Soviet Press* (CDPSP) 46, no. 30 (1994), p. 23.

79. Ibid., p. 74.

80. TASS, 20 December 1991, *FBIS-SOV-91-246*, p. 63.

81. See, for example, the view expressed in a letter from Ukrainian foreign minister Udovenko to Kuchma following Yeltsin's decree of 14 September 1994 on "The Strategic Course of Russia Toward CIS Countries," that "'Integration,' the necessity and usefulness of which is declared in the decree, in practice means the demolition of the sovereignty of CIS countries, subordination of their activities to Russian national interests, and the revival of the centralised superpower." Cited by Goncharenko in "Ukraine," in Allison and Bluth, *Security Dilemma*, p. 126.

82. Profil, 27 January 1992, *FBIS-SOV-92-018*, p. 60.

83. *Izvestiia*, 26 March 1994, in *The Current Digest of the Post-Soviet Press* (CDPSP) 46, no. 12 (1994), p. 24.

84. ITAR-TASS, 15 May 1992, *FBIS-SOV-92-099*, p. 20.

85. TASS International Service, 14 February 1992, *FBIS-SOV-92-031*, p. 14.

86. TASS, 14 February 1992, *FBIS-SOV-92-032*, p. 15.

87. On the role of Russian peacekeeping in the CIS, see Lynch, *Russian Peacekeeping Strategies in the CIS: The Cases of Moldova, Georgia and Tajikistan* (Basingstoke, UK: Macmillan, 2000).

88. Interfax, 21 December 1991, *FBIS-SOV-91-246*, p. 26.

89. *Nezavisimaia gazeta*, 12 January 1994.

90. Vadim Lukov, "Russia's Security: The Foreign Policy Dimension," *International Affairs* (Moscow) 41, no. 8 (1995): 7.

91. *Izvestiia*, 4 March 1993, in *The Current Digest of the Post-Soviet Press* (CDPSP) 45, no. 9, p. 17.

92. Statement to the conference of CIS and Baltic ambassadors, January 1994, quoted by Alexei Arbatov, "Russian Security Interests and Dilemmas: and Agenda

for the Future," in Alexei Arbatov et al., eds., *Managing Conflict in the Former Soviet Union: Russian and American Perspectives,* BCSIA Studies in International Security (Cambridge: MIT Press, 1997), p. 429.

93. ITAR-TASS World Service, 17 March 1993, *FBIS-SOV-93-050,* p. 7.

94. Andrei Kozyrev, "Russian Interests in the CIS," *International Affairs* (Moscow) 40, no. 11 (1994): 11–30.

95. *International Affairs* (Moscow) 39, no. 1 (1993): 14.

96. "The Basic Provisions of the Russian Federation's Military Doctrine," p. 11.

97. Ibid., p. 12.

98. *Rossiiskaia gazeta,* 25 February 1992, *FBIS-SOV-92-017,* p. 19.

99. *Krasnaia Zvezda,* 28 December 1991, p. 1.

100. *Krasnaia Zvezda,* 23 January 1992, *FBIS-SOV-92-016,* p. 24.

101. *Krasnaia Zvezda,* 5 February 1992, *FBIS-SOV-92-026,* p. 11.

102. This has, of course, remained a concern for other CIS member states in the period following the failure of the Joint Armed Forces project. One Ukrainian analyst, for example, has said that "contrary to previous agreements, Moscow has become the centre for all CIS activities: all of the organisation's major committees and ruling bodies are run by Russians; the completely Russified CIS Defence Council has evolved into a puppet body used to confer formal approval of the Kremlin's military operations within the CIS states" (Goncharenko, "Ukraine," in Allison and Bluth, *Security Dilemmas,* pp. 124–125).

103. Interview with *Moscow News,* no. 6, 21 February 1992, p. 4.

3

Nuclear Weapons:
Russia, Ukraine, and Belarus

On 1 January 1992, with the dissolution of the USSR, four nuclear states came into existence, replacing one nuclear superpower. Of all the security issues raised by the breakup of the Soviet Union, this was undoubtedly the one that caused the greatest immediate concern and interest internationally. Literally overnight, thousands of strategic nuclear warheads (and an unknown quantity of tactical nuclear weapons) that had previously been owned by a single state and subject to international arms control regimes became politically relocated to four new states in a region undergoing radical, destabilizing political and economic change. In addition to the nuclear weapons located on the territory of the Russian Federation, 81 SS-25 strategic missiles were on the territory of the independent state of Belarus, 1,410 warheads were in Kazakhstan, and 1,240 warheads and 44 strategic bombers were located in Ukraine.[1] Although the nuclear issue was resolved relatively quickly—all nuclear weapons had been removed from the territories of Belarus, Kazakhstan, and Ukraine by late 1996—its impact on relations within the former Soviet Union, and between these former Soviet states and the rest of the world (especially the nuclear powers), has been much longer lasting and more profound.

International concerns and intervention, above all on the part of the United States, focused primarily on two factors—the de facto proliferation of nuclear weapons caused by the emergence of four ex-Soviet states with nuclear weapons based on their territory; and the possibilities for proliferation through the export or theft of nuclear material and technology from these states. The priority for the United States and the other nuclear powers was the containment of nuclear technology and capability by restricting post-Soviet nuclear weapons possession as much as possible—in practice, to the Russian Federation. For the four ex-Soviet states in possession of nuclear weapons, the issues surrounding the former Soviet nuclear arsenal were broader and more complex. These states' nuclear weapons policies were focused not on the global security-specific concerns of proliferation but rather on the importance of nuclear weapons as symbols and bargaining chips within the wider framework of post-Soviet economic and security relations.[2] As became clear at a very early stage in the post-Soviet period, the nuclear weapons of the former USSR were negotiated over and talked about by political elites in a way that suggested that their central function was not as weapons but as a means of defining the place of former Soviet states as independent both within the wider international security arena and, in particular, in relation to one another.

As discussed in the previous chapter, sections of the Russian political and military elites—and the predominantly Russian-national CIS military elites—approached the idea of state sovereignty from an essentially Soviet perspective. This "nonsovereign" sovereignty was clearly not endorsed by Ukrainian political and military elites; the Belarusian position was somewhat different, moving over time toward an apparent readoption of the Soviet model. It is not surprising that this dispute about the possibility for sovereignty in the post-Soviet space should have emerged so strongly in the military arena as states attempted to resolve the question of what to do with the former Soviet armed forces, given the traditional primacy of military capability as a means of ensuring state sovereignty from external threats. In addition to the broader sovereignty functions of security policy and assets, however, the post-Soviet nuclear arsenal raised very specific issues concerning state sovereignty—both because of the nature of nuclear weapons and because of the particularities of the post-Soviet nuclear problem.

In this context, this chapter looks at the removal of strategic nuclear weapons from Ukraine and Belarus. It considers the way in which attempts to resolve the issue of the former Soviet nuclear arsenal were interlinked with the disputes between Russia and the other Soviet states over the development of state sovereignty in the sphere of military policy. It begins with an outline of some of the factors affecting the resolution of the post-Soviet nuclear weapons question. It then examines the denuclearization of Ukraine, then Belarus, in each case looking at both the key actions taken by their governments and parliaments and the Russian responses to them, and exploring the ways in which the conflicting assumptions about the nature and possible limits of the sovereignty of these two states influenced the manner and timescale of denuclearization.

The relationship between nuclear weapons and sovereignty is a complex issue, and one that will only be touched on briefly here. The existence of nuclear weapons has been seen as a fundamental challenge to the idea that a state can ever achieve full sovereignty in the absence of any means to protect the territorial integrity of a state from a nuclear missile attack. However, the possession of nuclear weapons has also historically been seen by states as both a guarantee and a marker of state sovereignty. Nuclear weapons are held, on a practical level, to be guarantees of sovereignty because of the deterrence value they possess, and thus, on a symbolic level, as markers of sovereignty—as a result, the possession of even a small number of nuclear weapons can act as a marker of state sovereignty. Conversely, the nonownership of nuclear weapons can be seen as a limitation of sovereignty; in particular, some analysts have viewed the Nuclear Non-Proliferation Treaty (NPT) as imposing a limitation on the state sovereignty of its nonnuclear signatories.[3] Finally, the frequently discussed symbolic function of nuclear weapons as prestige indicators is predicated on a conception of sovereign statehood. In this context, as Scott Sagan argues, nuclear weapons can also perform another, related, function for the state, as "an important normative symbol of a state's modernity and identity"; this, he suggests, can explain some aspects of nuclear policy that cannot be explained by viewing nuclear weapons solely as instruments of a narrowly defined security policy.[4]

The linkages between nuclear weapons and conceptions of state sovereignty are particularly evident in the post-Soviet case, where state independence and membership of the nuclear club occurred simultaneously. The debates within each state, and the bilateral discussions between Russia on the one hand and Belarus and Ukraine on the other, reflect the extent to which the nuclear weapons issue was constructed by all sides in terms of state sovereignty and the way in which the contrasting character of this debate in Belarus and in Ukraine reflected a radically different approach by these states to their newly acquired state sovereignty. Interestingly, and for reasons considered below, neither Belarus nor Ukraine conceived of the permanent ownership of nuclear weapons as a feature of their independent statehood, although a majority of Ukrainian and some Belarusian political actors viewed the establishment of claims to *temporary* ownership of these weapons as critical to the assertion of sovereignty, specifically sovereignty in relation to Russia.[5] Thus, the negotiations and disputes around nuclear weapons reflected and reinforced the ways in which different understandings of sovereignty and security emerged in the post-Soviet period, and the ways in which, in this period, key security assets had a symbolic value in relations between Russia and other successor states that far exceeded their material value, at least as security instruments.[6] As discussed in the introduction, the construction and therefore the practice of sovereignty cannot be separated from the issue of power relations involved in any interaction or relationship. In this case, however, and unlike the cases of the Black Sea Fleet and the use of military bases during the 1990s (although not subsequently), the impact of power inequalities between Russia and the other two states was moderated significantly by the engagement of actors external to the post-Soviet region, in particular the active engagement of the United States in the denuclearization process.

Obstacles to Denuclearization

Although the removal of nuclear weapons from three states, all of which were committed from the moment of their emergence as independent states to achieving nonnuclear status, seems like a relatively simple issue, it was in fact a highly opaque and complicated process of negotiations within and between states. All strategic nuclear weapons had been removed from these states by the end of 1996, and at no point during the five years it took to complete this process did it appear that the governments of any of these states would attempt to retain the missiles on their territory. Yet despite this absence of a serious threat to the denuclearization process, the presence of nuclear weapons on the territories of Belarus, Kazakhstan, and, in particular, Ukraine was the subject of acrimonious debate between Russia and these states and caused deep international concern, most visibly in the United States. This was, in part, a consequence of the number of issues that complicated the process, some of which were a consequence of the global interest in resolving this issue, and some of which were a function of the political, security, economic, and organizational turmoil of the period immediately following the collapse of the USSR. Factors that complicated any resolution of the nuclear weapons issue included the number of actors involved; the variety of forums in which they met to discuss it; the costs of denuclearization; the impact of the organizational turmoil that characterized the former Soviet armed forces in this period; and the interaction of the nuclear issue with other security problems, in particular the way in which nuclear weapons were used as instruments for addressing other security concerns.

As will be discussed below, it was clear that both the United States and Russia, positioning itself as inheritor of the Soviet Union's nuclear responsibilities, were keen to retain the bilateral structure of the existing international arms control agreements, despite the presence of three other post-Soviet states with nuclear weapons on their territory. However, Ukraine in particular was not prepared to accept this relegation of its status as newly independent state to that of de facto client state of Russia within the nonproliferation framework. Within the space of the former Soviet Union, the four inheritors of the Soviet nuclear arsenal were also required to engage with another actor in the nuclear weapons debate, the CIS Joint Armed Forces command and its subordinate strategic forces command, whose senior officers were not prepared to acknowledge any right to own, control, or determine the future of nuclear weapons on the part of Belarus, Kazakhstan, or Ukraine. Although we might expect to treat the CIS strategic forces as a distinct actor in these debates, their adherence to a strongly pro-Russian position (discussed in the previous chapter) means that it is very difficult to untangle their role from that of the Russian armed forces. In addition to these actors, the governments involved in these international agreements had to obtain the consent of their parliaments, who often adopted radically different positions on nuclear matters from their own governments. In the case of Ukraine, the demands by nationalist parliamentary deputies for greater security guarantees, and on occasion for the retention by Ukraine of nuclear weapons, stalled the process of treaty ratification, and exacerbated both US concerns and tensions with Russia.

A second complicating factor was the variety of international structures for the resolution of the post-Soviet nuclear issue, confusing the question of who had the authority to make decisions and sign agreements in this area. In addition to the bilateral Russian-US negotiating frameworks, the United States promoted its nonproliferation agenda through a series of trilateral and bilateral meetings with the other three states, leading ultimately to the Lisbon summit and the signing of the Lisbon Protocol to the START I Treaty, and to the Trilateral Agreement between the United States, Russia, and Ukraine in 1994. More confusingly, the question of denuclearization on the part of Belarus, Kazakhstan, and Ukraine was officially placed within the institutional framework of the CIS, through treaties and the arrangements for its strategic forces, but was in fact driven by bilateral relations between these states and Russia. This is particularly problematic because not all of the agreements reached bilaterally with Russia were compatible with the agreements signed within the CIS framework, or with the international agreements signed with the other nuclear states.[7]

Two other central problems in the attempt to resolve the issue of the former Soviet nuclear arsenal, both of which were direct consequences of the post-Soviet environment, were the economic costs of implementing agreements to denuclearize and the impact of the breakup of the former Soviet armed forces. The former Soviet states argued that, given the extent of economic collapse in the states concerned, they were unable to meet either the costs of removing and dismantling the nuclear missiles and their infrastructure or the costs of maintaining the weapons in secure conditions until their removal. Various funding arrangements were made by the United States under its Nunn-Lugar program, but the demands both for financial assistance and for compensation persisted throughout the denuclearization period. This was a problematic area, not least because of the perception on the part of some actors that states were seeking to profit from the denuclearization by demanding more money than the process itself required—an allegation rejected by those involved.[8]

A factor that greatly added to the difficulties of denuclearization was the uncertainty and confusion that accompanied the division of the former Soviet armed forces. From December 1991 until mid-1993 the CIS Joint Armed Forces had responsibility for command of all the strategic forces of the former USSR. With the failure of the project to retain a unified command within the CIS, the issue of which states had command of these forces became highly contentious. Even prior to the collapse of the project, however, the question was complicated by the disagreement—particularly between Russia and Ukraine, and largely in the context of the dispute over the Black Sea Fleet—over what was included in the CIS strategic forces and, as a result, which forces could be absorbed into the new national armies.

Finally, negotiations over nuclear weapons cannot be isolated from other security concerns, including the attempts to divide other assets of the former Soviet armed forces among the various CIS states and concerns over external security threats. The positions taken by the Ukrainian government and parliament, in particular, were explicitly linked at key points to the dispute with Russia over the ownership of the Black Sea Fleet, as well as to the claim made by the Russian parliament to Russian ownership of the Crimean peninsula. The Ukrainian government's linkage of nuclear weapons to other security issues, and the difference between Russia and Ukraine regarding the issue of control over the missiles, prompted Russian accusations that the fate of the former Soviet nuclear arsenal was being used as a political "trump card" in post-Soviet relations and in relations with extraregional states.[9] In the case of Belarus, deteriorating relations with NATO states after denuclearization was completed were marked by occasional threats to have Russia return nuclear weapons to its territory.

Ukraine and Russia

The process of Ukrainian denuclearization provides a clear example of the way in which security issues in the immediate post-Soviet period were treated by post-Soviet political and military elites as a site of debate over sovereignty. Although the Ukrainian government was committed from the outset to a complete removal of nuclear weapons from its territory, concerns about a perceived threat to Ukrainian territorial integrity and political sovereignty from Russia, and related concerns about the failure of the West to provide security guarantees to Ukraine in the face of this threat, contributed to a reluctance to comply with international expectations about the timescale and manner of weapons removal. In many of the debates between Ukraine and the other nuclear states, the denuclearization issue was explicitly linked to concerns about the central markers of state sovereignty—territorial integrity; noninterference in internal affairs; ownership of assets on state territory; and governmental control over events occurring within the borders of the state (specifically, the control over the movement and disposal of nuclear weapons). In contrast, the discourse of key sections of the Russian and CIS political and military elites challenged all these sovereignty principles as they applied to the Ukrainian nuclear issue. This dispute over nuclear weapons demonstrates the way that in the Ukraine-Russia bilateral relationship sovereignty and security concepts developed a negative interdependency—stronger Ukrainian assertions of sovereignty over the nuclear weapons issue were perceived as a threat to Russian security, while Russian attempts to increase its security (through control of the post-Soviet nuclear arsenal) were viewed as a challenge to Ukrainian sovereignty and, indeed, as an attempt to block it. Much of the debate revolved around two principles, closely linked to sovereignty—those of ownership and control. These in turn were linked to more pragmatic concerns—if Ukraine owned nuclear weapons, it had to be compensated for them; if Ukraine had "administrative" control of these weapons, its position had to be given greater weight in international negotiations.

One of the notable features of the Ukrainian nuclear weapons debate was that it occurred within the state as well as between Ukraine and other states. Unlike Belarus, where there was never a significant body of opinion opposed to the governmental position, Ukraine experienced divisions within its political elite on the subject, most dramatically in the form of resistance within the legislature to executive attempts to ratify international agreements on denuclearization. Some sections of the Ukrainian military and the political elite attempted to promote the idea that Ukraine should retain its nuclear weapons, which were seen as the best security guarantee in response to the perceived Russian security threat, and specifically in the face of Russian governmental claims to the Black Sea Fleet and Russian parliamentary claims to Crimea. In early 1993, both Kravchuk and Ukrainian foreign minister Anatoly Zlenko commented to the press on the growing levels of parliamentary opposition to the handover of nuclear weapons, while in the same period the chairman of the Congress of National Democratic Forces (CNDF) stated that Ukraine should retain its nuclear weapons; one of the CNDF parliamentary deputies compared the idea of handing nuclear weapons over to Russia to Kuwait handing over its weapons to Iraq.[10] In March 1993, during the opening session of hearings on START ratification, some deputies expressed the view that nuclear disarmament should only take place in conjunction with disarmament by *all* the former Soviet states.[11] The following month, Yuri Kostenko, head of the Ukrainian delegation to nuclear weapons talks, claimed that it would be less expensive for Ukraine to maintain nuclear weapons than to dismantle them; the following day, the Fourth Congress of the Ukrainian Officers' Union announced its support for continued nuclear status for Ukraine.[12] Although similar opinions continued to be expressed—in particular during 1993, when tensions with Russia over nuclear weapons were greatest—the government itself remained committed to a policy of denuclearization, contrary to the concerns of some analysts.[13] The path to eventual denuclearization, however, was not straightforward.

The Path to Ukrainian Denuclearization

At the start of the 1990s, Ukraine's commitment to nonnuclear status emerged as an important aspect of its identity as a post-Soviet, independent state. As in Belarus, which was also committed to nonnuclear status, the impact of the still-recent Chernobyl disaster on Ukraine contributed to this conception of a national identity bound up with the renunciation of nuclear weapons. In addition, nonnuclear status also served as a clear marker distinguishing Ukraine from the Soviet Union—evident in then foreign minister Zlenko's assertion that:

> Ukraine never played any role in the decision-making process which led to the creation of the third largest nuclear force in the world on its territory. . . . In fact, Ukraine is less responsible for the existence of these weapons on its territory than those countries which, through their multi-million dollar loans and credits to the former Soviet Union, helped, in part, to finance the Soviet military machine, including its nuclear component.[14]

The commitment to a nonnuclear Ukraine was given prominence in early documents relating to the emergent Ukrainian state. The Ukrainian SSR's mid-1990 Declaration of the State Sovereignty of Ukraine stated that: "The Ukrainian SSR solemnly declares its intention of becoming a permanently neutral state that does not participate in military blocs and adheres to three nuclear-free principles: to accept, to produce and to purchase no nuclear weapons."[15] A resolution "On the Nuclear-Free Status of Ukraine" was passed in October 1991, several weeks before the final dissolution of the USSR. Thus, the movement toward nonnuclear status developed with the movement toward independence, preceding the collapse of the USSR and thus also the moment at which Ukraine was forced to address the practical implications of a post-Soviet, nuclear inheritance. In the view of Ukraine's former defense minister Kostiantyn Morozov, this was one of the causes of what he regarded as a mistaken approach to the issue of nuclear weapons. He claimed that

> no one anywhere in the world had ever approached so important a problem as nuclear disarmament in such a declaratory fashion. Declarations were approved in Parliament without an examination of government programmes, without technical assessments, without financial estimates, and without many other necessary considerations.[16]

Nevertheless, declarations regarding Ukrainian denuclearization continued beyond the collapse of the USSR. Within days of the initial CIS founding agreement, Ukraine was committing itself both to complete elimination of nuclear weapons from its territory (within a period of not more than seven years and possibly in as little as three) and the retention of centralized command of strategic forces on its territory under the CIS.[17] By late December,

Zlenko had produced a "Summary of Measures Proposed for the Protection of the National Interests of Ukraine," which reaffirmed the commitment to denuclearization and stated that control over nuclear weapons should be transferred to the joint command of the four ex-Soviet nuclear states.[18] This conformed to the CIS agreement of 21 December 1991 on joint measures with respect to nuclear weapons, which committed Ukraine and the other three states to joint command of nuclear weapons under the CIS Joint Armed Forces; to the signing of the NPT by Belarus, Kazakhstan, and Ukraine as nonnuclear states; and to the removal of tactical weapons from all three states to Russia by 1 July 1992. It also gave the Russian president the authority to decide on nuclear weapons use, in consultation with the other three presidents.

Throughout the period leading up to the complete removal of nuclear weapons from Ukraine, the Ukrainian government repeatedly stated its commitment to denuclearization and entered into international agreements committing it to nonnuclear status. Yet from early 1992 onward serious disagreements emerged between the Ukrainian government and the Russian government and CIS military revolving around competing claims to determine the future of these nuclear weapons. An early manifestation of this dispute came with the Ukrainian response to Boris Yeltsin's apparently unilateral decision to make disarmament commitments to the international community in late January 1992. Interviewed about this move, Kravchuk stated that

> Yeltsin did not consult with me, he acted autonomously. His decisions are provoking considerable concern here and are giving rise to serious questions. First: he stated that strategic missiles no longer are targeted on America and the West. The question arises: On whom are they now targeted? We would like to know what the new targets are. . . . Whereas we decided to establish a national army, Russia did not. The strategic weapons belong to the Commonwealth of Independent States. So how can the Russian President cut weapons he does not have? . . . Why is Yeltsin speaking on our behalf without consulting us? This is not right. . . . Our strategic potential may not be very great but it is not up to him to decide its fate. Ukraine has its own policy: to eliminate all tactical nuclear weapons by this June and all strategic weapons in the course of 1994, thus achieving non-nuclear status.[19]

This sense that the Russian government and the CIS Joint Armed Forces command rejected not only the concept of Ukrainian authority to determine the future of nuclear weapons on its territory but even that the non-Russian CIS states should be involved in real joint control (as opposed to the nominal control set out in the CIS agreements on nuclear weapons) increased Ukrainian reluctance to cooperate in the agreed processes of denuclearization. In March 1992, Ukraine suspended its transfer of tactical nuclear weapons to Russia, pending guarantees from the Russian government that the transferred weapons were being destroyed, as agreed. Not surprisingly, this caused outrage among the Russian political elite and media, who accused Ukraine variously of violating the CIS agreement to remove all tactical nuclear weapons from Belarus and Ukraine by 1 July 1992, of manipulating the weapons transfer for political advantage in the run-up to negotiations over the division of the Black Sea Fleet at the March CIS Heads of State summit, and of the desire to become a permanent nuclear state.[20] Although the details of negotiations to resolve this problem are unclear—Ukraine, for example, repeatedly denied Russian claims that discussions on the matter had taken place at the CIS summit meeting or that Yeltsin and Kravchuk had spoken about it in a telephone conversation of 16 March—the transfer of tactical nuclear weapons resumed the following month.

This suspension of weapons transfer was one of the clearest possible signals of Ukrainian belief in its authority over the activities taking place in its territory, and specifically of the belief that Ukraine had sovereign decision-making powers in respect to the nuclear weapons on its territory. The suspension, it has been suggested, was one of the factors contributing to the establishment of a Russian Ministry of Defense (although with Russian troops still under joint CIS command).[21] Yeltsin's decree described this as means of "implementing my sovereign right to ensure security, with the purpose of perfecting the system of collective security and of implementing strict control over nuclear and other types of weapons of mass destruction."[22]

Although not explicitly linked by any of the parties involved, the timing of the weapons transfer suspension coincided with the negotiations over the proposed status of Ukraine, Belarus, and Kazakhstan in respect to the START I Treaty ratification, which reflected the competing Ukrainian and Russian perceptions of sovereignty in relation to nuclear weapons. Since the treaty was signed in July 1991, it was a bilateral treaty between the United States and the USSR. Russia argued that it should remain bilateral, with its formal commitments inherited solely by Russia and with the other three former Soviet states agreeing to let it act as sole nuclear inheritor of the USSR. Ukraine took a very different position, believing that all four of the states with nuclear weapons on their territory needed to be treated as parties to START and thus needed to ratify the treaty.[23] This was a problematic demand for the international nuclear community as well as for Russia, since the sovereignty over decisionmaking about nuclear weapons that would be implied by including the other three states in the official treaty processes would also formalize their positions as nuclear states, challenging the existing form of the NPT. Under pressure from the United States, this dispute was resolved by the agreement of all parties to a protocol to START I, known as the Lisbon Protocol, signed in May 1992. This recognized all four of the former Soviet states as successor states to the USSR for the purposes of the treaty and required all of them to ratify it, thus (though not explicitly) acknowledging the sovereignty of all four states over the former Soviet nuclear arsenal.[24] In return for this recognition, Belarus, Kazakhstan, and Ukraine were to ratify the NPT "as non-nuclear weapon states Parties in the shortest possible time."[25]

Despite the signing of the Lisbon Protocol by Ukraine, the issues of START I and NPT ratification and the related issue of Ukraine's nuclear status remained unresolved. The Ukrainian parliament's debate on START ratification was repeatedly delayed throughout early 1993, as it became apparent that the Ukrainian government's position was not shared by many parliamentary deputies. In closed hearings in April, parliament rejected the proposed Ukrainian military doctrine, reportedly after disputes over the doctrine's commitment to a nonnuclear status for Ukraine. The hardening of the Ukrainian parliamentary mood (and, to a lesser extent, that of the government) needs to be understood in the context of the deteriorating relations with Russia, connected to the nationalist orientation of the Russian parliament. Of most concern was the Russian parliament's position on the status of Crimea, in particular the May 1992 Russian parliamentary resolution that declared the 1954 transfer of Crimea to Ukraine to have been illegal and the July 1993 resolution giving Sevastopol Russian federal status.

Relations between Ukraine and Russia on the interlinked questions of nuclear weapons, Crimea, and the Black Sea Fleet, which were poor throughout the earlier part of 1993, reached a low point in September with a row about whether the Ukrainian text of the Massandra agreement had been modified after the summit to limit the scope of its application to the strategic nuclear missiles in Ukraine. In early September 1993, the Massandra summit between Ukraine and Russia produced a series of agreements on nuclear weapons—a general protocol on the dismantling of nuclear warheads, a more specific agreement on this dismantling, an agreement on the maintenance of nuclear weapons, and agreement on Russian compensation to Ukraine for the nuclear weapons it was handing over. Within a few days, however, a serious dispute erupted between the two states when a Ukrainian newspaper published the Ukrainian copy of the agreements with handwritten changes made by the Ukrainian side, removing the reference to "all" warheads and replacing it with a reference to nuclear warheads "covered by the treaty" (START). The changes meant that only around one-third of weapons on Ukrainian territory were still covered by the agreement, and it did not, therefore, include at least 460 warheads on SS-24 intercontinental ballistic missiles (ICBMs).[26] The Russian foreign ministry claimed that the handwritten changes were made after Russia had signed the treaty and that as a result the protocol was void. Ukraine, however, refused to remove the changes despite Russian protests, arguing that it had been altered by hand because the Russian side submitted incomplete versions for signing. The dispute was not resolved and the status of the Massandra agreement remained uncertain.

When the vote on START I was finally held in November 1993, it was ratified with thirteen qualifications, including both the removal of Article 5 of the Lisbon Protocol which required Ukraine to join the NPT as a non-nuclear state and an assertion that the weapons were the state property of Ukraine and that Ukraine therefore exercised administrative control over the strategic nuclear forces on its territory. Not surprisingly, these qualifications were denounced by a broad spectrum of organizations and states, including the Organization for Security and Co-operation in Europe (OSCE) and the US and Russian governments. The Russian government responded in more concrete terms, too, threatening to impose energy sanctions on Ukraine and, it was claimed, to halt the maintenance of nuclear weapons in Ukraine.[27] Following a further round of negotiations, however, the qualifications were removed in January 1994 after the signing of the Trilateral Agreement by Ukraine, Russia, and the United States. This agreement provided Ukraine with a reaffirmation of Russian and US recognition of Ukrainian sovereignty, including a commitment to refrain from the threat or use of force against its territorial integrity or political independence, and with a statement of US commitment to financial assistance with denuclearization. Security guarantees from both Russia and the United States and financial assistance from the United States had been consistent demands of the Ukrainian government; the involvement of the United States was critical not just for financial reasons but for its "honest broker" role on the fraught questions of sovereignty, security, and (given Russia and Ukraine's prior experience of the fragility of bilateral treaties) trustworthiness.[28] In November 1994, the Ukrainian parliament voted by 301 to 8 to accede to the NPT; with that, strategic nuclear weapons effectively ceased to be an issue in Russian-Ukrainian relations.

The Problem of Safety

Much of the dispute over the weapons revolved around the questions of ownership and control (both of the launch capability and of the command structures of the strategic forces). However, the safety of the warheads also proved to be a significant area of dispute between the two states, and one which also engaged the attention of the international community. As with the denuclearization issue as a whole, however, the safety dispute between Russia and Ukraine had an additional focus and function to the safety concerns of the wider international community. For Russia in particular, safety concerns appear to have been used instrumentally, to exert additional pressure at critical points in the wider dispute over nuclear weapons, particularly in response to Ukrainian claims regarding ownership and administrative control.

Throughout the denuclearization process, the Russian government and media repeatedly claimed that nuclear weapons under Ukrainian administrative control were unsafe because of Ukrainian failure to maintain them, in some cases asserting that the Ukrainian forces were blocking access to the weapons by Russian maintenance troops.[29] These accusations peaked in the first half of 1993, when Russian-Ukrainian nuclear relations had deteriorated and before the United States' policy reorientation toward an active role in the Ukrainian denuclearization process; in this context, they were clearly perceived by Ukraine as an attempt to pressure it into recognizing Russian authority over the missiles.[30] This view was given additional credibility by the timing and location of many of these claims, which appeared designed to exert maximum pressure on the Ukrainian decisionmaking process, but which often appeared to harden the Ukrainian position instead.

Thus, in February 1993, the period when the Ukrainian parliament was considering whether to ratify START I, *Izvestiia* published claims that Ukraine was unable to maintain the nuclear missiles on its territory due to lack of funding and governmental unwillingness to send them to Russia for repairs, and that consequently, "a second Chernobyl is brewing in Ukraine's missile silos" (significantly, the paper claimed that such problems did not exist in Belarus and Kazakhstan, both of which were more cooperative in agreeing to Russian demands over nuclear weapons).[31] Two days later, the Ukrainian parliament announced the postponement of the debate on START I ratification. In March 1993, during the Russian parliamentary hearings on START II ratification, and three days before the opening of Ukraine's parliamentary hearings on START I ratification, a senior Russian military official claimed that nuclear weapons in Ukraine were unsafe and leaking a thousand times more gamma radiation than those in Russia.[32] Later that month, at a meeting of the North Atlantic Cooperation Council in which the issue of Ukrainian denuclearization was being discussed, Pavel Grachev repeated the "second Chernobyl" allegation; in response, the Ukrainian defense and foreign ministries issued a statement attacking the claims and accusing Russia of manufacturing concern over nuclear weapons on Ukrainian territory in order to extend Russian control over the weapons and to block Ukrainian compensation claims regarding their components.[33]

Similar allegations appeared at other key moments in the negotiating process between Russia and Ukraine. The day after the publication of the Ukrainian copy of the Massandra agreement with handwritten changes, the Russian paper *Nezavisimaia Gazeta* published a report that a "critical situation" was developing at Ukrainian nuclear weapons storage facilities; this was followed by a similar article in *Izvestiia*.[34] In October 1993, as the Ukrainian parliament was considering the draft military doctrine (key aspects of which were clearly directed against Russian policy toward Ukraine), a senior Russian ministry of defense officer with nuclear weapons responsibility claimed that some warheads in Ukraine had exceeded their service lives and were unsafe—despite the signing by Russia and Ukraine of protocols on servicing and support for warheads in Ukraine a few days earlier.[35] In November 1993, the decision by the Ukrainian parliament to ratify the

START I treaty with qualifications led to a statement by the Russian government denouncing the ratification qualifications and again claiming that Ukrainian nuclear weapons were potentially unsafe. In addition, however, it threatened to halt the maintenance of nuclear weapons in Ukraine in response to the qualified ratification. This demonstrates perhaps most clearly of all the way in which the Russian government attempted to use the issue of weapons safety to pressurize Ukraine into accepting Russian demands.

The Question of Ownership

In addition to the various debates about safety, deadlines, and compensation for the removal of nuclear weapons from the territory of Ukraine—the issues that were of overriding concern to the United States and the rest of the international community—Ukraine and Russia were engaged in a protracted dispute about two questions that related directly to the issue of sovereignty in the security sphere, the questions of ownership of the nuclear weapons and of their control. Western analysis has generally only considered these questions in as far as they affected the timescale for Ukrainian denuclearization, yet they are equally important for an understanding of the underlying concerns driving the difficult bilateral relations between Russia and Ukraine on the nuclear issue.

Unlike Belarus, which never laid claim to ownership of the nuclear weapons on its territory, the Ukrainian government and legislature repeatedly stated that those nuclear weapons that were present within the territory of Ukraine at the time of independence belonged to the Ukrainian state. The question of ownership was not, initially, addressed explicitly by the Ukrainian government, but it structured many of the problems that arose in agreeing a denuclearization program for the post-Soviet states. Initially, the issue of ownership was confused by the contradictory nature of national laws and international agreements that addressed issues of post-Soviet inheritance and ownership of assets formerly owned by the USSR. Two positions emerged on the issue of ownership of those nuclear weapons on Ukrainian territory at the moment of independence. Ukraine argued that it owned the nuclear weapons on its territory, as it did all other assets on Ukrainian territory at the time of independence. On 2 July 1993, the Ukrainian parliament adopted a resolution on the main guidelines of foreign policy which stated that Ukraine was the owner of nuclear weapons inherited by it from the USSR. The basis for this position was the law passed by the Ukrainian Supreme Soviet on 10 September 1991 that determined that all property on Ukrainian territory belonged to Ukraine—a point that Kravchuk and others made repeatedly in public during 1993.[36] The most straightforward version of the Ukrainian argument was given by Kravchuk, who stated that "in accordance with our legislation, everything that there is on Ukrainian territory belongs to Ukraine. That is also the case with Russian legislation: every-thing that is situated on Russian land belongs to Russia. This is stated in the adopted CIS documents."[37] This appeared to contradict the claims made on other occasions (in response to Russian ownership claims) that the weapons belonged to the CIS; it also, of course, raised serious questions about Ukraine's nonnuclear status. These apparently contradictory positions appear to have been resolved in the position that although the weapons belonged to the CIS *as weapons,* the component parts belonged to Ukraine. In either case, however, a critical concern seems to have been to oppose Russian claims to ownership.

The Russian position, most frequently expressed in response to Ukrain-ian ownership claims, was that all nuclear weapons that had previously belonged to the USSR now belonged to Russia, because Russia was the legal, nuclear successor of the USSR, as recognized in international agree-ments, including those that had been signed by Ukraine. One of the most detailed statements to this effect was released in April 1993, at the height of the Russian-Ukrainian dispute:

> Ukrainian representatives plainly declare that these nuclear weapons belong to Ukraine. Such statements can only be interpreted as a claim by Ukraine to the possession of nuclear weapons. The stance adopted by the Ukrainian leadership indicates direct violation of the decision adopted by the CIS heads of state on 6 July 1992 about the participation of CIS mem-ber states in the treaty on non-proliferation of nuclear weapons. According to this decision, which had also been signed by Ukraine's President Leonid Kravchuk, the Russian Federation is the only state out of all the legal suc-cessors of the USSR to possess nuclear weapons. . . . Kiev's claims to the possession of nuclear weapons stationed on the territory of Ukraine also violate the Lisbon Protocol to the START I treaty. . . . The written state-ment of the Ukrainian side with regard to the signing of that protocol clearly states that the "right and responsibility of possessing nuclear weapons of the former USSR have been given solely to the Russian Fed-eration with the express agreement of Ukraine and all the other legal successors of the former USSR." . . . The government of the Russian Fed-eration would like to draw attention to the undisputed fact that nuclear wea-pons cannot belong to a nuclear-free state. Only a nuclear state can possess such weapons.[38]

As might be expected, given the position of the CIS Joint Armed Forces senior staff (discussed in the previous chapter), this was an interpretation shared by Shaposhnikov as the commander of the CIS Joint Armed Forces, who considered Russia to be the undisputed inheritor of the Soviet nuclear arsenal.[39] Shaposhnikov was cited as taking the position that the nuclear weapons of the former USSR "belong to no state, while judging by all doc-uments they belong to Russia."[40] During his tenure as commander in chief of the Joint Armed Forces, he repeatedly expressed the view that all the nuclear weapons on the territory of the former Soviet Union either belonged already, or should be handed over, to Russia. In October 1992, at a summit of the CIS heads of state, he proposed that the four CIS nuclear states agree to recognize Russia as the sole inheritor of the Soviet nuclear arsenal. Speaking in an interview, he commented that all CIS nuclear weapons should be placed under Russian ownership and that he was prepared to hand over his "nuclear briefcase" to the Russian ministry of defense immediately.[41] In the same period, he also commented on more than one occasion that the nuclear weapons should be handed over to Russia because the CIS was not a state and that nuclear weapons must belong to a state.[42]

This dispute about ownership also needs to be seen in the context of the uncertainty about the status of a large section of the former Soviet armed forces, which was created by the attempts to retain a joint CIS strategic force. The question of ownership was already problematized, as Shaposhnikov's comments acknowledge, by the fact that the CIS was agreed to have strategic forces even though it was neither a state nor a suprastate organization, which raised questions—not least among the Ukrainian political and military elites—about its ability to have armed forces of any kind. Thus the former Soviet nuclear arsenal in Ukraine existed in a legal limbo, claimed by two states and apparently the joint property of the CIS states under the command of a non-suprastate international organization. As at other points in the sequence of disputes over former Soviet military property, the battle over ownership of the weapons on Ukrainian territory appears strange from a Western security perspective; at no point was it suggested by the government that Ukraine intended to remain a nuclear power permanently, nor was there any open disagreement on the part of the Ukrainian government with the internationally agreed timetables for denuclearization. There was also general agreement for most of the time in this period that in order to denuclearize, Ukraine had to allow the weapons on its territory to be transported to Russia for decommissioning, since the only nuclear weapons decommissioning facility in the former Soviet Union was in Russia. Russian governmental statements and proposals regarding these weapons did not change significantly over this period. Yet despite this, the question of ownership was fiercely contested, with the Ukrainian claim to own nuclear weapons cited by the Russian government as one of the primary reasons for the breakdown of bilateral negotiations over START I implementation and nuclear security measures in March 1993.[43]

The intensity of the struggle over the question of ownership reflects the number of central concerns to which the issue was connected. Ownership of nuclear weapons was closely connected to demands for financial assistance for the process of weapons removal and for compensation. It was also linked to the desire to obtain security guarantees from other nuclear states, in particular the United States. This continued to be the case throughout the period leading up to the eventual ratification of the NPT. The January 1994 Trilateral Agreement, which provided both financial assistance and security guarantees, was sufficient to allow START I to be ratified in full by the Ukrainian parliament. The guarantees were not, however, enough to prevent parliament ratifying the NPT in November 1994 with the provision that the nuclear warheads on its territory would remain the property of Ukraine and with the implication that Ukraine would withdraw from the NPT if another nuclear state (unnamed but clearly intended to refer to Russia) threatened its territorial integrity or political sovereignty.[44] As discussed in the next chapter, claims to ownership also appear to have been seen as a mechanism for obtaining leverage in discussions with Russia on other issues, such as the Black Sea Fleet, creating a highly complex cycle of interaction between a range of nuclear and nonnuclear security concerns.

The question of the ownership of nuclear weapons on Ukrainian territory at the point of independence connects to the problems of sovereignty in different ways, raising questions about both internal and external sovereignty. First, the Russian ownership of nuclear weapons in Ukraine would have meant, according to Kravchuk in one interview, that "if we declare that these weapons belong to Russia, the 43rd Army will no longer be a CIS army but a Russian army. This would mean the presence of occupying forces on the territory of Ukraine."[45]

Second, claims to ownership had important implications for Ukraine's internal sovereignty, since at stake was the principle that assets on the territory of Ukraine were Ukrainian (and, at least as important, not Russian). Critical to this issue was the dispute over which state had rights, as the USSR's legal successor, to inherit assets—in this case, military assets. Both Ukraine and Russia claimed succession rights to the nuclear weapons on Ukraine's territory—Ukraine on the basis that assets collectively owned by the constituent republics of the USSR, including Ukraine, that were on its territory when the USSR ceased to exist were, logically and legally, their property. Ownership was claimed by Ukraine because it was an independent state, the missiles were on its territory at independence, and the state to which they previously belonged and of which Ukraine had been a part no longer existed. Nuclear weapons were understood to be inherited by them in the same way that all other former Soviet property in Ukraine was held to be Ukrainian. The claim of any other successor state to ownership of property in Ukraine, particularly automatic ownership, posed a fundamental challenge to sovereignty.

The Russian claim, in contrast, invoked international arms control agreements, asserting that Russia was the internationally recognized nuclear successor to the USSR. This claim reflected the emergent post-Soviet understanding of sovereignty—that the other successor states had sovereignty over those issues not reserved by Russia for itself (here, as most frequently, a security issue), that the successor states were not legally equal, and that Russia had claims to sovereignty over aspects of post-Soviet security that extended beyond its own borders. This recalled the Soviet constitutional principle of sovereignty resting with the republics only in those areas not reserved by the center, to which these elites regarded Russia as the successor in matters extending well beyond the issue of legal successor status. The apparent assumption that Russian authority extended to the security policy of, and assets inside, other states posed a clear challenge to their external sovereignty—thus, the Russian claim to automatic ownership of the nuclear weapons was described by Ukrainian political elites as a threat to Ukraine's sovereign status.

The Question of Control

In addition to the issue of ownership, one of the most problematic issues related to the nuclear missiles on Ukrainian territory was the question of control, which was the subject of protracted disputes and negotiations, both between Ukraine and Russia, and Ukraine and the wider international community. Two principal control issues dominated Ukrainian and Russian concerns—who controlled the "nuclear button," which authorized the launch of the weapons, and who controlled the weapons on the ground (to whom were the strategic forces in Ukraine answerable and who controlled the mechanics of the denuclearization process), often referred to as "administrative control."

With the breakup of the Soviet Union, the most pressing nuclear weapons question for the international community was who had control of the USSR's nuclear missile launch systems. The CIS nuclear weapons agreement signed by the four nuclear states in December 1991 gave launch control to the Russian president, but under the terms of the agreement, the weapons could only be used with the consent of the other three signatories to the agreement. This agreement, then, did not give the other three states control over the nuclear weapons on their territory, simply the right to be consulted about their use. However, this was an extremely impractical procedure, since the limited time available to respond to a first strike by another nuclear force (at that time still the only conditions under which the former Soviet nuclear missiles were to be launched) made a four-way telephone consultation about the decision to use nuclear weapons impossible.[46]

Within days of the signing of this agreement, however, it was clear that this arrangement—which, given its impracticality, gave de facto control of both the launch codes and the decision to launch to the Russian government—was not going to be accepted by Ukraine.[47] TASS news agency quoted Kravchuk as rejecting "both the short-term and the long-term probability that the Russian leader or any other person will be given the individual right to be in charge of strategic weapons situated in Ukraine." Instead, he advocated a collective responsibility for nonuse of the nuclear weapons on the territory of the former USSR in the transitional period leading to their removal from Ukraine and the two other states committed to denuclearization.[48] Nevertheless, despite Ukrainian objections, the Soviet-era practice of having three "nuclear briefcases" was maintained, placing the nuclear button under effective Russian control since one briefcase was in the possession of the Russian president, another with the outspokenly pro-Russian Shaposhnikov, and the third (held by Gorbachev until the end of 1991) put into storage but under the custody of the CIS strategic forces command.

Throughout 1992 and 1993, the issue of control of nuclear missile launch capabilities was a subject of dispute between the Ukrainian government on the one hand and the Russian government and CIS command on the other. Of particular sensitivity were the claims made periodically by the Russian government and media that Ukraine was attempting to obtain operational control over the weapons. The Ukrainian denial of these claims was complicated by the fact that Ministry of Defense officials occasionally claimed to have control over their nonuse—in other words, that despite having ceded operational control to the CIS command, Ukraine had established a technical means of preventing use of the nuclear button without its authorization.[49] Despite the uncertainty generated by these assertions, however, the CIS command and the Russian president retained control of the launch mechanisms.

Although the combination of the December 1991 treaty framework and the possession of the nuclear button by the head of the CIS Joint Armed Forces (acting, at least in theory, under the direction of the CIS heads of state rather than simply the Russian executive) gave some limited institutional guarantees of control over the use of nuclear weapons to Ukraine and the other states, these were removed by the collapse of the CIS Joint Armed Forces in mid-1993. With the move of Shaposhnikov from his post as commander in chief of the Joint Armed Forces to the Russian Security Council in June 1993, the policy of joint control of the nuclear button by Shaposhnikov and Yeltsin ended, making the status of the CIS states' nuclear weapons even more opaque than it had been before. An additional problem for Ukraine was that with the end of the Joint Armed Forces the operational control of all former Soviet nuclear weapons was transferred to the Russian Ministry of Defense, giving the Russian president ultimate control of both the nuclear button and the strategic forces maintaining and carrying out the removal of nuclear weapons on the territory of the other three post-Soviet nuclear states. Despite the de facto transfer of operational control to Russia, the Ukrainian government insisted that the CIS continued to have de jure operational control, that the absence of a commander in chief did not affect this, and that this was the only basis on which Ukraine had agreed to relinquish operational control over the weapons on its territory. Although these claims did not reflect the reality of operational control, they were, arguably, a necessary fig leaf to cover the damage to Ukrainian independence caused by the unilateral action of a more powerful state in relation to security assets it claimed to own and over which it had joint legal control. Thus, from mid-1993, control of the missile launch capability for the nuclear weapons on Ukrainian territory—theoretically under joint CIS control—resided exclusively with the Russian Ministry of Defense.

At about this time, and during the negotiations over the ratification of START I, the Ukrainian Ministry of Defense began moves to extend its authority over all nuclear weapons–related troops on its territory. Ukraine had already asserted that it had, or had the right to, administrative control over the nuclear forces on its territory, on the principle that it could not have foreign troops (or "occupying forces") stationed within its borders. The Ukrainian position, before the dissolution of the Joint Armed Forces command, had been that the CIS command had operational control of the nuclear missiles, and that Ukraine had administrative control, at least in theory; with the end of the joint command and the assumption of de facto, unilateral control by Russia, the exercise of administrative control became a more serious issue for both states.

In April 1993, the Russian government had alleged that Ukraine was taking over the nuclear warhead maintenance teams and facilities on its territory and that strategic bomber crews had sworn the Ukrainian oath of allegiance.[50] Ukraine rejected the Russian claims but asserted that administrative control lay with Ukraine; in any case, by August the process of Ukrainian allegiance-swearing had apparently been completed. The collapse of the CIS Joint Armed Forces structure made the question of control over the strategic troops in Ukraine particularly important, because if such troops were not subordinate to the Ukrainian government then they were subordinate to Russia, which the Ukrainian cabinet considered unacceptable and which Kravchuk claimed would mean the presence of occupying forces in Ukraine.[51] One issue of dispute during this period was over a Russian proposal in July to subordinate some of the personnel working in Ukrainian missile installations to the Russian ministry of defense, apparently to ensure safe storage of the missiles until their elimination. This was allegedly in response to an order from Ukrainian minister of defense Morozov rescinding Russian orders to disband some of these facilities, placing them under the command of Ukraine's 43rd Missile Army. According to a Russian government statement, this was part of an attempt by Ukraine to "bring the [nuclear] weapons under national physical control," which, as with previous, similar statements, Ukraine denied.[52]

Both the Russian assertion of full operational control and the possibility of Russian administrative control through Russian nationalization of the strategic forces in Ukraine were profoundly threatening to the Ukrainian sense of emergent, Western-style state sovereignty. Although the initial arrangements for operational control through the CIS Joint Armed Forces command were impractical, they represented a recognition that Ukraine (and Belarus and Kazakhstan) had the theoretical right to joint control of the nuclear weapons on its territory. The dissolution of the Joint Armed Forces command and the unilateral appropriation of operational control by the Russian Ministry of Defense represented (at best) a disregard for Ukrainian claims to authority over the missiles on its territory. With the end of the CIS joint command structures, the forces in Ukraine had to be under the command of one of the states concerned; the dispute was thus about which one could claim them. The fact that Ukraine assumed that forces within its territory could be incorporated into the Ukrainian armed forces, and the fact that the Russian political and military elites appeared to believe that not only was this incorrect but that any attempt by Ukraine to do this was profoundly threatening to Russia's rights and security, reflected profoundly different understandings of sovereignty—specifically, of Ukraine's sovereignty and what its limits might be.

Conclusion: Ukraine and Russia

Several key concerns emerge from a consideration of the complex and often contradictory series of negotiations, agreements, and disputes that ultimately produced the final withdrawal of nuclear weapons from Ukraine in May 1996. It is clear that the nuclear weapons represented leverage to obtain specific aims (compensation, security guarantees, and a stronger negotiating position in relation to Russia over the Black Sea Fleet and Crimea). It also appears that for Ukraine, as for other states, what analysts have described as the political prestige of nuclear weapons was an important factor, particularly in its dealings with other states.[53] Perhaps one of the most interesting aspects of the debate about the Ukrainian nuclear weapons, however, was the disparity between international and Russian concerns. As noted earlier, the Ukrainian government was committed throughout this period to the ultimate removal of nuclear weapons from its territory, and international interest was concentrated on ensuring that this was achieved as rapidly and safely as possible. In order to achieve this, the US government was prepared to provide financial assistance and security guarantees (albeit of limited scope).

What appeared to dominate much of the bilateral Ukrainian and Russian negotiations, however, was the issue of who owned and controlled the missiles—in other words, who had sovereignty over this aspect of the former Soviet military. In the course of the arguments over these issues, both sides employed serious threats to achieve their goals—in the case of Ukraine, the suspension of missile transfers; in the case of Russia, the threat to suspend safety maintenance work at the weapons installations. Both sides also made use of allegations as well as threats, which appeared to be designed to influence international—as much as domestic—opinion. The competing claims about safety risks, and the Russian allegations that Ukraine was attempting to seize operational control of the weapons, were effective mechanisms for exerting pressure through increasing international concern.

On the face of it, the bitter Ukrainian-Russian dispute over the nuclear weapons in Ukraine was curious since not only had Ukraine committed to denuclearization even before independence, but its political identity *as* a newly independent, post-Soviet state appeared to be bound up with the twin security commitments to neutrality and nonnuclear status. Although financial assistance ultimately emerged from the United States, the likelihood of it in the earliest period of the negotiations did not appear great.[54] In order to make greater sense of the dispute, we need to understand the ways in which it related to profound anxieties about state sovereignty, including the contested understandings of what sovereignty meant in the post-Soviet space. The nuclear weapons negotiations and disputes between Russia and Ukraine touched on the issue of Ukrainian sovereignty in fundamental ways. The relationship between these two concerns was exacerbated both by the issues raised by the nature of nuclear weapons, and by the vulnerability of the newly independent Ukrainian state—as Sherman Garnett notes, for the Ukrainian denuclearization negotiators, "there were no technical matters that were not somehow connected to strategic decisions about Ukrainian security policy and even the consolidation of the Ukrainian state."[55] Russia's claim to automatic ownership of property in Ukraine was clearly felt to pose a serious challenge to Ukrainian internal sovereignty, since it would undermine the attempt by the new Ukrainian state to assert authority within its borders—in effect, another state would have precedence in matters of ownership of state assets inside Ukraine.

A second, equally urgent problem raised by the Ukrainian nuclear issue concerned external sovereignty—specifically, recognition of Ukraine's right to independence and territorial integrity by the international community of states in general, and by Russia in particular. Concerns about the potential security threat posed by Russia were heightened by particular aspects of Russian domestic politics and of foreign and security policy, including the 1993 political crises and the subsequent election of a "red-brown" Duma; Russian military intervention in Moldova, Tajikistan, and Georgia; and, of most immediate concern, the reluctance of significant sections of the Russian political elite to relinquish claims to Crimea, which threatened Ukrainian sovereignty through a challenge to its territorial integrity. Taken together, these developments created a climate in which Ukrainian politicians and military personnel could speak with some credibility about the potential threat posed by Russia to Ukrainian independence and territorial integrity. In response to these challenges, some members of parliament sought to retain what they saw as the deterrent effect of continued possession of nuclear weapons, which would guarantee sovereignty. In this climate, it was argued, it made little sense for Ukraine to give up nuclear weapons, and none at all for it to hand them over to Russia. Thus, a critical element in the disputes and negotiations over Ukraine's nuclear weapons became the provision of security guarantees by both Russia and other nuclear states, in particular the United States.

Examining the debates and standoffs over Ukrainian nuclear weapons, it appears that two distinct sets of negotiations were taking place—one between Ukraine and the international nuclear community, in particular the United States, and the other between Ukraine and Russia, both bilaterally and within the broader framework of the CIS. The negotiations with the international community revolved around the need on the part of the Ukrainian government to obtain international recognition of Ukrainian sovereignty, and, as a result of this recognition, security guarantees from other nuclear states and financial compensation for denuclearization. In the case of the negotiations with Russia, the debates and disagreements similarly revolved around a recognition of Ukrainian sovereignty, but rather than seeking a recognition of sovereignty as one state among many in the international community, as such a demand required in the case of the other members of the nuclear club, the sovereignty Ukraine asserted was based primarily on a recognition of independence from the former Soviet Union as a whole and from Russia in particular. As noted earlier, the attitude of the Russian political elites and the pro-Russian CIS military command was one of acceptance of the Western model of state sovereignty in theory but a resistance in practice to the idea of non-Russian state sovereignty over military issues. This underlying tension helps to explain the manner of the negotiations over Ukrainian denuclearization and the reason why a state committed from the outset to achieving a nonnuclear status appeared at times to be so resistant to the idea of giving up its nuclear weapons.

Belarus and Russia

The role of nuclear weapons in the shaping of Belarusian relations with Russia and with the West was more ambiguous than their role in the emergent security-sovereignty relations between Ukraine and Russia. This, I will argue, is a function of several factors—the impact of Chernobyl as a factor in the identity formation of an independent Belarusian state, fundamentally linking the principles of denuclearization and Belarusian statehood; the comparatively weak nature of national identity and commitment to sovereignty among the Belarusian political elite and the wider population in the immediate post-Soviet period; the shift away from this already limited commitment to sovereignty and neutrality toward an apparent policy of sovereignty rejection under the presidency of Alyaksandr Lukashenka; and the Lukashenka government's changeable approach to these issues.[56] Thus the removal of nuclear weapons played a key role in the signaling of contradictory and changing understandings of Belarusian state sovereignty—both underpinning state sovereignty and, in other respects, indicating the limited interest in Western-model sovereignty on the part of key Belarusian actors. Of course the nature and meaning of these changing approaches to security and sovereignty are made all the more opaque to analysts because of the authoritarian and secretive nature of decisionmaking in contemporary Belarus, which prevents any real domestic scrutiny of governmental policy.

Despite these difficulties, however, it is still possible to trace out a relationship—or rather a series of contradictory relationships—between nuclear weapons and attitudes to sovereignty in Belarus in the early and mid-1990s. Despite indications in the months immediately following the breakup of the Soviet Union that nuclear weapons and ideas about state sovereignty were linked by some members of the Belarusian political elite (most frequently by the acting defense minister, Pyotr Chaus), the subsequent period until mid-1996 when the last strategic nuclear weapons were removed from Belarusian territory was characterized by a renunciation of claims to any active role in the fate of the weapons, reflecting a similar movement away from claims to state sovereignty as understood in the Western tradition. One analyst has noted that "Belarus paid more attention than any other CIS nation to Russia's position on settling disputes concerning the reduction and limitation of nuclear and conventional weapons," and this reflects a broader willingness to recognize Russian claims to leadership on security matters.[57]

Perhaps surprisingly, in contrast to the situation in Ukraine, it has been Lukashenka, rather than the more prosovereignty and proindependence administration before him, who disrupted the previously smooth disarmament process by suspending weapons transfers to Russia in mid-1995. However, it would be misplaced to view his actions as an assertion of Belarusian sovereignty in the defense sphere; his halting of the transfer of warheads to Russia may in fact be understood in a variety of different ways—as a mechanism to obtain more financial aid; as a signal of potential support for a more conservative Russian security policy; and as an attempt to assert personal authority in relation to Russia (rather than a commitment to the sovereignty or independence of the Belarusian state).

The Process of Belarusian Denuclearization

The breakup of the Soviet Union meant that Belarus emerged into independence with 1,220 nuclear warheads on its territory, giving it the smallest nuclear arsenal of the four post-Soviet nuclear states.[58] From the outset—and indeed before independence, through the Declaration of State Sovereignty—Belarus was committed both to neutrality and to denuclearization. Although the issue of neutrality proved to be one of the most contentious issues of the early post-Soviet period, culminating in an acrimonious debate over the decision to join the CIS collective security treaty, the commitment to nonnuclear status was never seriously challenged. This appears curious at first glance, but Belarus's continued commitment to nonnuclear status needs to be understood, at least in part, as a response to the Chernobyl disaster, which was a foundational event for the Belarusian nationalist movement of the late Soviet period and thus for the emergent identity of an independent Belarus.[59] As a result of this commitment to denuclearization, and as a result of the apparent willingness on the part of Belarus to dispose of its nuclear weapons as rapidly as possible, the issue of Belarusian nuclear weapons was never viewed with the same concern as the issue of Ukrainian or Kazakh nuclear weapons either by Russia or by the United States and the rest of the international nuclear community.

In contrast to the Ukrainian case, Belarus's attitude toward denuclearization was clearly regarded by most analysts as uncontentious.[60] However, there were signals in the early, key period following the collapse of the Soviet Union—the period up to the signing of the Lisbon Protocol in May 1993—that some members of the Belarusian political elite considered the nuclear weapons on Belarusian territory as a subject for Belarusian decisionmaking rather than as objects to be handed over without question. In particular, two members of the executive, the acting defense minister and the foreign minister, adopted a more robust position with regard to control over the nuclear weapons on its territory than has usually been associated with Belarus.

Pyotr Chaus, the acting Belarusian defense minister from December 1991 until April 1992 (when he became deputy defense minister), consistently made public statements that, while never challenging the idea that Belarus should seek to become a nonnuclear state, implied the desire for a more assertive approach to the nuclear issue on the part of the Belarusian state, in particular in its dealings with Russia over this issue. Within days of the signing of the CIS founding agreement, he commented that "there is no point being hasty to hand over nuclear weapons to anyone, whomever they are, and this statement in no way contradicts the goal to make Belarus a neutral and nuclear-free power," a view that he had previously expressed to the Belarusian Supreme Soviet.[61] In February 1992, although noting that the timetable for the removal of tactical nuclear weapons from Belarus was being adhered to, he stated that a decision on the strategic nuclear weapons stationed in Belarus had yet to be reached—an issue on which he was quoted as saying, "I don't think we want to be too hasty."[62] This implied possibility of halting the weapons transfer to Russia was reiterated the following month when Chaus was quoted as saying that he approved of Ukraine's decision to halt the transfer of nuclear weapons to Russia and that he was considering the issue of the transfer of nuclear weapons from Belarus to Russia.[63] Elsewhere he expressed the view that Belarusian experts should be involved in the monitoring of the destruction of nuclear weapons removed from Belarus.[64] Chaus continued to express his ambiguous views on nuclear weapons following the appointment of Pavel Kozlovskiy as Belarusian defense minister, and his own appointment as deputy defense minister, in April 1992. In July, *Krasnaia Zvezda* reported that although he remained committed to the ultimate denuclearization of Belarus, he felt that "in the interests of the republic, we must not be hasty in the withdrawal of strategic nuclear missiles. The presence of such a powerful weapon in our country will at first help Belarus to establish itself. The whole world treats us as a nuclear power."[65]

A similarly robust position was taken in late 1991 by the Belarusian foreign minister Pyotr Krauchanka, who was reported as saying that Belarus intended to control the nuclear weapons on its territory directly because "the people of Belarus are tired of being pawns to someone else's military decisions."[66] He was also reported as saying that the monitoring of nuclear weapons should be carried out on a centralized, unified basis for the CIS as a whole and that the nuclear weapons in Belarus should be destroyed in Belarus rather than redeployed elsewhere.[67] Strikingly, these arguments, made by two of the key government actors involved in nuclear weapons policy, are very similar to those used by Ukrainian actors in the context of Ukraine's dispute with Russia; yet in the case of Belarus, they failed to lead to the same treatment of nuclear weapons as bargaining chip or symbol of sovereignty.

This is even more surprising given that this approach appears to have been reflected to some extent in the Belarusian legislature. As with the two ministers, there is evidence of concern about the disposal of nuclear weapons, not because of a desire to retain them as an arm of the defense capability of an independent state, but because the manner of Belarusian nuclear disarmament indicated an absence of independence and sovereignty over actions taking place within Belarusian territory, which was felt to be unacceptable. One Supreme Soviet deputy, for example, complained that

> its [Belarus's] opinion had ceased to be taken into consideration . . . [and] that removal of tactical nuclear arms from its territory was carried out without its knowledge and without any agreement with the republic of Belarus. . . . We [Belarus] are not going to threaten anybody, but we are responsible for the nuclear arms which were situated on our territory, whereas its removal is carried out in such a way that we don't even know what, where, and in what quantities was carried away.[68]

As a result, Belarus would not speed up the process of weapons removal (although the deputy did not explain how, in any case, it would be possible for Belarus to do so if this process was being conducted outside Belarusian control). The position of Chaus, Krauchanka, and others on the question of disposal of nuclear weapons does not, however, appear to have been shared by Supreme Soviet chairman Stanislau Shushkevich, and this may be one reason why the official position of Belarus in this period differed so markedly from that of Ukraine.

Nevertheless, this early period of Belarusian debate on nuclear weapons shares with the situation in Ukraine the linkage by different participants of external sovereignty and the possession of nuclear weapons. As noted earlier, US and Russian actors both linked questions of international recognition of sovereign statehood to a commitment to nonnuclear status. Since the commitment to denuclearization appeared to be fundamentally linked to emergent Belarusian identity as an independent state, this appeared to be broadly unproblematic. There are also indications, however, that this same linkage was, on at least one occasion, made in Belarus in reverse order to the denuclearization-then-recognition proposals made by others. In mid-December 1991, as US secretary of state James Baker was visiting Minsk, Shushkevich was reported to have said that although Belarus reaffirmed its commitment to becoming a nuclear-free neutral state, the length of time this process would take depended on the international recognition of Belarus, including by the United States.[69] This is a rare example of such use of nuclear weapons by Belarus; as will be discussed below, the subsequent approach taken by the Belarusian government, rather than linking nuclear weapons to ideas of state sovereignty, suggests in fact that the attitude toward nuclear weapons can be taken as a marker of low levels of commitment to any ideas of Belarusian state sovereignty.

Although such views continued to be expressed on occasion, from the start of 1992 it was clear that the drive toward nonnuclear status was the primary goal of the Belarusian government. The commitment to the removal of nuclear weapons from Belarus was frequently given in interviews by members of the Belarusian executive. In at least one instance, when Shushkevich reiterated the commitment to removal before the agreed international deadlines at the height of the dispute over Ukraine's halting of the weapons transfer to Russia, this policy of restatement seems to have been at least in part intended to draw a favorable comparison with the policy of Ukraine.[70]

At a meeting with CIS Joint Armed Forces commander Shaposhnikov on 2 January, Shushkevich confirmed that all strategic nuclear forces in Belarus were to be placed under CIS unified command. This confirmation was, however, given at the same time as the announcement of plans to establish the Belarusian Armed Forces and a Ministry of Defense, thus it would clearly be incorrect to view this move as a part of a wider relinquishment of all claims to any independent military position during this period. Instead, both moves can be seen as attempts to carry through the commitments to neutrality and nonnuclear status that underpinned the emergent identity of a sovereign, post-Soviet Belarus. However, in retrospect, these commitments in themselves posed problems for the future independence of Belarusian security policy. In particular, the fact that the Belarusian executive was prepared to renounce all ownership and control claims over the weapons on their territory, which arose from the commitment to nonnuclear status, meant that the executive's position became the same as that of the Russian political and military elites and the CIS command—that the weapons, on Belarusian territory at independence and the property of a state to which Belarus was a successor, were Russian. This assumption of automatic Russian ownership suggests that the dominant understanding of Belarusian sovereignty was, from an early point in the post-Soviet period, fundamentally compromised as a reflection of international sovereignty norms and open to the post-Soviet "nonsovereign sovereignty" of the Russian political and military elites.

In contrast to the position of the Ukrainian government, the question of administrative control over nuclear weapons was not raised, and no attempts were made in this period either to halt or to slow their removal to Russia. By the start of May, all tactical nuclear missile warheads had been declared to be removed from Belarusian territory, and throughout 1992 the commitment to the removal of strategic nuclear weapons from Belarus within the seven-year period was reiterated. In the case of both tactical and strategic weapons, in fact, Belarus committed itself to completing removal before the agreed deadlines. In February, Krauchanka claimed that "Belarus will not only adhere to the principle it has assigned itself and to which it has bound itself, but it will even fulfil it ahead of schedule," while during the same period, Leonid Privalov, the deputy chairman of the Supreme Soviet's Commission for Matters of National Security, claimed that "Belarus will be free of strategic nuclear weapons in approximately 1996 or 1997"—potentially a year ahead of schedule.[71] However, in the same interview he stressed that after the withdrawal of nuclear weapons the only armed forces stationed on the territory of Belarus would be those of the republic of Belarus.

In December 1991 and early 1992, then, the attitude of members of the Belarusian executive toward the nuclear weapons on its territory appeared to coexist with, rather than be used to explicitly support or draw attention to, commitments to Belarusian state sovereignty, and particularly sovereignty in the sphere of military policy. Nonnuclear status was one of the two key planks of Belarusian military policy in this period—the other being neutrality—and given that the commitment to both was fundamental to an independent Belarus's identity and was reiterated by figures such as Shushkevich, Krauchanka, and Chaus, it is probably more useful to view the absence of attempts to control or retain nuclear weapons as part of an independent military policy rather than a lack of engagement with the idea of sovereignty over military issues. Nevertheless, one consequence of the executive's position on denuclearization was that it logically implied a position—automatic Russian ownership of assets on Belarusian territory—that at least raised a question about the sovereignty of Belarus in relation to Russia.

By mid-1992, this view of the Belarusian approach to nuclear weapons was reinforced by the signing of a number of agreements, including the Treaty on Cooperation in the Defense Sphere, signed by Russia and Belarus in Moscow on July 20. Although in theory still under the unified command of the CIS during this period, the treaty and other agreements signed with Russia handed over all the strategic nuclear weapons on Belarusian territory to Russian control. In addition, the agreement set a seven-year deadline for the withdrawal of these Russian-controlled weapons from Belarus—a deadline that clearly contradicted the timetable of·Russian withdrawal by 1993 agreed in CIS documentation.

The July 1992 agreements with Russia are important to an understanding of the shifting Belarusian approach to nuclear weapons because they mark a definitive break with Belarus's earlier commitments both to sovereignty and neutrality in defense matters. One of the few Western analysts to comment on these agreements argues that they were the product of concerns on the part of the Russian Defense Ministry about the possibility that the Belarusian parliamentary elections would produce a stronger nationalist bloc that might lay claim to, and demand the retention of, nuclear weapons.[72] It seems, in any case, hard to avoid connecting these agreements to the replacement of the more assertive Chaus with Kozlovskiy, who was seen on appointment as the generals' candidate.[73] One indication of the way in which this represented a move toward a more dependent position in relation to Russia was the way in which Kozlovskiy echoed the positions and rhetoric of the Russian military in his comments on the agreement, in which he claimed that the treaty meant that Russia and Belarus would coordinate their military activity but that this did not mean that Belarus had entered a military alliance with Russia (which would contravene the neutrality principle).[74]

From this point on, too, it became clear that the question of ownership had been resolved as far as the Belarusian executive was concerned. Shushkevich's position on the issue was unequivocal: "Only Russia has the moral right to possess nuclear weapons on the territory of the former Soviet Union."[75] At the CIS Heads of State summit in Minsk in January 1993, Shushkevich commented that:

> We understand that the nuclear weapons on our territory belong to Russia and are under Russia's command. We would like to reach agreement on all these questions not with some kind of abstract military structures but with

> Russia. . . . After all, the nuclear troops on our territory are Russia's troops. They are under Russia's command, and I believe to think otherwise would create a great many unnecessary complications.[76]

Shushkevich condemned those members of the political elite who sought to retain nuclear weapons, describing denuclearization as the best way to enhance Belarus's international position.[77]

In contrast to the concerns of Ukraine in this period, the Belarusian executive and legislature in late 1992 and 1993 demonstrated a lack of concern with the potential sovereignty issues surrounding nuclear weapons and a commitment to their rapid removal from Belarusian territory. In November 1992 the Belarusian parliament adopted a military doctrine that called for the removal of nuclear weapons from Belarus within two and a half years instead of the seven given by the Lisbon Protocol. In 1993, in contrast to the Ukrainian delays and disputes, parliament ratified START I on 4 February, and the NPT the following day.

The Lukashenka Period

As in other areas, the election of Lukashenka in 1994 led to further moves away from Belarusian sovereignty in the defense sphere, with nuclear weapons becoming one of the most obvious indicators of this.[78] The first Lukashenka-Yeltsin summit in early August 1994 raised the issue of a Russian nuclear missile early warning radar facility on Belarusian territory, which contravened the Belarusian constitution of the time. The summit also discussed the possibility of extending the presence of Russian strategic forces in Belarus, a proposal at odds with both the constitution and with the Lisbon Protocol, which had committed Russia to withdrawal of troops from Belarus by 2000.

However, in the period between the election of Lukashenka and the final withdrawal of nuclear weapons from Belarus in late 1996, it was the suspension of weapons removal to Russia that provoked the most attention. This provides an interesting point of comparison with the suspension of the weapons transfer to Russia from Ukraine three years earlier. As discussed above, the Ukrainian position was clearly signaled as a demonstration of independence. In the case of Belarus, similarly explicit reasons were given for halting the transfer, but they demonstrate a radically different approach to relations with Russia. In announcing this suspension of the withdrawal of the remaining eighteen missiles, Lukashenka described the decision to remove nuclear weapons from Belarus as a mistake by the previous government and as an unnecessary action given the possibility that Russia and Belarus might unite in the near future.[79] Although this statement obviously indicates a reluctance to pursue a military policy independently of Russia, the fact that neither the Russian Ministry of Defense nor the Russian president were informed of this decision in advance suggests that this suspension was less an indication of Belarusian governmental weakness in the face of Russian defense priorities than another in a series of apparently arbitrary and unilateral decisions taken by Lukashenka as a means of asserting personal authority as president.

Although weapons transfers were resumed, and were finally completed by November 1996, Lukashenka again placed a question mark over the nonnuclear future of Belarus in January 1996, when he stated that Belarus might be forced to redeploy nuclear weapons on its territory if NATO expansion took place.[80] In June, the withdrawal of the last of the nuclear weapons was again delayed, despite a Russia-Belarus agreement in December 1995 to complete withdrawal by the end of May. In this instance, various explanations were offered by commentators, including a further response to proposed NATO expansion and a desire on the part of Lukashenka to halt withdrawal until the outcome of the Russian presidential election.[81] Later reports attributed the delay to Belarusian financial difficulties and a desire for compensation. It is notable that Lukashenka's dramatic announcements about the future of the nuclear weapons in Belarus do not appear to have been agreed with the Russian military or executive, nor to have been welcomed by them. Thus, the presentation of these suspensions as an anticipation of future union or as part of an anti-NATO (and thus by implication pro-Russian) defense policy is problematic, not least because no attempt appears to have been made to maintain this position.

Despite these repeated, high-profile interventions in the withdrawal of nuclear weapons by the Belarusian government, none of the periods of delay was long lasting, and there were, in fact, questions about whether the withdrawal process had been halted at all, or merely slowed. In any case, they ultimately delayed the process by no more than six months. Yet although they proved to have a negligible impact on the future of nuclear weapons in Belarus, they are interesting both as a point of comparison with the Ukrainian suspension of withdrawals to Russia, and as an indicator of the way in which even a government as seemingly reluctant to develop an independent military posture as that of Belarus saw nuclear weapons as a means of asserting a clear international position. By the mid-1990s, in an inversion of the sovereignty-marker and prestige functions that are attributed to nuclear weapons, nuclear weapons were being used by the Belarusian president to emphasize that Belarus was *not* independent from Russia on critical matters of security, that there was no sovereignty boundary between Russian and Belarus.

Conclusion

Between the dissolution of the USSR in 1991 and the final removal of nuclear weapons from their territories in 1996, Belarus and Ukraine became de facto nuclear states. How these two states managed their temporary nuclear status and the process of denuclearization—to which both were committed from the outset—illustrates the very different approaches that they took to their status as sovereign states. For Ukraine, the idea that property of the USSR that it believed itself to have inherited was not owned by it, and was thus placed outside its control, was unacceptable. Its protracted dispute with the international community and above all with Russia about its ownership of these weapons and its consequent nuclear status was clearly in part connected to a desire for financial assistance and international recognition as an independent actor. This was also about the attempt to assert sovereignty over its military policy and, at a practical level, over the assets and military activities within its borders. This in turn arose from the perception that it was not regarded as possessing sovereignty in these matters by Russia or, until the collapse of the Joint Armed Forces project, by the senior officers within the CIS military structure. This perception of the Ukrainian government and members of its parliament appears justified when the statements and actions of Russian and CIS actors are examined. This Russian/CIS perspective is not, of course, surprising given the way in which the understanding of sovereignty on the part of these actors appears to derive from Soviet theory. As a result, in the case of Ukraine, the issue of denuclearization became linked to a wider security concern in respect to Russia, which could only be resolved with the intervention of the United States.

In contrast, the government and parliament of Belarus did not react to the issue of sovereignty raised by nuclear ownership and control questions in a manner that resulted in disputes with either Russia or the rest of the international community. With the exception of some figures in the government and parliament in the very earliest stages of independence, members of the Belarus political and military elite appeared entirely willing to cede ownership and control of the nuclear weapons on its territory to Russia. Strikingly, even when the transfer of missiles to Russia was halted in 1995, the reasons given implied a desire for even less sovereignty over security policy than it already possessed. This provides an instructive comparison with the reasons for Ukraine's decision to halt weapons transfer in 1992.

Another noticeable difference is that unlike Belarus, Ukraine consistently maintained a distinct, independent position on the status of the nuclear weapons on its territory—a further marker of the divergent attitudes toward sovereignty. Although early Belarusian commitments to removing nuclear weapons can be viewed as part of a coherent position on nonnuclear status stemming from the 1990 Declaration of State Sovereignty, an increasingly close military relationship with Russia and the erratic behavior of Lukashenka on the issue of nuclear withdrawal meant that Belarus effectively renounced any coherent position in the post-Soviet nuclear debate in favor of presidential grandstanding and acquiescence to Russian preferences. Lukashenka's comments aside, at no point did Belarus demonstrate a determination to adopt a stance on the nuclear weapons on its territory that differed significantly from the Russian government's position on nuclear weapons on Belarusian territory. This is evident both at the executive level—through the government's repeated statements of its commitment to denuclearization, through a readiness to sign agreements favorable to the Russian position, and through the failure ever to lay claim to ownership of the nuclear weapons on its territory—and in the legislature, which ratified START, including the Lisbon Protocol, and the NPT without incident. In the case of Ukraine, sovereignty over nuclear weapons and the use of the nuclear weapons issue to demonstrate sovereignty over military policy and over the property and activities on its territory were the subject of concern throughout the executive and legislatures, and despite changes to both following elections. In the case of Belarus, the issue of nuclear weapons can be seen as an indicator of the way that the state progressively renounced an interest in its own sovereignty (as that term is generally understood in the Western tradition) and reverted to a Soviet model of understanding about and practices of sovereignty in relation to Russia (a move considered in Chapter 4).[82]

Notes

1. Nuclear Threat Initiative country profiles for Belarus, Kazakhstan, and Ukraine, available from www.nti.org/ e_research/profiles/index.html. A different (although not incompatible) set of figures for strategic and tactical warheads is given in Marco De Andreis and Francesco Calogero, *The Soviet Nuclear Weapons Legacy,* SIPRI Research Report 10 (Oxford: Oxford University Press, 1995), p. 5, table 2.1. This puts the total per state at 1,120 warheads for Belarus, 2,050 for Kazakhstan, 4,335 for Ukraine, and 17,275 for Russia.

2. Pavel K. Baev identifies three coexisting functions of nuclear weapons in the Soviet and then the Russian approach: symbols, bargaining chips, and weapons (*The Russian Army in a Time of Troubles* [London: Sage, 1996], pp. 41–46). The use of nuclear weapons as symbols and bargaining chips is arguably even more evident in the case of Ukraine, not least because they performed both these functions primarily in relation to Russia itself, as well as the United States. Baev notes the Ukrainian use of nuclear weapons as bargaining chips (p. 42), but not as symbols.

3. See, for example, George Quester, *The Politics of Nuclear Proliferation* (Baltimore: Johns Hopkins University Press, 1973).

4. Scott D. Sagan, "Why Do States Build Nuclear Weapons? Three Models in Search of a Bomb," *International Security* 21, no. 3 (Winter 1996–1997): 55. Sagan argues that this symbolic function explains key aspects of French policy, such as the *"tout azimuts"* commitment and the continuation of testing in the 1990s, since nuclear weapons acted as symbols of continued great power status after the loss of empire (pp. 79–80). Although he argues that the Ukrainian commitment to denuclearization is evidence of the force of nonproliferation norms, I argue here that the Russian-Ukrainian disputes over ownership and control also need to be seen in the context of the symbolic function of nuclear weapons as status markers.

5. Some Ukrainian military and political groupings *did* argue for Ukraine's retention of nuclear weapons, but this position was not adopted by the Ukrainian government or parliament.

6. As discussed below, the successful claim to ownership of nuclear weapons did, however, have an important financial function, as US funding for denuclearization demonstrated.

7. The 1992 Russia-Belarus agreement, discussed below, contradicted previous agreements made within the CIS framework.

8. See, for example, the article by the then–foreign minister of Ukraine, Anatoly Zlenko, "Ukrainian Security and the Nuclear Dilemma," *NATO Review* 41, no. 4 (August 1993): 11–14.

9. A. G. Arbatov, "Conclusion," in *Iadernye Vooruzheniia i Respublikanskiĭ Suverenitet* (Moscow: Mezhdunarodnye Otnosheniia, 1992), pp. 65–66.

10. Interfax, 15 January 1993, *FBIS-SOV-93-012*, p. 2.

11. *FBIS-SOV-93-043*, p. 56.

12. ITAR-TASS, 11 April 1993, *FBIS-SOV-93-068*, p. 50.

13. One proponent of this view was John Mearsheimer, who asserted in mid-1993 that "Ukraine is likely to keep nuclear weapons, regardless of what other states say and do" ("The Case for a Ukrainian Nuclear Deterrent," *Foreign Affairs* 72, no. 3 [Summer 1993]: 58). Unusually for a US analyst (although entirely consistently with his other post–Cold War security analyses during this period), Mearsheimer argued that international security would be best served by Ukraine retaining nuclear weapons.

14. Zlenko, "Ukrainian Security," p. 13. He also notes the impact of Chernobyl on Ukrainian attitudes toward nuclear weapons.

15. "Declaration of the State Sovereignty of Ukraine," Clause 9.

16. Kostiantyn P. Morozov, "Current Ukrainian Military Policy and Issues in Its Formation," in *The Military Tradition in Ukrainian History: Its Role in the Construction of Ukraine's Armed Forces* (Cambridge, MA: Ukrainian Research Institute, 1995), p. 29.

17. Commitments appear in *Radio Moscow World Service*, 13 December 1991, *FBIS-SOV-91-241*, p. 70, and TASS, 13 December 1991, *FBIS-SOV-91-241*, p. 69, respectively.

18. *Uradovyy Kuryer*, 28–29 December 1991, *FBIS-SOV-92-006*, p. 61.

19. Interview with Kravchuk in Italian newspaper *La Stampa*, quoted in *Izvestiia*, 4 February 1992, *FBIS-SOV-92-025*, p. 59. In an interview two days later, however, the Ukrainian deputy defense minister (and leader of the Ukrainian group of experts in military negotiations with Russia), Ivan Bizan, commented that Yeltsin's initiative was welcome because it coincided with the Ukrainian position.

20. See, for example, A. A. Pikaev, "Respublikanskaia Bomba: Iadernye Illuzii i Real'nosti," in Alexei Arbatov et al., eds., *Managing Conflict in the Former Soviet Union: Russian and American Perspectives*, BCSIA Studies in International Security (Cambridge: MIT Press, 1997), p. 58. Examples of contemporary Russian media comments include *Kuranty*, 20 March 1992, p. 1, *FBIS-SOV-92-056*, p. 1, and *Kommersant*, 12, 16–23 March 1992, p. 22, *FBIS-SOV-92-057*, p. 1.

21. Richard Woff, "A Russian Army," *Jane's Intelligence Review* 4, no. 5 (May 1992): 200.

22. TASS International Service, 16 March 1992, *FBIS-SOV-92-052*, p. 31.

23. In an interview on Radio Ukraine World Service, the Ukrainian foreign minister Anatoly Zlenko outlined the Ukrainian proposal to maintain the bilateral structure of START I by treating the four ex-Soviet states as a single collective party to the treaty. He regarded the Russian rejection of this approach as evidence of the fact that Russia was less concerned about nuclear weapons reductions than about asserting superiority over the other three states (*FBIS-SOV-92-073*, p. 42).

24. Protocol to the Treaty Between the United States of America and the Union of Soviet Socialist Republics on the Reduction and Limitation of Strategic Offensive Arms (Lisbon Protocol), Article 1.

25. Lisbon Protocol, Article 5.

26. John W. R. Lepingwell, "Ukraine, Russia, and Nuclear Weapons: A Chronology," *RFE/RL Research Report* 3, no. 4 (28 January 1994): 24.

27. *Izvestiia,* 23 November 1993.

28. On the importance and role of the United States in the Trilateral Agreement, see, for example, Nadia Schadlow, "The Denuclearisation of Ukraine: Consolidating Ukrainian Security," in Lubomyr A. Hajda, ed., *Ukraine in the World: Studies in the International Relations and Security Structure of a Newly Independent State* (Cambridge, MA: Harvard University Press for the Ukrainian Research Institute, Harvard University, 1998), pp. 81–88.

29. For example, an Ostankino news report on 6 April 1993; see *FBIS-SOV-93-067, p.* 13.

30. On the mid-1993 change in US policy to greater engagement in the negotiations over Ukrainian nuclear weapons, and the subsequent willingness of the United States to offer security and financial incentives to Ukraine, see Sherman W. Garnett, "U.S.-Ukrainian Relations: Past, Present, and Future," in Hajda, ed., *Ukraine in the World,* pp. 103–124.

31. *Izvestiia,* 6 February 1993, p. 2.

32. Interfax, 2 March 1993, *FBIS-SOV-93-040,* p. 37.

33. *Izvestiia,* 2 April 1993, p. 3. The Ukrainian deputy foreign minister, Boris Tarasyuk, went further, implying that if the Ukrainian missiles were unsafe this could be because Russian maintenance specialists were tampering with them.

34. See *Nezavisimaia Gazeta,* 10 September 1993; *Izvestiia,* 14 September 1993.

35. Interfax. 19 Octover 1993, *FBIS-SOV-93-201,* p. 8.

36. This basis for the statement was given both by the chair of the Ukrainian parliament's foreign affairs committee, Dmytro Pavlychko (*Cesky Denik,* 7 August 1993, p. 5, *FBIS-SOV-93-153,* p. 39), and by Kravchuk (Radio Ukraine World Service, 29 July 1993, *FBIS-SOV-93-146,* p. 51). In a contradictory comment, a characteristic feature of the debate on nuclear weapons among the post-Soviet states, Kravchuk claimed in this interview that "the Supreme Council's resolution did not say that Ukraine was a nuclear state. It said that Ukraine was the owner of nuclear weapons deployed on its territory due to historical circumstances."

37. *Holos Ukainy,* 23 January 1993, p. 3, *FBIS-SOV-93-017,* p. 36.

38. ITAR-TASS, 5 April 1993, *FBIS-SOV-93-064,* pp. 21–22. For other examples of the Russian government's use of this argument, see also the statement in ITAR-TASS World Service, 4 August 1993, *FBIS-SOV-93-149,* pp. 4–5.

39. Interfax, 25 January 1993, *FBIS-SOV-93-015,* p. 6.

40. ITAR-TASS, 4 November 1992, *FBIS-SOV-92-214,* p. 3.

41. *Nezavisimaia Gazeta,* 8 October 1992.

42. *Izvestiia,* 17 November 1992, p. 2, and ITAR-TASS World Service, 25 January 1993, *FBIS-SOV-93-015,* p. 6.

43. Interfax, 5 March 1993, *FBIS-SOV-93-043,* pp. 2–3.

44. Statement by the Ukrainian parliament "On Ukraine's Entering the Nuclear Non-Proliferation Treaty," 16 November 1994, *Uradovyi Kuryer,* 22 November 1994, in Michael Mihalka, "Ukraine: Salvaging Nuclear Arms Control," *Transition* 1, no. 7 (12 May 1995): 35.

45. Interview in Hungarian newspaper *Pesti Hirlap,* 3 May 1993, *FBIS-SOV-93-084,* p. 41.

46. See, for example, the transcript of the television debate about the treaty in *FBIS-SOV-91-248,* p. 41. In the course of this debate, Yeltsin claimed that four-way control of the nuclear button, by each of the presidents, was technically impossible.

47. On the Russian control of launch capabilities, see Pikaev, "Respublikan-skaia Bomba."

48. TASS International Service, 25 December 1991, *FBIS-SOV-91-248,* p. 62.

49. For example, statements made on 11 January 1993 and 18 August 1993.

50. Statement published by ITAR-TASS, 5 April 1993, *FBIS-SOV-93-064,* pp. 21–22.

51. An assertion made more than once by Kravchuk in media interviews (see, for example, Interfax, 7 April 1993, and *Pesti Hirlap* interview, 3 May 1993, *FBIS-SOV-93-084,* p. 41). See also the statement by the Ukrainian cabinet of ministers of 7 April 1993, *FBIS-SOV-93-067,* pp. 57–58.

52. *FBIS-SOV-93-141,* p. 7.

53. See, for example, Quester, *The Politics of Nuclear Proliferation;* Sagan, "Why Do States Build Nuclear Weapons?"; and Arbatov, *Iadernye Vooruzheniia.*

54. Garnett, "U.S.-Ukrainian Relations."

55. Ibid., p. 105.

56. On the weakness of Belarusian national identity, see Steven M. Eke and Taras Kuzio, "Sultanism in Eastern Europe: The Socio-Political Roots of Authoritarian Populism in Belarus," *Europe-Asia Studies* 52, no. 3 (May 2000): 523–547; and David Marples, *Belarus: From Soviet Rule to Nuclear Catastrophe* (Basingstoke, UK: Macmillan, 1996).

57. Anatolii Rozanov, "Belarus: Foreign Policy Priorities," in Sherman W. Garnett and Robert Legvold, eds., *Belarus at the Crossroads* (Washington, DC: Carnegie Endowment for International Peace, 1999), p. 30.

58. This figure includes both tactical and strategic warheads. See De Andreis and Calogero, *The Soviet Nuclear Weapons Legacy,* p. 5, table 2.1.

59. On this point, see, for example, Marples, *Belarus: From Soviet Rule to Nuclear Catastrophe;* Helen Fedor, ed., *Belarus and Moldova, Country Studies* (Washington, DC: Federal Research Division, Library of Congress, 1995). As noted earlier, the Chernobyl disaster also seems to have influenced the Ukrainian commitment to denuclearization. However, it appears to have played a more limited role in post-Soviet Ukrainian identity formation because of the much greater number of important political and historical factors in Ukrainian nationalism—the comparatively weak and limited nature of Belarusian nationalism, with fewer foundational myths, afforded greater prominence to Chernobyl.

60. In fact, the nuclear weapons stationed in Belarus have been the subject of very little analysis, even within more general considerations of the problem of post-Soviet proliferation. See, for example, Phillip A. Petersen, "Control of Nuclear Weapons in the CIS," *Jane's Intelligence Review* 5, no. 7 (July 1993): 297–300, which makes no mention of the denuclearization process in respect to Belarus. This absence of interest in the fate of the nuclear weapons in Belarus is presumably a result of the absence of any consistent attempt on the part of the Belarusian government to challenge the terms of the denuclearization process as set by the United States and Russia.

61. TASS International Service, 13 December 1991, *FBIS-SOV-91-241,* p. 57.

62. ADN, 9 February 1992, *FBIS-SOV-92-027,* p. 74.

63. Interfax, 16 December 1991, *FBIS-SOV-91-242,* p. 57.

64. ITAR-TASS World Service, 17 April 1992, *FBIS-SOV-92-076,* p. 2.

65. *Krasnaia Zvezda,* 16 July 1992, *FBIS-SOV-92-139,* p. 48. Also reported by Postfactum, 8 July 1992, *FBIS-SOV-92-132,* p. 63.

66. Radio Rossii, 16 December 1991, *FBIS-SOV-91-242*, p. 57.
67. Interfax, 16 December 1991, *FBIS-SOV-91-242*, p. 57.
68. Postfactum, 12 February 1992, *FBIS-SOV-92-030*, p. 81.
69. TASS International Service, 18 December 1991, *FBIS-SOV-91-244*, p. 41.
70. Radio Rossii Network, 21 March 1992, *FBIS-SOV-92-056*, p. 2.
71. *Hospodarske Noviny,* 5 February 1992, p. 14, *FBIS-SOV-92-029*, p. 80; TASS International Service, 27 January 1992, *FBIS-SOV-92-017*, p. 59.
72. Frank Umbach, "Back to the Future?—The Security Policy of Belarus," *Jane's Intelligence Review* 5, no. 9 (September 1993): 413.
73. *Nezavisimaia Gazeta,* 24 April 1992, pp. 1, 3.
74. *Krasnaia Zvezda,* 25 July 1992; ITAR-TASS, 24 July 1992, *FBIS-SOV-92-144,* p. 2.
75. ITAR-TASS, 1 September 1993, *FBIS-SOV-93-169,* p. 48.
76. Interview with Stanislav Shushkevich, *Kuranty,* 23 January 1993, p. 2, *Current Digest of the Post-Soviet Press* (CDPSP) 45, no. 3 (1993): 8.
77. *Nezavisimaia Gazeta,* 23 September 1992, *FBIS-SOV-92-187,* p. 37.
78. As under the previous administration, a weak position on military sovereignty in respect to nuclear weapons did not prevent attempts by the Lukashenka government to obtain financial compensation. This was one of the areas discussed at the first Yeltsin-Lukashenka summit in early August 1994. Financial issues continued to be treated separately from the broader approach toward nuclear weapons; in May 1995, the Lukashenka administration's increasingly anti-Western position did not prevent Belarus receiving an additional $6 million from the United States to dismantle the launching pads for Russian SS-25 missiles deployed on Belarusian territory.
79. "Belarus Stops Arms Reductions," *OMRI Daily Digest,* 7 July 1995, available from http://archive.tol.cz/ archive.html.
80. "Belarusian President Criticised over Statement on Nuclear Weapons," *OMRI Daily Digest,* 22 January 1996.
81. "Russian Press Speculates on Belarus's Delay in Nuclear Withdrawal," *OMRI Daily Digest,* 14 June 1996.
82. Hrihory Perepelitsa, "The Belarus Factor in the European Policy of Ukraine," in Margarita M. Balmaceda, James I. Clem, and Lisbeth Tarlow, eds., *Independent Belarus: Domestic Determinants, Regional Dynamics, and Implications for the West* (Cambridge, MA: Ukrainian Research Institute and David Centre for Russian Studies, 2002), p. 306, also comments on the weakness of the Belarusian commitment to state sovereignty compared with that of Ukraine.

4

The Black Sea Fleet: Russia, Ukraine, and Georgia

The five-and-a-half-year dispute among Russia, Ukraine, and Georgia in the 1990s over the Black Sea Fleet appears to present observers with a puzzle: Why did these states vigorously contest ownership of an asset that had lost most of its strategic value and that none of the claimants could afford to maintain? With the end of the Cold War, the emergence of fundamental changes to forms and technologies of warfare, and during a period of economic crisis for all three states, the acrimonious, occasionally violent, pursuit of competing claims to an obsolete and expensive security asset appears irrational. This is not an issue on which analysts have often focused, but it is one that was clear from the outset of the dispute and that is fundamental to any attempt to understand it.[1] Citing an observation made by the *Financial Times*, *Izvestiia* commented in 1992 that "the paradox is that this Fleet does not, in reality, have any strategic significance, while its maintenance is now clearly beyond the capabilities of Ukraine and Russia."[2] This was still an issue puzzling the Russian press in January 1993, when one paper commented that "the Fleet's physical deterioration through wear and tear, now obvious, makes it increasingly costly to maintain, and the aims driving Russia to cling stubbornly onto the Fleet (after the departure from the Mediterranean and the reduction in Russia's shoreline) are not clear."[3] Then–Ukrainian president Kravchuk also noted that the fleet's ships were old and no longer of any real strategic value.[4] In order to make sense of a dispute that at points looked as if it might spill over into conflict, and that reemerged almost a decade after the signing of the supposedly definitive agreement in 1997, the ways in which the Black Sea Fleet's importance exceeded its value as a security asset need to be considered. In particular, Russia and Ukraine's dispute over the Black Sea Fleet needs to be understood as a struggle for control over a historic symbol of national identity and, as with the nuclear weapons dispute, as a struggle for sovereignty in relation to post-Soviet security.

101

Prior to the breakup of the USSR, and in particular before the end of the Cold War, the Black Sea Fleet occupied a position of considerable strategic significance. Based principally at a number of sites on the Crimean peninsula, but with additional bases both within the USSR and on the Bulgarian coast, the fleet patrolled the only area where the Soviet Union shared a border with a NATO member state (Turkey) and had the ability to operate in the Mediterranean, both factors that made the fleet a key part of the overall Soviet defense capability. With the end of the Cold War, however, the strategic importance of the Black Sea declined dramatically, leaving a fleet of approximately 400 vessels spread across three former Soviet states and with no function that could justify its size or cost.[5] The purpose of the Black Sea Fleet in a post–Cold War world was unclear.

There was, however, a second serious threat to the post-Soviet Black Sea Fleet: in addition to the fact that the end of the Cold War had deprived the fleet of the strategic function for which it was designed, the states on whose territory the fleet was principally located—Ukraine, Russia, and Georgia—were faced with severe economic difficulties, which meant that they were (to varying degrees) unable to maintain the fleet in anything approaching an operational state. This, as much as the dispute over ownership that developed in the early 1990s, created a situation in which the fleet was able to undertake only one large-scale exercise over a two-year period, and in which more routine exercises lasted for two days rather than the weeks that had been normal in the Soviet era. Even when the fleet was able to undertake exercises, the financial resources did not exist to ensure that its vessels and equipment were updated, resulting in what one analyst described as the "virtual loss of combat readiness and modern character by the Black Sea Fleet."[6] By 1994, according to the Russian Defense Ministry, the newest vessels in the fleet were seventeen to eighteen years old, and it was clear that there was no prospect at that point of the average age reducing, since work on new vessels started before the collapse of the USSR had been suspended.[7] One of the most dramatic symbols of this financing crisis for the fleet was the ship in the process of construction at the time of the breakup of the USSR (the *Varyag*), which remained uncompleted in dry dock throughout most of the mid-1990s and was eventually sold to China in 1996. In 2001, four years after the final agreement on the Black Sea Fleet, most of the vessels Ukraine had received in the division of the fleet were considered nonoperational.[8]

More routine financial problems affecting the Black Sea Fleet, some of which were common to many parts of the post-Soviet armed forces, were routinely cited by naval officials and politicians and indicate the depth of the problems in which the fleet found itself. Throughout the period of the dispute over ownership, the fleet's electricity supply was regularly cut off by Ukraine for nonpayment of energy bills. In 1994 the fleet's then-commander

Eduard Baltin asserted that disruptions to the supply of material and technical provisions to the fleet were due to the economic situation of both Russia and Ukraine.[9] In addition and, again, as elsewhere in the post-Soviet armed forces, the issue of pay for the fleet's personnel was seriously affected by the collapse of the defense budgets of these states, with erratic salary payment and the different value of the wages of those paid by Ukraine and those paid by Russia causing unrest.

Taken as a whole, the Black Sea Fleet's numerous financial problems and the inability of any of the states involved to resolve them adequately given their own economic problems, the fleet's aging vessels and infrastructure, and its decline in strategic value raise the question of why any of the states bordering the Black Sea would seek to claim ownership rights over the fleet. The answer appears to lie in three areas. First, as was noted throughout the dispute, the sale of part of the fleet's hardware would provide additional revenue, although there was a perception that (even to states in such difficult economic circumstances as Ukraine and Russia) this would always have been of marginal benefit.[10] In fact, the sale of assets in the period up to the 1997 agreement on the fleet proved to be a highly contentious issue, with all parties accusing one another of the covert sale of equipment, the ownership of which was still disputed.

A second, more important, factor underpinning the dispute was the perception of both the continued military and the growing economic and geopolitical significance of the Black Sea region. Despite the post–Cold War decline in the importance of the Black Sea as a military theater, both Russia and Ukraine viewed control of the fleet, and specifically of the fleet's Crimean bases, as a significant strategic asset in the region. In particular, the loss of part of the fleet, and the decline in the fleet's capability as a whole, was a subject of concern for those Russian actors and analysts concerned by the changes to the regional balance of power and by the issue of NATO's eastward expansion. During the period of the dispute over the fleet, several Russian commentators drew attention to concerns over the potential expansion of the Turkish naval presence in the Black Sea (and in particular its increased size relative to the depleted Russian Black Sea Fleet) and to a growth in US naval activity in the region. Of at least equal importance for both Russia and Ukraine from the early 1990s onward was the issue of the economic significance of the Black Sea region for both states. As several analysts have noted, the Black Sea region is critical for both states because of its key role in the development of regional economic integration and in the development of energy pipelines.[11] In addition, the strategic value of the Black Sea coastline for Russia was clearly a key factor in Russian military and foreign policy toward Georgia. None of these factors has diminished in the decade since the signing of the final agreement on the Black Sea Fleet. The period since 1997, and especially since the start of the United States'

"War on Terror" and after the elections of Viktor Yushchenko in Ukraine and Mikhail Saakashvili in Georgia, has seen increased NATO engagement in the region and the rapid growth of the region's importance in the politics of energy pipelines (including the opening of the Baku-Ceyhan pipeline, which crosses Georgia). Russia's continued strategic interest in Georgia has reflected concerns about the Western orientation of the Saakashvili administration and the United States' security engagement in Georgia.

Just as important, however, the issue of the ownership of the Black Sea Fleet was connected to a number of fundamental issues of national identity and emergent state sovereignty, and specifically to the sovereignty and national identity of these three states as understood in relation to one another. In the immediate post-Soviet period, for Russia and Ukraine, the Black Sea Fleet represented an important national symbol, connected to originary myths of Russian and Ukrainian nationhood. As with the issue of nuclear weapons, ideas of sovereignty in relation to the Black Sea Fleet are important in a number of respects. First, the approaches taken to the questions of the ownership of the fleet, control of its bases, and the loyalties or national sympathies of its command are, in themselves, indicative of attitudes within military and political elites toward their state's sovereignty, and toward the sovereignty (and limits to sovereignty) of the other states involved.

Second, and critically, the nature of the dispute over the fleet reflects the particularly interdependent conception of sovereignty in the post-Soviet space—sovereignty as a zero sum game played between Russia and the other states involved, in this case played over questions of security assets and territory (in particular, Crimea and Abkhazia). Finally, sovereignty has played an important role in the issue of the Black Sea Fleet in a more tangible way—as a commodity to be traded by Georgia and Ukraine (with varying degrees of success) for internal stability or assets such as energy supplies. Although in a relatively weak position for a number of reasons considered below, Ukraine was able to assert a strong negotiating position in relation to Russia; Georgia, in contrast, was unable to pursue its claims to a significant part of the fleet because of the extremely weak nature of key features of its state sovereignty (specifically, territorial integrity and the ability to prevent external interventions) in relation to Russia. Thus, the process of division itself can be used as a yardstick by which to assess the sovereignty of the states concerned. The dispute over the fleet reflected a more fundamental difference between positions informed by a broadly Western model and a Soviet model of sovereignty.

Statements made by politicians and military personnel involved in the dispute clearly connect the Black Sea Fleet to ideas about national identity, with both the Russian and Ukrainian sides invoking images of a historic tradition of naval innovation and dominance in the Black Sea. A second, related factor in the dispute, therefore, has been the way in which, as with the dispute over nuclear weapons, the issue of ownership of the assets and control of the associated bases has been linked to tensions over sovereignty and post-Soviet independence. Clearly, one of the issues of greatest concern for a number of the groups involved was the way in which the issue of the ownership of the Black Sea Fleet became linked by various actors to the issue of Ukrainian sovereignty over the Crimean peninsula.

The dispute over the ownership of the Black Sea Fleet began simultaneously with the breakup of the USSR and was not substantively resolved until 1997; even after this date, however, it has continued to surface as a source of discontent among sections of the political and military elites of Russia, Ukraine, and Georgia, emerging after the election of Yushchenko as a subject of renewed dispute between Ukraine and Russia, and within the Ukrainian political elite. Although the ownership and possible division of the fleet did not remain continuously at the top of the diplomatic and security agenda of Russia and Ukraine throughout this period, the nature of the negotiation process and the different perspectives and objectives of the various actors involved in the debate over the fleet's future meant that it was never marginalized for long. This was not, however, the case in Georgia, where the future of the Black Sea Fleet occupied a relatively lowly place on the country's security agenda as the Tbilisi government attempted to establish more fundamental attributes of state sovereignty, in particular its territorial integrity.

Looked at as a whole, the complex and generally unsuccessful process of negotiation over the Black Sea Fleet, which ran from independence up to the May 1997 agreement, takes on a repetitive, cyclical appearance, with frequent, official-level meetings to discuss the negotiating framework, followed by regular presidential bilateral meetings, leading to the annual signing of apparently definitive agreements, which were then either revoked by ministers or not ratified (or ratified with significant amendments) by the national parliaments. Simultaneously with the process of negotiation, the defense ministries and the fleet command were engaged throughout this period in a process of asset seizure and low-level, aggressive maneuvers, which reflected the military elites' attempts to reconfigure the position on the ground in reaction against, rather than in accordance with, the political agreements on the future of the fleet. In both of these respects—the annual renegotiation of supposedly definitive agreements because prior agreements did not (and perhaps were not expected to) reflect actual intentions, and the gap between official agreements or statements and actual practice—the process recalls the experiences of the Soviet era, in which the expectation that official theory and actual practice were not necessarily directly, causally, connected, underpinned structures and processes. A third strand of the process was the repeated intervention by politicians outside the state governments, often in the form of visits or attempted visits to Sevastopol (the main base of the Black Sea Fleet)—a phenomenon that has again increased fleet-related tensions between Russia and Ukraine in recent years. Once again, these visits track the process of negotiation—indicating, as does the scale and persistence of disruption to the political negotiations by the military elites, the extent to which the various political and military elites within each state were acting independently in what would normally be expected to be a process in which states presented themselves as unitary actors. For both Russia and Ukraine, the combination of conflicts among executive and legislature and strong interest groups (above all, the states' armed forces) proved to be particularly problematic for the resolution of the fleet issue. In the case of Georgia, the absence of a consolidated state structure and the failure of the center's political authority over much of the state's territory proved to be the critical block to establishing a sustained and recognized claim to part of the fleet.

Ukraine and Russia

The dispute between Ukraine and Russia over the ownership of the Black Sea Fleet started with the collapse of the USSR and—despite the supposedly definitive 1997 agreement—appears to remain unresolved. Its duration and severity—at points, involving asset seizure and the threat of a more sustained use of force—needs to be understood as a result of the way the fate of the fleet touched issues of state building, sovereignty, and national myth. The first significant negotiations over the future of the Black Sea Fleet were held in the first week of January 1992 and already reflected some of the issues that would dominate the dispute for the next eighteen months. These talks between the Black Sea Fleet command on the one hand and President Kravchuk and Ukrainian defense minister Morozov on the other, were unsuccessful because of the conflict between Ukraine's claim to the fleet and the fleet command's position that as part of the former Soviet Navy, the CIS agreements required the Black Sea Fleet to be classified as strategic and therefore part of the Joint Armed Forces. Ukraine was apparently offered a limited number of ships and some port facilities, consistent with the view of the Black Sea Fleet command/CIS Joint Armed Forces that Ukraine only required a navy for the purposes of coastal protection and customs enforcement. Talks held shortly afterward apparently reached agreement on the principle that some of the armed forces on Ukrainian territory should be classified as strategic forces of the CIS but that this would not include that part of the fleet that would form part of the armed forces of Ukraine.

Two other dominant features of the dispute over the fleet also emerged—the fact that the CIS Navy Main Staff claimed that, legally, the Black Sea Fleet should fly the Russian flag "since Russia is recognised by the world community as the rightful heir to the former Union," and the claims by Russian sources that officers of the Black Sea Fleet had been ordered to take an oath of allegiance to Ukraine and to fly the Ukrainian state flag on the fleet's ships.[12] These two issues of the flags and oaths of allegiance were points of tension for Russia and Ukraine throughout the early period of the dispute. As discussed below, an interesting feature of these—and many subsequent—talks was the absence of clear demarcation between the representatives of the Black Sea Fleet and of the Russian Federation. Both on this occasion and at other points in the dispute, reports of negotiations were unclear as to whether the Ukrainian delegation was negotiating with the Black Sea Fleet command, representatives of the Joint Armed Forces of the CIS, or the Russian government. At subsequent negotiations, these three organizations were frequently grouped into a single delegation in what effectively became bilateral negotiations with Ukraine.

In the first quarter of 1992, talks over the Black Sea Fleet appeared to be moving forward in principle. However, the process was disrupted in April with the issue of conflicting decrees (quickly withdrawn) by Presidents Kravchuk and Yeltsin, in which each asserted their state's exclusive ownership of the fleet. The decrees followed the visit of Russian vice president Alexander Rutskoi to Sevastopol, during which he suggested both that Russia could incorporate Crimea and that the Black Sea Fleet was Russian.[13] In response, the Ukrainian Foreign Ministry accused both Rutskoi and Yeltsin of a deliberate attempt to undermine Ukrainian sovereignty.[14] According to Shaposhnikov, in late May 1992, after the cancellation of the conflicting Russian and Ukrainian presidential decrees, the CIS defense ministers decided that the Black Sea Fleet would not be considered as part of the CIS strategic forces.[15] By mid-June, however, the CIS Joint Armed Forces were apparently reconsidering this—at least one Russian report appeared to imply that this was because of the extent to which it weakened the Russian negotiating position.[16] Official-level talks continued throughout May and June, culminating in late June with a summit meeting at Dagomys, which produced one of the key agreements on the fleet. Various versions of this agreement appeared in the press, but all noted that there had been agreement on the principle of dividing the Black Sea Fleet, and there appeared to be agreement on short-term joint use of shore installations and on joint financing. The Dagomys agreement was followed in August by a more specific agreement at the Yalta summit, which agreed on the withdrawal of the Black Sea Fleet from CIS Joint Armed Forces control and on the fleet's eventual division. The Yalta agreement also provided for a transitional period until 1995, during which the fleet would be under the joint command of Russia and Ukraine.

Throughout the rest of 1992 and early 1993 the Russian and Ukrainian negotiators met at regular intervals; no agreement on specifics was reached, however, and the agreement in mid-June between Kravchuk and Yeltsin was effectively little more than a restatement of earlier agreements. The Massandra summit in September 1993—the focus of international attention because of the agreement signed on nuclear weapons—produced an agreement on the Black Sea Fleet, under the terms of which Ukraine would nominally receive 50 percent of the fleet but would then exchange it for energy debt forgiveness from Russia. Almost immediately, however, the agreement was being described by the Ukrainian government as merely a proposal put forward by the Russians, rather than an agreed strategy; not surprisingly, the deal collapsed. The principle of exchanging part of the Ukrainian share of the fleet for energy debt forgiveness remained, however, and became a feature of all subsequent agreements, including the (supposedly) definitive one.

Throughout this period, as the dispute over the division and basing of the fleet was negotiated at a governmental level, and debated by the legislatures, attempts were clearly being made by the various military bodies involved to provide a favorable resolution on the ground. These attempts at gaining de facto control over portions of the fleet involved the seizure of individual vessels and parts of the infrastructure, including the seizure of key buildings in the main Sevastopol base by personnel who had taken the oath of loyalty to Ukraine in July 1992, and the seizure of facilities in Odessa by Ukrainian troops in April 1994. The seizure of vessels and other assets (including the fleet's aircraft), the alleged sale of some of these assets by the Black Sea Fleet command, and the repeated unauthorized raising of national flags on vessels by both Ukrainian and Russian groupings seriously complicated the negotiation process, not least because of the uncertainty created about total assets of the fleet.[17] This uncertainty was compounded by the apparent reluctance on the part of the fleet command and the Russian negotiators to provide a complete inventory of the fleet's assets as of December 1991.

Despite a series of meetings and agreements in 1994 and 1995, the definitive presidential agreement on the Black Sea Fleet was not signed until May 1997, together with the bilateral Russian-Ukrainian Treaty on Friendship and Cooperation, the signing of which had been conditional on agreement on the fleet. The friendship treaty was an important document because, among other things, it provided a formal, mutual recognition of sovereignty and territorial integrity—the first Russian-Ukrainian bilateral treaty to do so in the post-Soviet period. The 1997 agreement nominally awarded 50 percent of the fleet to Ukraine, but Ukraine in fact only retained 12 percent (124 surface vessels and one submarine) with the other 38 percent, valued at US$526 million, handed over to Russia as payment of a proportion of Ukrainian energy debts to Russia.[18] The rent payments for basing facilities in Sevastopol were similarly offset against Ukrainian debts. Although this appeared to bring the dispute over the fleet to an end, both the friendship treaty, providing mutual recognition of sovereignty and territorial integrity, and the agreement on the fleet required ratification by the Russian and Ukrainian legislatures. The Friendship and Cooperation Treaty was ratified by the Ukrainian Rada in an overwhelming vote in January 1998, but the vote on the fleet agreement was postponed and only ratified in March 1999, following the treaty ratification by the Russian Federation Council (which, in turn, was not to take effect until the Ukrainian ratification of the fleet agreements).

For several years, the 1997 agreement appeared to have provided a definitive resolution to the dispute over the fleet. This period (from the late 1990s until 2004) also saw a gradual lessening of the tensions between Russia and Ukraine over the issue of Russian influence in the post-Soviet space—in large part, a consequence of the Ukrainian domestic political crisis that developed in this period. By the start of the twenty-first century, the Ukrainian executive was engulfed by the twin crises of catastrophic economic mismanagement and allegations of corruption and other forms of criminality. In response, the Ukrainian executive appeared to be compensating for its unpopularity at home and the distancing of Western European states and the United States by improving ties with the other CIS states in general and with Russia in particular.[19] In this context, the division of the Black Sea Fleet, the number and nature of its assets, and the Russian lease of the Sevastopol facilities did not appear to be matters for further dispute.

This changed, however, as Ukrainian-Russian relations worsened in the aftermath of the "Orange Revolution," since the newly elected president was widely understood to represent a break with the increasingly Russia-dependent Leonid Kuchma administration and to favor improved ties with European Union (EU) and NATO states. The perception of active Russian involvement in the election and its aftermath, with the purpose of ensuring the appointment of his eastward-oriented opponent, Viktor Yanukovych, soured relations from the very start of the Yushchenko administration. In keeping with the anticipated foreign and security policy shift away from Russia by the new Ukrainian government, and within a few weeks of Yushchenko's confirmation as president, Foreign Minister Boris Tarasyuk had first denounced the Russian Black Sea Fleet's presence in Ukraine and then asserted that the basing agreement would probably not be renewed after 2017.

As before, the dispute over the fleet appeared to be focused on a wide range of political aspects in addition to matters directly related to the fleet itself. Issues of Ukrainian sovereignty in general, and its relationship to the status and politics of Crimea in particular, featured prominently, as did the instrumentalization of the fleet in relation to financial and energy questions. After a period in which the issue of the Black Sea Fleet appeared to have been resolved, the future of the Russian fleet in Ukraine again appeared to be uncertain and a matter of serious dispute between the two states.

By the end of March 2005, both Yushchenko and the head of the Ukrainian security services had raised questions about the fleet, with the security service head claiming that its deployment in Ukraine was inconsistent with Ukrainian national interests.[20] In the following months, a variety of issues relating to the fleet agreements were raised, often at the same time other contentious issues were dominating Russian-Ukrainian relations, although once raised, the Ukrainian government tended to downplay them. By December 2005, the status of the 1997 treaty and the continued presence of the Russian Navy in Ukraine were raised in the context of the Russia-Ukraine gas dispute, although the Ukrainian government denied that there was an attempt to link the two issues. A number of Ukrainian politicians indicated in this period and later that the rent paid by Russia for the base should be revised to reflect what they described as commercial rates, although Yushchenko said that there would be no revision to the existing agreements, and Russia refused to consider any increase.[21]

The renewed dispute took a more dramatic turn in January 2006, when Ukrainian officials took over the Yalta lighthouse, which both Russia and Ukraine claimed belonged to them under the terms of the 1997 treaty. This highlighted a broader dispute over the disposition of various shore-based assets under the treaty, with Ukraine claiming that Russia was illegally occupying territory and facilities, and Russia maintaining that it was adhering to the agreement.[22] Ukraine repeatedly demanded both a complete inventory of assets used by the Russian fleet and that the fleet provide details of weapons located on Ukrainian territory. In the aftermath of the confrontation over the lighthouse, the issue of renegotiating the agreement, including the rent and the date of withdrawal, was raised in a series of bilateral talks, but no agreement was reached. In June 2006, in what appeared to be part of a pattern of steady escalation in the dispute since early 2005, protests erupted in Crimea over the proposed visit of a US ship to Crimea in preparation for joint military exercises. This extended beyond an internal Kiev-Crimea dispute, since Russian politicians and journalists were involved in the protests, and this in turn drew in the Russian government when Yushchenko issued a decree expelling foreigners (in practice, Russians) who were taking part in the Crimean, anti-NATO protests.[23] Several months later, in February 2007, Russian political activity in Crimea again drew condemnation from the Ukrainian Foreign Ministry and nationalist Ukrainian politicians; on a visit to Sevastopol, the mayor of Moscow, Iurii Luzhkov, spoke of Sevastopol and Crimea having been "torn away" from Russia—an assertion that caused nationalist politicians to accuse Luzhkov of interference in Ukrainian internal affairs.[24]

Although the contours of this revived dispute over the fleet were generally similar to the pre-1997 arguments over assets, basing, and Russian political intervention in Crimea, one notable, new aspect was the division within the Ukrainian political elite between, on the one hand, Yushchenko and his political allies and, on the other, Yanukovych, the Ukrainian prime minister (and unsuccessful 2004 presidential candidate) and his allies. Yushchenko and, more forcefully, his allies in government and parliament consistently represented the Russian naval presence as unwelcome and Russian comments regarding both its role and its future in Crimea as attempts to interfere in Ukraine's affairs. In October 2006, for example, Putin suggested that the basing of the Russian fleet in Crimea could be prolonged beyond the 2017 deadline, that its presence increased regional stability, and that it could be used to defend Ukraine in the event of "outside interference." The response of Yushchenko was to state that Ukraine was capable of defending itself, while the Ukrainian defense minister, the first deputy foreign minister, and others (although not, explicitly, Yushchenko himself) asserted that the Russian fleet would not remain beyond 2017.[25] The dominance of this view of the fleet within the Ukrainian Foreign Ministry appeared to outlast the tenure of Foreign Minister Tarasyuk, who was dismissed by parliament in early December 2006; in January 2007, the Foreign Ministry stated that a failure on the part of Russia to obey a Ukrainian court order demanding the return of navigation facilities in Crimea would produce a response of "measures stipulated by international law." This followed a failed attempt by Ukraine to seize one such facility earlier that month.[26]

In contrast, Yanukovych and other Ukrainian politicians who regarded Russia with less—and the EU and NATO with more—suspicion than Yushchenko and the Ukrainian nationalists did, were much more sympathetic to the Russian position. Thus, Yanukovych appeared to support Putin's October 2006 proposal to extend the Russian lease beyond 2017 as potentially beneficial to both Ukraine and Russia.[27] With the dismissal of Tarasyuk and the increased dominance of Yanukovych and his allies, by early 2007 political conditions within Ukraine appeared to favor Russia and thus the possibility of a continued presence in Ukraine; by spring, however, the constitutional standoff between Yushchenko and Yanukovych made the prospects appear much less certain.

The Basis of Claims to the Fleet: Laws, Money, and History

Throughout the period of the dispute over the Black Sea Fleet in the early and mid-1990s, the positions of Russian, CIS, and Ukrainian participants were dominated by rhetoric connecting state sovereignty and national identity to the fleet. The basis of these claims to the fleet tended to fall into one (or sometimes both) of two categories—legal/financial or historical.

Legal/financial claims. Arguments about the ownership of the fleet in the early period of the dispute (before Russia and Ukraine had agreed in principle on the division of the fleet) often turned around competing interpretations of laws and international treaties, and sometimes on the competing claims of different documents. Broadly, it is possible to trace three positions: that the legal position confirmed Ukrainian ownership, that it confirmed Russian ownership, and that it confirmed that the fleet was the property of the CIS. Various actors on all sides of the debate treated these last two positions as interchangeable.

As with the debate about the ownership of nuclear weapons, the Ukrainian legal position on the ownership of the Black Sea Fleet derived from the law passed on 10 September 1991 by the Ukrainian Supreme Soviet on property on Ukrainian territory. Thus, in April 1992 the Ukrainian National Information Agency (Ukrinform) Diplomatic Information Service issued a statement saying that "Ukraine's position at the negotiations . . . on the issue of the BSF will be built on the right of every state to inherit the property located on its territory."[28] In addition to this law on property, the Ukrainian government invoked the December 1991 law specifically concerning the armed forces on Ukrainian territory. A statement released by Ukrinform in April 1992, in relation to the dispute over the Black Sea Fleet, asserted that:

> As is known, on 24 August 1991, all military formations deployed on the republic's territory were subordinated to the Ukrainian Supreme Soviet by a resolution of the Ukrainian parliament. Any attempt by another state to transfer the Black Sea Fleet deployed in Ukraine to its jurisdiction will be regarded as interference in the internal affairs of independent Ukraine and contradicts the norms of international law, including the treaty between Ukraine and Russia of 19 November 1990 and the agreements reached within the framework of the CIS.[29]

Not surprisingly, this claim based on the right of a state to ownership of and control over assets on its territory was not a position that was accepted by all the other parties in the dispute over the fleet. The deputy commander in chief of the CIS Joint Armed Forces, Yuri Rodionov, interviewed on Russian television, stated that "to divide the Armed Forces on a territorial principle, that what's on my territory is mine—well, that's an unacceptable option."[30] The same view was taken by Admiral Ivan Kapitanets, who—in a fusion of the legal arguments about ownership and the arguments based on national identity and history—commented that "the question of the formation of armed forces on the territorial principle introduced by the Ukrainian delegation is invalid. This is because the grouping in Ukraine was created by the whole country during more than fifty years."[31]

As with other property disputes, such as that over the nuclear weapons in former Soviet states, the dispute over the Black Sea Fleet was further complicated by the fact that contradictory agreements and laws appeared to support the claims of different parties. The legal basis of the Ukrainian claim to the fleet was the legislation passed by the Ukrainian parliament in 1991. There were, however, two other claims to the fleet (Russian and CIS), both apparently supported by international agreements.

The second ownership claim was that the fleet was in fact the property of the CIS—a claim advanced by both the senior officials within the CIS military structures and the Russian government (and occasionally politicians in other CIS states).[32] A key point of disagreement over the ownership of the fleet turned on its classification within the overall structure of the former Soviet armed forces. Under the terms of the Minsk agreements of December 1991, to which Ukraine was a signatory, all those units of the armed forces of the former USSR with a nuclear capability were classified as strategic, and all strategic forces were incorporated into the CIS Joint Armed Forces. The Black Sea Fleet included vessels with a nuclear capability and thus, it was argued, the Black Sea Fleet as a whole was under the command of the JAF. Senior military officers, including naval officers and figures in the JAF command, argued that Ukraine was thus in violation of the Minsk agreements in its attempts to claim the part of the Black Sea Fleet located on its territory, even though the agreement contained a provision for the formation of Ukrainian naval forces based on (an unspecified) part of the fleet.[33]

Thus, in his statement to the Russian Supreme Soviet on the negotiations over the fleet, the head of the Russian delegation, Iurii Yarov, was able to state that the Russian position was "based on the generally accepted principles and norms of international law, CIS documents, and bilateral treaties and agreements. More specifically, the protocol signed by the CIS heads of state 16 January says: 'The former USSR Navy is part of the Commonwealth Strategic Forces.'"[34] Russian ambassador Iurii Dubinin also claimed that the protocol adopted by CIS heads of state on 16 January 1992 was the basis for the Russian position and complained that the Ukrainian delegation rejected any mention of the CIS documents as a basis for the negotiations.[35] In an interview with *Krasnaia Zvezda,* Admiral Kapitanets described the Ukrainian delegation to talks on the fleet as adopting "a unilateral interpretation of the agreements reached at Minsk" and stated that the issue of the fleet should be resolved "in the interests of the whole of the CIS."[36] The fleet's commander, Vladimir Kasatonov, took the position that "legally, it is obvious: the Black Sea Fleet forms part of the CIS forces."[37] This was a view apparently shared in early 1992 by Yeltsin, who reportedly described the fleet as an indivisible part of the CIS strategic forces, and by Russian defense minister Pavel Grachev, who supported the position that the fleet should belong to the CIS.[38] As with other disputes surrounding the breakup of the former Soviet security structure, a shared view was evident in the positions adopted by the Russian government and by members of the CIS military structures.

Although this line of argument was effectively made redundant by the 1992 Yalta agreement, which provided for a transitional joint command of the fleet by Russia and Ukraine, thus cutting the CIS structures out of the process, it was occasionally utilized by some actors as part of a broader challenge to Ukrainian sovereignty over the fleet or the Crimean peninsula. Crimean president Yuri Meshkov, for example, claimed in early 1994 that the issue of the fleet should be resolved in the interests of all CIS members, taking into account the wishes of the populations of Crimea and the Crimean executive and legislature.[39] During the same period, Shaposhnikov expressed the view that the fleet should be divided between all the CIS states, rather than simply split between Russia and Ukraine. He also commented that because Ukraine had not joined the CIS Collective Security Treaty, it should only receive one-eleventh of the fleet and that the rest of the fleet should be used to protect CIS interests in the region.[40]

The third position taken by some actors during this period was that the Black Sea Fleet was in fact the property of Russia, as the internationally recognized legal successor to the USSR. One *Rossiiskaia Gazeta* article commented that "Russia [is] recognized by the world community as the legal heir to the former Union. If you follow logic, then the Russian Federation is also the legal heir to its Armed Forces."[41] In early January 1992 several Russian deputies wrote an open letter to Yeltsin on behalf of the Russian National Union and the Rossiia faction that complained about "the attempts to seize the Black Sea Fleet from Russia."[42] More serious for Russian-Ukrainian relations, of course, were the April 1992 comments of then–vice president Rutskoi about Russian ownership of the Black Sea Fleet and the subsequent, short-lived decree by Yeltsin transferring the Black Sea Fleet to Russian ownership.[43]

Thus, the legal basis of the claims to the Black Sea Fleet can be seen to reflect the wider disjunction between understandings of sovereignty in the former Soviet states. On the one hand, Ukraine claimed ownership on the basis of a commonly understood assumption about sovereignty—that a state owns the state assets located on its territory. On the other, and suggesting a set of assumptions based on a conception of sovereignty inherited from the USSR, the Russian government and the CIS military command viewed rights to ownership and control over military assets by the center (the CIS Joint Armed Forces and Russia, in its capacity, as successor state to the USSR) as prior to any other states' claims to sovereignty in this area.

A second basis for competing claims to ownership of the fleet was financial. A number of Ukrainian politicians gave this as one of the primary reasons for Ukrainian claims to the fleet. In April 1992, the Ukrainian ambassador to Moscow stated that in principle Ukraine could claim 16 percent of the whole of the former Soviet navy (more than the whole of the Black Sea Fleet) because, he said, it had assumed 16.4 percent of the USSR's foreign debt. He stated that Ukraine was in fact only claiming the non-nuclear-carrying Black Sea Fleet warships registered in Ukraine—about 70 percent of the fleet, or 10 percent of the former USSR's navy.[44] A variant of this Ukrainian claim to the fleet was made by presidential foreign affairs adviser Anton Buteyko, who stated that Ukraine had contributed between 20 and 25 percent to the building of the Soviet navy, while the whole of the Black Sea Fleet represented only 17 percent of the total navy, with the part of the fleet based in Ukraine representing only 10 percent. According to Buteyko, this meant that the part of the fleet based in Ukraine was already automatically Ukrainian property, and that talks were therefore only to discuss the proportion of the fleet to be transferred to the CIS strategic forces.[45] During the same period, Ukrinform Diplomatic Service stated that "the Black Sea Fleet amounts to a little under 10 per cent of the entire composition of the Navy, which is considerably less than the expenses of Ukraine on its construction and maintenance."[46] A statement by the Ukrainian Republican Party on the fleet division in January 1992 claimed that Ukraine owned 30.2 percent of the former Soviet navy.[47]

Claims to ownership arising from financial obligations and contributions were not confined to activities of the Soviet period, however. Both Russia and Ukraine claimed at various points to be the sole source of financing for the fleet. One of the most significant features of the dispute between Russia and Ukraine over the fleet was the fact that, despite their serious economic problems and, even more strikingly, despite the commitments of both governments to cut their military budgets, both states competed to finance the fleet and to block one another's attempts to do so. Members of the fleet command and the Russian delegation to the talks on the fleet repeatedly claimed that Ukraine had frozen the accounts in which Russian money intended for the fleet had been deposited, and that they refused to forward Russian funds to the fleet. In April 1992, the Russian delegation raised the issue of 250 million rubles of Russian funding for the fleet which it claimed Ukraine had not transferred.[48]

After the agreement on transitional arrangements for the fleet, which included arrangements for joint funding, there were repeated claims by both states of attempts to gain control of the fleet through unilateral funding, and in particular through the payment of fleet service personnel. Yeltsin's April 1992 decree placing the fleet under Russian jurisdiction stated that "the activities of the BSF are financed out of the Russian Federation budget."[49] In May 1993, the head of the Russian navy's finance and economics directorate claimed that the Ukrainian government was trying to finance the fleet via the Ukrainian navy financial service rather than through the joint funding mechanisms. He also claimed that the Ukrainian Ministry of Defense had more than doubled the pay of fleet servicemen since 1 November 1992, but only for those who had taken the Ukrainian oath.[50] At the same time, there were reports that Russia had ordered that fleet personnel were to start being paid at Russian rates. In June, Baltin, then-commander of the Black Sea Fleet, signed a directive to transfer fleet personnel to the pay conditions of the Russian Ministry of Defense, over the strong objections of senior officers of the Ukrainian navy, who described this move as interference in Ukraine's internal affairs.[51]

Historical claims. However complex and contradictory the various competing legal or financial claims to the fleet may have been, they were at least, by their very nature, open to some form of negotiation. The second set of claims, however, was not open to negotiation and compromise because it located the basis of ownership of the fleet at the level of history and national identity.

Both Russia and Ukraine invoked ideas of a historically based national identity to claim that the Black Sea Fleet was not only legally theirs but also essentially theirs. These claims drew on national myths about the history of these states from the Kievan Rus' period onward. A typical example of this approach is outlined in a paper by Zenon E. Kohut, who argues that an indigenous Ukrainian fleet originates in the early Kievan Rus' period and thus predates Ukrainian statehood.[52] He also notes the claim that links the Black Sea Fleet to the Cossack exploration of the Black Sea. This was also an image used by Kravchuk, who spoke of the Zaporizhian Cossack fleet sailing in the Black Sea.[53] The promotion of this founding myth relating to the fleet persisted beyond the dispute; in mid-2002, for example, the Ukrainian navy's website provided an overwhelmingly Ukrainian account of the history of the Black Sea Fleet (and failed to make a single reference to either Russia or the Soviet Union despite mentioning the Crimean War and World War II):

> Our navy has a history of over a thousand years. Historical sources have well established that Kievan princes had carried out successful naval campaigns against Byzantium, Khazaria, Volga, Bulgaria. . . . In the centuries during and following the Middle Ages the name of Ukraine had been glorified by the victorious naval campaigns of [the] Cossack Hetmans of the Zaporizhian Sich. . . . The Ukrainian navy has a glorious past and a bright future. To build the national navy is one of the most important missions of our country.[54]

The claim that the nationality of the Black Sea Fleet has been clearly defined since its creation is not, of course, exclusively a Ukrainian one. The assumption that the Black Sea Fleet (and, closely connected to this argument, Crimea) is essentially Russian and has always been so, was a recurring view in the early 1990s among a number of senior military officials in the fleet command and in the CIS command structures (all of whom were at this point officially serving the CIS states as a whole rather than exclusively Russia).[55] Vladimir Chernavin, for example, stated in an interview that, although the fleet served the whole CIS, the navy (including the Black Sea Fleet) "has always been Russian, as we know from history."[56] A less-explicit comment by Kasatonov linked the creation of the fleet to both the Russian empire and the Soviet Union.[57] A more outspoken proponent of the view that the Black Sea Fleet was historically and essentially Russian was Russian vice president Rutskoi, who commented on his infamous April 1992 visit to Sevastopol that "Russia decided to have a fleet in the Black Sea a long time ago, and it will have a fleet there," as well as asserting that the fleet should be flying either the St. Andrew's flag (the traditional flag of the Russian navy) or the Soviet flag.[58] This position continued to be asserted more than a decade later; in 2006, as tensions revived between Russia and Ukraine over the fleet's presence in Crimea, a Russian analyst writing in *Military Thought* asserted that Sevastopol's

> status as the main base of the Russian Black Sea Fleet both in the past 200 years and in the future should remain immutable. . . . Sevastopol was not built and equipped as a naval base for centuries, enduring two heroic blockades for [it] to be used as a base for US navy warships or those of Turkey as a NATO member that has more than once been routed by the Russian navy. This is in fact the principal objective for Russian diplomacy in the "process" of Russian-Ukrainian relations.[59]

A Unified or a Divided Fleet?

The dispute over the Black Sea Fleet can be divided into several phases, determined both by the changing personnel involved and by the nature of the specific points under dispute. One of the issues that structured the nature of the dispute from 1993 onward was the question of bases, discussed in a later section of this chapter. The issue that dominated the first period of the dispute, however, was whether the fleet should be divided at all.

The question of whether the fleet should be divided or whether it should remain unified was of critical concern to the Black Sea Fleet command and officers, and the commanders of the CIS navy and JAF. It was complicated, however, by the additional assumption held by many of these actors that a unified CIS fleet was, essentially, a Russian fleet.[60] Whether driven by Russian nationalism or organizational survival instincts, or a combination of the two, the CIS military personnel overwhelmingly supported the retention of a unified fleet; in contrast, the Ukrainian military and political actors in the dispute vehemently opposed the idea of a unified CIS fleet—as they had done with the idea of a CIS Joint Armed Forces in general.

This Ukrainian hostility was grounded in the perception that such a structure would represent a continuing threat to their sovereignty over matters of security, not least because of their view that the structure would necessarily not perform the function for which it had in theory been established (the security of all the CIS member states). As with debates over the future of other parts of the former Soviet military, the Ukrainian government held the view that an army (or navy) cannot be stateless, and that therefore—particularly since the CIS had been declared not to be a supranational body—the CIS armed forces must in reality be answerable to a particular state, which they identified as Russia. There was another objection too, voiced by Kravchuk in January 1992:

> Take the problem of the unified armed forces, for instance. That is not a technical but a political problem. Let us think of its possible consequences. . . . If the armed forces are unified and there are 11 civilian bosses, the troops listen to one man. Then—like it or not—a military man, a commander in chief, will rise above all 11 republics. The armed forces will rise above politics. . . . Unified armed forces herald the end of democracy and the end of independence.[61]

In the same period he also commented both on the fact that the CIS could not have a Joint Armed Forces since it was not a state, and on the need for "other republics" to extend their power within the CIS framework.[62] He also described the JAF as "a serious problem for the Commonwealth. I, the leader of an independent state, am nobody for the supreme command of the JAF. I can control these forces only by telephone. And not control, rather ask. For example, I ask Shaposhnikov to do something and he answers: 'I disagree.' So, it turns out that the supreme authority in Ukraine cannot resolve important issues on its own territory."[63]

The call to preserve a unified Black Sea Fleet was made most strongly by the fleet's officers and by Russian and Crimean deputies. Early in February 1992, the Russian parliament passed a resolution in favor of preserving a united Black Sea Fleet "defending, in the Mediterranean area, the interests of all CIS member states as a single whole, in line with the provisions of the treaty on the formation of the CIS of December 8, 1991."[64] At an emergency session in June 1993, the Crimean Supreme Soviet adopted an appeal to the Ukrainian and Russian presidents, calling on them to preserve the Black Sea Fleet as a single military unit belonging to both states, as suggested by Baltin.[65] Not surprisingly, the most vociferous proponents of the retention of a unified Black Sea Fleet were the fleet's officers and the CIS naval command. In February 1992 the Black Sea Fleet military council and representatives of officers' assemblies issued a joint statement declaring their allegiance to the CIS and stating that the fleet should be a single strategic force for the defense of the CIS's southern waters.[66] The previous month, a letter had been sent to Kravchuk by senior CIS naval officers stating that "the Black Sea ocean fleet . . . can be controlled only from a single centre, namely the apparatus of the Commander in Chief of the CIS Armed

Forces. . . . To exclude the BSF from the unified system of the country's [sic] naval forces and transfer it to Ukrainian jurisdiction would mean undermining the defence of the Commonwealth."[67] Kasatonov commented in this period that "it was clearly established that the . . . components of the navy are subordinated to a single command. . . . The leadership of the Defense Ministry and the navy consider that the fleet cannot be divided into strategic and nonstrategic force"; he also asserted that the personnel of the fleet opposed its division.[68]

Apparently in response to these attempts to retain a unified fleet under the command of the JAF, members of the Ukrainian military promoted the idea of retaining a unified Black Sea Fleet under Ukrainian command (on the grounds that the fleet was the property of Ukraine). In January 1992, the Ukrainian deputy defense minister, Ivan Bizhan, reportedly stated that his country's future navy should incorporate all units of the Black Sea Fleet, except for its strategic components, and that the whole of the Black Sea Fleet staff should be made Ukrainian in order to keep it united.[69] At the Third Congress of Ukrainian Union of Officers, the chairman demanded that Ukraine immediately take the fleet under its jurisdiction. During the Dagomys talks in 1992, an (unnamed) adviser to the commander of the Ukrainian navy stated to journalists that the fleet should not be divided at all, because Ukraine had the indisputable right to ownership.[70] Once again, however, the attitudes of military officials were notably more radical in their nationalism than those of the politicians, who repeatedly denied that Ukraine laid claim to the whole of the fleet.

Closely linked to the Russian/CIS officers' desire to retain a unified fleet was the view that Ukraine was entitled to a proportion of the fleet but that the Russian/CIS military personnel had the authority to determine both its size and role. As noted earlier, the Minsk agreements categorized all units of the armed forces of the former USSR with a nuclear capability as strategic, and it incorporated all strategic forces into the Joint Armed Forces of the CIS. There was, however, a separate provision made in the agreements for the creation of a Ukrainian navy, and it was the tension between these two aspects of the foundational military agreements that structured the dispute over the future of the Black Sea Fleet until the agreement in principle to withdraw the fleet from CIS control and divide it was taken at Yalta.

The provision for a Ukrainian fleet was interpreted by the CIS naval command and the Black Sea Fleet command in an extremely restricted sense. Speaking in January 1992, for example, Admiral Chernavin, commander in chief of the former Soviet navy, commented that, as a sovereign state, Ukraine of course had the right to a navy, but that its navy should be restricted to the capability to undertake border patrols and smuggling-prevention operations. He commented that "you have to determine what Ukraine needs a navy for and what its tasks are. And I took the liberty to formulate the tasks."[71] This was also the view of the deputy commander in chief of the CIS Joint Armed

Forces, Boris Pyankov, who contrasted the border patrol requirements of a Ukrainian navy with the strategic capability of the Black Sea Fleet.[72] In an interview at the start of 1992, Kasatonov commented that "the leadership of the [USSR] Defence Ministry and the Navy . . . agreed to transfer part of the formations of the light surface forces [as opposed to any of the fleet's warships or submarines] to the Ukrainian Defence Ministry's control. In the long term that state's naval forces would be formed from them."[73] In an interview in April 1992, Shaposhnikov expressed the opinion that "Ukraine does not need the great Black Sea Fleet. Just 20–25 per cent of it is more than enough"; earlier he had apparently expressed the view that Ukraine should receive only 7 percent of the fleet.[74] In a radio interview, Rear Admiral Nikolai Yelenin (assistant to the commander in chief of the CIS navy) gave the Russian/CIS perspective on Ukraine and the fleet—"What does the Ukrainian leadership need the Black Sea Fleet for? What task does it fulfil?"—and said that "our military leaders consider that it is quite sufficient" for Ukraine to have 20–22 percent of the fleet.[75] The assumption that non-Ukrainian politicians and officers had both the capability and the right to determine the future character of the emergent Ukrainian navy is significant in what it suggests about their views of Ukrainian state sovereignty over security policy and assets and, indeed, about their conception of *Russian* authority in relation to Ukrainian security affairs.

The nature of this debate over the future of the fleet was characterized, as with other such issues, by the belief on all sides that there was no clear distinction between the structures of the JAF and the Russian government. Despite a number of statements that the JAF represented the security interests of the whole CIS, on several occasions officials within its structures made statements that clearly indicated that the Black Sea Fleet was in fact Russian. In an interview in February 1992, Admiral Kapitanets, first deputy commander of the CIS navy, twice described the navy (then under the command of the CIS JAF) as Russian and asked, "Why should we surrender it to anyone?"[76] When asked in March 1992 which flag the Black Sea Fleet should sail under, Kasatonov said of the St. Andrew's flag that "it will be a great honour to put out to sea under such a flag" and that he would be the first to raise the flag if a decision were taken on it.[77] In May 1993, Kasatonov (then no longer the fleet's commander) stated that "in the position of Black Sea commander . . . I came forward to defend Russia's interests and managed to defend the Fleet."[78] In April 1992, the Ukrainian parliament passed a resolution attacking JAF interference in the internal affairs of a sovereign state, in response to the apparent order by Shaposhnikov to execute Yeltsin's decree of transfer of the Black Sea Fleet to Russia. Talking about his view that the fleet should be maintained under a common operational command, Feliks Gromov, its first deputy commander, stated that the fleet should maintain its capability to work in cooperation with the Baltic and Northern fleets, "all the more so since Russia is not only one of the countries of the CIS to have signed the treaty on collective security but is also in essence its guarantor."[79]

The perception that the JAF, including the fleet, was indistinguishable from Russian security structures was necessarily exacerbated by the fact that the lines of command during the fleet's transitional period (until 1995) did not appear to reflect the structures agreed to by the Russian and Ukrainian presidents for joint command. Although nominally a joint command that bypassed the two defense ministries and was under the direct command of the presidents, the fleet's structures never appeared to acknowledge the authority of the Ukrainian president or the role of any Ukrainian governmental structures. The Ukrainian navy repeatedly complained that the fleet command was attempting to bypass the provisions of joint command—in early 1995, for example, the commander of the Ukrainian navy complained that the fleet commander had sent all documents regarding the handing over of a base at Balaklava to the Sevastopol city council rather than to the Ukrainian naval structures who were supposed to receive them.[80] In April 1993, Kravchuk complained that:

> What is happening today in the Fleet under the command of the Russian Defence Ministry—and I consciously emphasise this—this proves that no one reckons with the facts that the Fleet is in Ukraine and the land is ours; the coast is ours and the people who serve in the Fleet are our people as well. No one reckons with this, because the Fleet is completely financed at the expense of Ukraine and the Fleet is commanded by the Russian Defence Ministry.[81]

This was highlighted by the process of replacing Kasatonov as fleet commander, when the decision to appoint Baltin appeared to be taken by the Russian Ministry of Defense, without prior consultation with Ukraine. The impression of partisanship was strongly reinforced by the fact that during the period leading up to the Yalta agreement, members of the fleet and CIS command regularly appeared as part of the Russian state delegation in negotiations. Although the Ukrainian delegation reportedly raised no objection to the presence of two CIS admirals in the Russian delegation in April 1992, since their position was classified as that of nonvoting experts, the fact that they were apparently advising only one of the two states which they were supposed, as CIS officers, to represent is an important indication of the role that they saw for themselves in this dispute.[82]

Bases

Of all the issues involved in the dispute over the Black Sea Fleet, the issue of the allocation of bases, and in particular the Sevastopol bases, proved to be the most intractable. In the period immediately following the breakup of the Soviet Union, this was not apparent, since other issues, including the question of whether the fleet would actually be divided, dominated the debate. Once agreement had been reached in principle that it would be divided, however, the question of which bases would be occupied by the Ukrainian navy and which by the Russian fleet became critical to the wider dispute. This question was clearly linked to issues of sovereignty—specifically, the wider question of the status of Crimea (and Sevastopol, in particular) and the question of the right of the Ukrainian state to determine the use of facilities on its territory. As with other issues surrounding the Black Sea Fleet, such as the ownership of ships and the attempts to preserve a unified fleet, the disagreement over where Russian and Ukrainian fleets would be based, and on what terms, reflects the contested understandings of state sovereignty underpinning the different positions.

The dispute over the allocation of bases began to emerge as one of the dominant issues in the negotiations over the fleet following the June 1993 agreement, which raised the issue of the fleet's coastal infrastructure. According to some reports, the agreement provided for Russian use of the Sevastopol bases, in return for which Russia would formally acknowledge an absence of territorial claims on Ukraine.[83] It became clear that the question of basing arrangements was one of the key areas of contention between these two states (and, importantly, a similarly contentious issue within these states, between the governmental structures, the legislatures, and the military). One of the reasons most commonly given for the failure of talks on the fleet's division, and for the inability to convert the general provisions of presidential agreements to concrete arrangements, was the lack of agreement over the Black Sea Fleet bases. By the end of the period up to 1997, it was clear that despite continued press reports of disagreement over the fleet's division, the only significant dispute remaining about the division of fleet assets was over the bases, since Russia and Ukraine had already agreed upon a formula for the division of the fleet's vessels.

The specific areas of disagreement varied over the course of the period 1993–1997 but most commonly turned around the question of whether one or both of the two states would retain use of the extensive basing facilities within the Sevastopol city limits. On the Ukrainian side, many members of the Ukrainian military (including Morozov) resisted the proposal to lease all of the basing facilities to Russia. However, the proposal that both the Ukrainian and Russian navies be based at Sevastopol was strongly rejected by Russian negotiators and military officials, who wished to secure exclusive use of the Sevastopol facilities. In addition, there was serious disagreement about how many other bases would be allocated to the Russian fleet, where they would be situated, the length of the lease, and what the wording of the arrangement regarding the Sevastopol base would be. At several points, both states' negotiating bodies and supporters stated an intention to see the other state's naval forces entirely removed from Crimea.

Claims by Russian politicians and military personnel on the Sevastopol bases were clearly connected to the claims that the Crimean peninsula generally and Sevastopol in particular, were essentially Russian. In an interview in March 1993, for example, Gromov spoke about the "ties with Sevastopol, the main base of the Fleet, historically dear to Russia."[84] The issue of the status of Crimea—the most direct challenge to Ukrainian sovereignty, since it raised the question of its territorial integrity—was repeatedly raised by members of the Russian legislature during the dispute, often at points immediately before negotiations over the fleet. In May 1992, for example, five days before the opening of a CIS defense ministers meeting at which the fleet issue was to be discussed, the Russian Supreme Soviet held a closed session on the 1954 transfer of Crimea to Ukraine. In October 1996, the Russian Duma adopted a resolution calling on the Ukrainian Rada to alter its position on the Black Sea Fleet and referring to Sevastopol as under Russian jurisdiction; it also described the 1954 transfer of Crimea to Ukraine as "arbitrary." It stated that Sevastopol "has been, and will be the main base of the Russian Black Sea Fleet."[85] In December, the Russian Federation Council overwhelmingly passed a resolution that described Sevastopol as part of Russia and not under Ukrainian jurisdiction. In April 1997—the month before the final agreement on the fleet—the Federation Council made another intervention on the subject, requesting that Yeltsin consider whether Sevastopol could be jointly governed by Ukraine and Russia, and asking him to insist that Ukraine recognize the existence of problems with the legal status of Sevastopol.[86]

One consequence of this conception of the status of Sevastopol was the view that Ukraine should not base its own navy within the city limits. Following the creation of the Ukrainian navy in April 1992, headquarters were established in Sevastopol, existing in parallel to the Sevastopol headquarters of the Black Sea Fleet command. This Ukrainian naval presence in Sevastopol was opposed both by the Black Sea Fleet command and members of both the Crimean and Sevastopol City Soviets. In late January 1993, the coordinating council of Black Sea Fleet officers issued an appeal to Yeltsin and Kravchuk to move the Ukrainian naval headquarters out of the city and stated that if the two presidents failed to resolve this and other problems by mid-February, they reserved the right to solve them "by the means they have at their disposal."[87] This appeal to the presidents to remove the Ukrainian navy from the Sevastopol base was repeated in March by the Sevastopol City Soviet. The view that Ukraine should be prevented from basing part of its armed forces on a given part of territory within its borders represented a clear challenge to Ukraine's internal sovereignty.

One of the points of dispute in the negotiation over the Sevastopol bases was the wording of the proposed agreement. Having agreed in principle to the Russian use of some or all of the basing facilities in Sevastopol, the Ukrainian negotiators objected to the proposed Russian formulation that "Sevastopol is the main base of the Russian fleet," insisting on a variant. In 1994, Interfax reported that the proposed Ukrainian formulation was that "the main Russian navy base in Crimea will be stationed in Sevastopol"; at the June 1995 Sochi summit, this appeared to have changed slightly to "the Russian fleet will be based in Sevastopol."[88] The significance of such an apparently trivial difference in wording can only be understood in the context of Ukrainian concerns to assert its sovereignty over Sevastopol and concerns that Russia was seeking to downplay or undermine this sovereignty; in this context, the proposed Russian wording could be understood as implying that Sevastopol was in some way the property of the Russian fleet.

Another significant area of disagreement was the issue of leasing. Not only did some Russian politicians and members of the Russian military object to the proposed length of the lease—regarding the leases proposed by the Ukrainian negotiators as too short—they objected in principle to the idea of leasing what they regarded as their bases. As one unnamed member of the Russian negotiating team commented:

> As regards the shore, Ukraine believes that it is its territory and that it may only lease it out. However, we are asking that it also be divided. Not the land, because we agree that it is Ukrainian, but just what is directly pertinent to the functioning of the Fleet.[89]

During negotiations over the wording of the agreement on basing arrangements, one member of the Russian delegation commented that the Ukrainian formulation—opposed by Russia—meant that all the infrastructure in Sevastopol belonged to Ukraine; he also noted that the Russian delegation wanted to avoid the use of the term *lease,* preferring the term *utilization* instead.[90] Such implicit Russian assertions of ownership of bases on Ukrainian territory (perhaps especially because of the contested status of the Crimean peninsula more generally) were regarded by many Ukrainian officers and politicians as a challenge to the internal sovereignty of the Ukrainian state. In response to such perceived threats to their state sovereignty, some Ukrainian politicians and Ukrainian military officials adopted an extremely robust position on the continued Russian naval presence on Ukrainian territory. In his period as Ukrainian minister of defense, Morozov was particularly outspoken on this issue (as on other subjects related to the fleet, often more so than the president or foreign minister).

A key obstacle to the resolution of the basing problem was the existence of the conflicting demands for the two navies to be based separately from one another and for both to be based in Sevastopol (although the final agreement allowed for the continued use of Sevastopol by both navies). The Ukrainian attitude toward the Sevastopol bases was neither uniform nor consistent during the long negotiation process. The position of the Ukrainian Defense Ministry in early 1994 was that the main base of the Ukrainian navy was and would remain in Sevastopol.[91] It was unclear at this stage whether the Defense Ministry envisaged Russia also retaining a base in Sevastopol, but at a presidential meeting, following the incident at the Odessa base in early April, it was agreed that the two states' fleets needed to be based separately to avoid conflict between them. This decision automatically raised the question of what would happen to the Sevastopol base. This question was not clarified by the respective statements of the Ukrainian president, who commented on the need for Ukraine to withdraw from the base and lease it to Russia, and the Ukrainian defense minister, who instructed the Black Sea Fleet command that Sevastopol was to be the base of both the Ukrainian and Russian fleets.[92] On the same day, he apparently stated that the Russian fleet should actually be based at two naval bases in Crimea but outside Sevastopol.[93] These conflicting positions reflect the fact that senior Ukrainian military figures in this period frequently adopted a more strongly nationalistic position than the president or other members of the executive.[94] Morozov stated on several occasions that Ukraine was only prepared to consider the division of the fleet's ships, not bases, and that at the end of the transitional period, Russia would have to entirely withdraw its navy from Ukrainian territorial waters. He reportedly declared that "no treaty can make us share Ukrainian land with another state."[95] In a speech to the Union of Officers of Ukraine in April 1993, he reportedly said that he saw no chance that Sevastopol or other ports would be leased to the Russian Black Sea Fleet.[96]

One of the central issues in this dispute over basing arrangements was the perception that the Russian government, in conjunction with the fleet command, was attempting to dictate to Ukraine over arrangements for bases on Ukrainian territory—much as the fleet and JAF commands had appeared to be doing over the character of the Ukrainian navy in early 1992. As Ukrainian deputy defense minister Bizhan said, "I do not see at all how one can dictate such conditions to a state, in which the other state would like to be based. I think that the problem of where the navies will be based is, after all, not Russia's problem, but Ukraine's problem."[97] The chief of staff of the Ukrainian army, General Anatolii Lopata, explained the failure to implement any of the agreements on the fleet as the result of the fact that Russia continued to view all of the fleet's infrastructure, including the bases, as Russian property, which Ukraine could not accept.[98] After talks broke down in April 1994, the Ukrainian Defense Ministry released a statement claiming that the Russian delegation had insisted that the Russian fleet should have all the Crimean bases and that the Ukrainian fleet should be based outside Crimea altogether. It blamed the breakdown of these talks specifically on the failure of the Russian delegation "to understand Ukraine's legitimate position concerning the deployment of the Ukrainian Navy on its own territory."[99] It was precisely this sense, that Russia did not recognize the right of Ukraine to determine the location of its own (and other states') forces on its own territory, that lay at the root of this protracted dispute over the location of bases. The problem was compounded by the fact that while the statements of the Russian government on the issue of Sevastopol related entirely to the question of the bases, other actors, including members of the Russian legislature, the military, and the Black Sea Fleet command itself, connected the basing issue to the question of the status of Sevastopol and of the legitimacy of the 1954 transfer of Crimea to Ukraine.

The conception of the Crimean bases as Russian property, the view that Russia had a right to determine the use of these bases, and the linkage of both these issues to the question of the status of Crimea within Ukraine directly challenged not only the Ukrainian parliamentary declaration on property on its territory but also the usual international understanding of internal sovereignty—the idea that states have the right to control what happens on their territory and in particular that they have the right to delimit the activities of other states within their borders. In the same way, the idea of Ukrainian sovereignty was implicitly thrown into question by the attempts on the part of non-Ukrainian military officials to determine the future size and purpose of the Ukrainian navy. Sovereignty, as generally understood in international political exchange, and indeed as apparently understood by the new Ukrainian political and military elites in the early 1990s, precludes the determination of policy or the prior claim to territory by an external state. However, such a view runs counter to the post-Soviet understanding of sovereignty evident in the assumptions of CIS officers and sections of the Russian political and military elites. Ukrainian security and sovereignty policy, in this conception, were not clearly delimited in relation to Russia—particularly when, as here, the dispute involved a region that many Russian political and military figures appeared to regard as essentially Russian.

Georgia and Russia

If the dispute between Russia and Ukraine over the Black Sea exposed the complex and contested sovereignty interrelationship between these two states, the role (or absence of a role) of Georgia in the division of the fleet demonstrates an almost complete failure of both internal and external sovereignty as broadly understood in Western analysis. The inability of Georgia to secure a place at the negotiating table—let alone a share of the fleet— demonstrates this failure in a number of respects: specifically, a failure to assert ownership or control over assets on its territory or over much of the territory itself. The failures to assert internal sovereignty over its territory or, in large measure, external sovereignty in relation to Russia were closely connected to its inability to assert its claim to a portion of the fleet in the same way that Ukraine was able to do. Thus, the division of the Black Sea Fleet can be seen as an indicator of extremely weak state sovereignty. Unlike the voluntary abdication of sovereignty over military policy by Belarus, however, the case of Georgia demonstrates a failed attempt to assert external sovereignty, caused by the collapse of attempts to assert internal sovereignty.

After the breakup of the Soviet Union, Georgia, occupying roughly one-third of the former Soviet Black Sea coastline, emerged as a state with a substantial proportion of the Black Sea Fleet based on its territory; however, following the signing of the May 1997 agreement between Russia and Ukraine, it owned only one vessel from the fleet, which it had been given by Ukraine.[100] An earlier agreement, in 1992, had given Georgia the two Black Sea Fleet bases on its territory, one at Ochamchire, the other at Poti; however, Ochamchire is located in Abkhazia and the Poti base suffered serious damage and lost many of its movable assets in the early 1990s, as a combined result of the Russian withdrawal and of looting. In order to understand why Georgia was unable to assert a claim to these assets on its territory, it is essential to understand the collapse of what must be described as a project to assert state sovereignty (rather than the collapse of an extant state sovereignty, since, as will be discussed below, this never fully existed in Georgia). This was a double failure to build sovereignty—a failure to assert internal sovereignty, above all to assert territorial control, and to establish external sovereignty in relation to Russia. This had two principal consequences for Georgian efforts to obtain a share of the Black Sea Fleet. First, these sovereignty problems—in particular in relation to Abkhazia and the challenges to the Shevardnadze government by the supporters of the deposed president Gamsakhurdia—meant that the Georgian government was not able to regard the issue of the Black Sea Fleet as a security priority in the way that the Ukrainian government did. Second, the failure to assert external and internal sovereignty deprived Georgia of the capability to assert what it perceived to be its rights in relation to the fleet—above all in relation to Russia, the state in relation to which Georgian external sovereignty had failed.

Georgia's role in the debate over the division of the Black Sea Fleet in the 1990s is characterized more by its absence than by its presence. For obvious reasons, the issue was not at the top of the Georgian security agenda during the period when the debate between Russia and Ukraine was taking place. Equally, there was little interest in Georgia's putative claim to a portion of the fleet, either on the part of the other participants in the negotiations or among analysts and commentators. Most analysis of the Black Sea Fleet division, both by CIS and non-CIS observers, fails to mention the Georgian claim altogether. This is not entirely surprising given the relatively low priority accorded to Georgia by Western European and North American analysts in the early and mid-1990s and the almost exclusive focus on the Abkhaz and South Ossetian conflicts among those who did comment on it.

By mid-April 1992 it had become clear that Georgia, despite a presidential decree in December 1991 apparently indicating a lack of interest in the fleet, did in fact consider itself to have a claim to that part of the fleet based at Poti and Ochamchire, and that the Georgian government was unhappy with the way in which the division of the Black Sea Fleet was being treated as a matter for resolution on a bilateral basis between Russia and Ukraine.[101] Georgian deputy defense minister Nodar Giorgadze stated in May 1992 that:

> In line with the principles of justice, the Black Sea Fleet should be divided between three states—Russia, Ukraine, and Georgia. Of course we shall not be laying claim to a large part of it, only that part which will be needed by the republic in order to guarantee the territorial integrity and inviolability of its borders. . . . When the Black Sea Fleet came under discussion, certain circles literally "forgot" that a part of our national income is invested in it, that the republic has a 320 kilometre coastline and, finally, that there are naval bases on our territory in Poti and Ochamchira.[102]

An alternative proposal by the Georgian government was apparently that the fleet should either be divided equally among the Black Sea littoral states of the former USSR, or on a proportional basis, relative to the extent of Black Sea coast occupied by each claimant state.[103] At around this time, the commander in chief of the Ukrainian navy stated that Ukraine was prepared to share the fleet with Georgia as well as Russia and that each state should create their navies on the basis of the ships based on their territory.

In early June 1992, the Georgian and Russian governments agreed to the transfer to Georgian control of the two fleet bases on Georgian territory, together with a number of small ships. It was noted at the time that the agreement was to form part of a broader military agreement between Russia and Georgia, although the nature of that agreement was not made explicit. It was also agreed that Georgia would abide by the understandings on the fleet reached that May, with a Georgian navy being created from Black Sea Fleet units on Georgian territory. The precise status of the base at Poti remained unclear, however, with reports in October that Black Sea Fleet personnel and property were being withdrawn from it, a process that was expected to be completed by the end of 1992. The status of the base at Poti was complicated in this period by the conflict in Abkhazia, with Russian military personnel claiming that Georgia had imposed a blockade on the port; Georgia denied this but acknowledged an attempt to impose some control over movements into and out of the port because of the war.

Throughout the period from the end of 1992 to the May 1997 agreement on the fleet, the Georgian government periodically restated its claim both to a portion of the fleet and to the right to take part in the bilateral Russian-Ukrainian negotiations over the division of the fleet. In September 1993, following a visit by Grachev to Tbilisi, primarily to discuss the future of Russian troops in Georgia, it was reported that the issue of Georgia's claim to a portion of the fleet would be resolved following the signing of the Russian-Georgian Treaty on Friendship and Cooperation, and that in the intervening period no military equipment would be removed from Georgian territory.[104] Despite these claims, however, Georgia did not take part in the negotiations over the fleet and, rather than securing some or all of the part of the Black Sea Fleet based on its territory, witnessed the wholesale removal of fleet vessels to bases outside Georgia. Interestingly, one explanation for this action given by Gromov, the Russian navy commander in chief, was that the withdrawal of one brigade of ships from Poti was necessary "in connection with the formation of the independent states"—by implication, specifically Georgia.[105] The most common explanation given was that the removal of the fleet's ships from Georgia was precipitated by security concerns arising from the Abkhaz conflict.

Despite previous intermittent statements on ownership of the Black Sea Fleet, the Georgian government began to make more concerted claims only in the second half of the 1990s. In February 1996, the Georgian government stated its intention to negotiate with Russia and Ukraine for a portion of the fleet. Foreign Minister Irakli Menagarishvili told a press conference that Georgia had the "logical and legal right to lay claim to its share in the former USSR's Black Sea Fleet." In stating this, he acknowledged that it would have been more useful for Georgia to have asserted its claim earlier (clearly referring to the period when the main negotiations over the fleet between Ukraine and Russia began) but said that Georgia had previously "lacked the appropriate conditions."[106] Georgian claims to part of the fleet were dismissed by one Black Sea Fleet officer in a Russian newspaper article on the grounds that Georgia had already been given control of the Poti naval base and its coastal infrastructure, and that since the value of such naval base infrastructure was more than double that of any ships based there, Georgia had already received the majority (in value terms) of that part of the fleet that had originally been located on its territory. The article also raised the question of whether Georgia, were it to receive any additional part of the fleet, would be able to maintain and man it.[107]

The series of presidential-level agreements between Russia and Ukraine in this period are notable for their systematic exclusion of any reference to a Georgian claim on part of the fleet; such agreements represented the division of the fleet as a two-way split. The Russian-Ukrainian agreement on the fleet in May 1997 provoked an angry denunciation by the Georgian government, which, as in previous agreements between Russia and Ukraine, had not had their claims to a portion of the fleet recognized, despite apparent Ukrainian support for Georgian claims to vessels previously stationed at the Poti base. By spring 1997, Georgia was claiming either twenty or thirty-two vessels, but neither claim resulted in the transfer of ships to Georgia, despite expectations shortly before the Russia-Ukraine summit that twenty ships previously removed from Poti would be returned to Georgia by Russia.[108] In a statement made at the time of the agreement, Shevardnadze linked the development of Georgian-Russian relations to Russian assistance in resolving the conflict in Abkhazia and to Georgia receiving a part of the fleet, a linkage he repeated in a statement made the following month.[109] In an echo of comments made by Shaposhnikov during the negotiations with Ukraine, the Russian deputy foreign minister was cited as saying that Georgia had no right to part of the fleet because the original agreement to divide the fleet had been taken at a CIS heads of state meeting in January 1992, at a time when Georgia was not a member of the CIS.[110] An apparently simultaneously held Russian position was that Georgia was not entitled to any further part of the fleet because it had already received vessels from the Ukrainian share; both were positions that Georgia rejected. A variant of the Russian position, repeating the argument used in the press the previous year, was given by Russian Defense Council secretary Iurii Baturin, who stated that the value of the Poti base handed over to Georgia far exceeded that of the vessels previously stationed there—the clear implication being that as a result, Georgia had no further claim to fleet assets.[111] Despite these Russian statements, vessels were handed over to Georgia by Russia in October 1997—interestingly, after an apparent withdrawal of the Georgian claim to a further share of the fleet's assets.[112] Discussion over Georgian claims to Black Sea Fleet ships continued, as part of the wider debate over Georgian claims to those military assets of the former Soviet Union located on its territory, or to compensation for military assets removed from Georgia by the Russian army since 1991.[113]

The sequence of events outlined above indicates several factors relating to the Georgian position in the debate over the fleet's division, the most obvious of which is that for the other parties involved in the process, Georgia did not have a position of any significance. As noted earlier, the various meetings held with Georgian politicians and military personnel all took place outside, and in response to, the structured sequence of negotiations between Russia and Ukraine. At no point was Georgia involved in these negotiations, and its position was not acknowledged in the documents that emerged from them. A second feature of the meetings with Georgia was that, until 1997, most of them were conducted not at a state-to-state level with Russia, but with the personnel of the Black Sea Fleet command. This was in contrast to the negotiations with Ukraine, which, although often involving the participation of the fleet's command as part of the Russian delegation, were clearly treated as a bilateral, state-level activity. The fact that the Russian government did not consider it necessary to negotiate with the

Georgian government over its claims to part of the fleet suggests both that it did not take the claims seriously and that it did not consider Georgia a sufficiently significant actor on this issue to devote direct attention to its position. Shevardnadze commented in early 1993 that the Russians "do not want to negotiate with us on what we will receive from the federal property situated on our territory: military bases, military factories, telecommunication infrastructure . . . we would like to get a share of the BSF . . . and they are mistaken in thinking that we do not see that most ships have already been directed to Russian ports."[114] Skepticism about Georgian claims to the fleet was not confined to Russian actors, however; while reiterating Georgian claims to a part of the fleet in November 1992, the commander of the Georgian navy gave a commitment not to "conduct any nationalisation [or] undertake any illegal actions with respect to the Poti brigade of the Russian fleet."[115] This is an interesting statement because of its implication that, despite Georgia's claim to that part of the fleet located on its territory, the Black Sea Fleet was regarded as Russian. This in turn indicates that Georgian claims over the fleet were regarded as weak and limited not only by other parties involved but by the Georgian military structures.

Weak Sovereignty, Weak Claims

To understand why the Georgian claim to a share of the Black Sea Fleet was so unsuccessful, it is essential to understand both the impact of the failure of the Georgian state to establish internal sovereignty, and the dissolution of internal and external sovereignty as discrete categories in the case of Georgia. As noted earlier, there is an extremely close theoretical and practical interconnection between a state's internal and external sovereignty. This is particularly evident in the case of the former Soviet states, which have been required to define both their internal and external sovereignty primarily in relation to one another, and specifically in relation to Russia. Throughout the 1990s, this was particularly evident in the case of Georgia, in the relationship between its internal sovereignty problems in Abkhazia and South Ossetia and its external sovereignty problems with Russia. The Abkhaz and South Ossetian separatist conflicts, the conflict in Megrelia, and (before his resignation in May 2004) Russia's ties to the Adjarian leader Aslan Abashidze have had fundamental consequences for the relationship between Georgia and Russia, in particular on security questions, and in the way that the demarcation between internal and external sovereignty has become blurred.

As discussed earlier, the distinction between internal and external sovereignty is not absolute, most obviously because freedom from intervention by another state (external sovereignty) is also a condition of internal sovereignty, since it pertains to the exercise of authority within the territory of a sovereign state. Georgian internal sovereignty was never convincingly established in a number of key respects. The two aspects of failed Georgian internal sovereignty that are important for an understanding of the situation in relation to the Black Sea Fleet are the failure by the structures of the Georgian state to assert control over all the territory within the boundaries of the Georgian state (in Abkhazia and South Ossetia in particular) and the failure to establish the state's monopoly on the legitimate use of force. From the point of independence onward, Georgia has been unable to assert control over all of the territory within its borders. Even excluding the autonomous region of Adjaria (which has improved its relationship with Tbilisi since Abashidze's resignation), a large proportion of the country has never been under the control of the government in Tbilisi. Abkhazia and South Ossetia declared their independence from Georgia at or before Georgia's emergence as an independent state, while other areas of the country were periodically under the control of armed groups loyal to the deposed president Gamsakhurdia, or—as in the case of the predominantly Armenian province of Javakheti—in practice, beyond the reach of Tbilisi's authority. Georgia, then, has never managed to attain territorial integrity in any sense; the failure to do so has had serious implications for other aspects of its sovereignty. This has been most evident in the Russian relationship to Abkhazia. In particular, the initial Russian support for the Abkhaz secession, the later reliance on the deployment of Russian peacekeeping troops along the border between Abkhazia and the rest of Georgia, the reestablishment of transport links between Russia and Abkhazia, and Russia's preferential visa policies in respect to Abkhazia (and compared with Georgia) have seriously weakened Georgian external sovereignty in relation to Russia.[116]

Georgia's failure to establish a claim to part of the Black Sea Fleet is linked directly to the failure of Georgian internal sovereignty, specifically to the failure of sovereignty in relation to Abkhazia. The mid-1992 bilateral agreement between Georgia and Russia on the fleet gave Georgia the bases at Poti and Ochamchire. However, Georgian control of both these bases was undermined by the Abkhaz conflict—particularly in the case of the Ochamchire base, which was located inside Abkhazia, and thus out of the control of the Georgian government. As well as the practical failure to extend Georgian control over the base, the Abkhaz government had challenged the legal right of Georgia to own a base on Abkhaz territory, on the basis that "the naval port of Ochamchire, as well as all the property and adjoining territory, belong to the republic of Abkhazia and its people and to no one else. This right is fixed in Article 11 of the [Abkhaz] constitution and by a resolution of the Republic of Abkhazia Supreme Council." It also rejected the legitimacy of Russia-Georgia negotiations over the base, which did not take into account "the interests of the Republic of Abkhazia and with participation of representatives from Abkhazia."[117] The de facto loss of Abkhazia and the legal counterclaim asserted by its government made any attempt to claim the Ochamchire base impossible, given the failure of the Georgian state to establish authority over its territory.

Given the level of Russian involvement in internal Georgian security and the failure to assert central government control over areas such as Abkhazia and South Ossetia, it is difficult to maintain any clear distinction between the internal and external aspects of sovereignty in the Georgian case. What is clear, however, is that as a result of this, Georgia did not have the international political influence to successfully demand that Russia and Ukraine take its claims to a portion of the Black Sea Fleet seriously; it was equally unable to prevent the Black Sea Fleet from removing those ships to which Georgia had laid claim from Georgian territory. The failure of Georgia to fully establish either the structures or the attributes of state sovereignty not only had an impact on its government's ability to secure a place at the negotiations over the division of the fleet, but also was explicitly invoked as a factor undermining Georgian claims. In an interview in early 1992, Baltin commented that:

> The Black Sea is geographically, physically, and politically a watershed in which Russia's interests have always predominated. The situation which is taking shape on its shores now is in many ways the result of the indeterminate international legal status of the changed political realities. Georgia, for example, having appropriated part of the Fleet, continues to live without the definition of the borders of its territorial waters and other attributes of maritime statehood.[118]

In understanding why Georgia was unable to pursue a successful claim to a share of the Black Sea Fleet, it is important to recognize the fact that Russia was able to act in two ways to minimize the significance of Georgian claims: first, by ensuring a favorable structure to the negotiations (bilateral, not trilateral, and with Russian governmental officials and members of the fleet command acting apparently interchangeably in negotiations); and second, by avoiding tying the fleet to negotiations around Abkhazia. Most important, however, Russia has been able to minimize Georgian claims to the fleet precisely because Russia itself was a critical factor in the failure of Georgia to establish internal sovereignty in the 1990s. The weakness of Georgian external sovereignty—the basis on which states interact with one another on issues such as the division of the Black Sea Fleet—is, above all, a weakness of sovereignty in relation to Russia.

It is also clear that the Georgian position was critically undermined by the comparatively low priority that a claim to the Black Sea Fleet had for the government during the key period of negotiation over the fleet's division. Although the issue of the fleet was not resolved until 1997, the most intensive period of negotiation, when the details and mechanics of division were agreed in principle by Russia and Ukraine, took place between early 1992 and mid-1994. This was precisely the period during which the Georgian government was overwhelmingly engaged by the conflicts within its borders, particularly in Abkhazia and with pro-Gamsakhurdia forces. The Georgian problem stands in contrast to the case of Ukraine, where the major challenge to its internal sovereignty, in Crimea, was in key respects coincident with the dispute over the division of the fleet; the two issues were seen as interrelated by all the key actors. This was clearly not the case for Georgia, where engagement with one of these issues necessarily meant a diversion from the other. The failure of Georgia to assert its claim to a share of the fleet was, in part, a result of the Georgian government's inability to address the issue given the far more urgent security problem of state survival posed by the conflicts within its borders. As a result, the issue of the Black Sea Fleet was rarely discussed at ministerial or presidential bilateral meetings with Russia, which were, inevitably, focused on Abkhazia in this period and on the closely related issue of the Russian military presence in Georgia.[119] At presidential meetings in May 1993 and February 1994, for example, the issue of the Black Sea Fleet appears to have been left off the agenda entirely.[120] As a result, the failure of Georgia to assert a clear and consistent claim to a share of the fleet can be understood, in part, as the result of the comparatively low priority of the fleet as an issue compared with the issues of war within its borders and the presence of a foreign army on its territory. Thus, the Georgian failure to lay claim to the fleet was not only the result of weak sovereignty in relation to Russia as evidenced in negotiations over the issue, it also needs to be understood as the consequence of the attention demanded by two more important sovereignty-related issues—the attempt to preserve territorial integrity and the multifaceted challenge to a Western model of sovereignty posed by the presence of Russian troops.

The issue of Georgia and the Black Sea Fleet also needs to be placed in the broader context of negotiations over all military assets. Although the division of the Black Sea Fleet was in some ways a discrete issue, for Georgia it was also part of the wider question of ownership of military assets. One of the most persistent accusations of the Georgian government in the 1990s was that the Russian armed forces had withdrawn large quantities of military equipment from Georgian territory despite the fact that Georgia claimed equipment on its territory as the property of the Georgian state. The removal of Black Sea Fleet ships from the bases in Georgia was, in this sense, a (particularly dramatic) manifestation of a wider Russian policy. Thus, the failure of Georgian attempts to assert ownership or control over the assets of the fleet, which were on its territory at the point of independence, needs to be understood as part of a wider failure on the part of the Georgian government to assert a successful claim to military assets more generally.

One further, important explanation for the lack of Georgian success over the Black Sea Fleet is the fact that the issue was not located within the wider negotiating framework between Russia and Georgia, in which bargaining over issues took place. This can best be understood by comparison with Ukraine. During the process of negotiating the division of the fleet, it became clear that the Ukrainian portion of the fleet was perceived to be part of a trading arrangement, in which ships and the leasing of Crimean bases were exchanged for the cancellation of energy debts. This was possible because the assets that the Russian government wanted were on the territory of, and at least partially under the control of, Ukraine. In the case of Georgia, the key security trade attempted with Russia was that of the use of Georgian military bases in exchange for Russian assistance in the resolution of the situation in Abkhazia, rather than a trade involving the fleet.[121] An additional, and critical, problem for Georgia was that given its lack of control over the portion of the fleet based on its territory, Georgia was essentially negotiating with Russia to be *given* part of the fleet rather than being in a position to trade it in exchange for benefits such as energy debt forgiveness and formal recognition of state sovereignty, as Ukraine was. In order to be part of any exchange of security benefits, the fleet would have to have been identified as a benefit sought by Georgia rather than exchanged by it (as in the case of Ukraine). However, given the far more urgent need to resolve the Abkhaz conflict with Russian assistance and the perceived need for Russian withdrawal from the military bases on Georgian territory, ownership of part of the fleet was pushed to a comparatively low position on the list of Georgian security demands, and consequently did not feature in such a trade. The fact that no security advantages would result for Russia from agreeing with Georgian ownership claims to part of the fleet— to offset the perceived security loss from any increase in Georgian security independence—meant that there was no reason for Russia to recognize Georgia's claims. Thus. Georgia's failure to establish a claim to a key security asset on its territory at independence reflected the multiple failure of its attempt to establish a state based on a Western model of security.

Conclusion

The protracted dispute over the Black Sea Fleet cannot be fully understood without an engagement with the questions surrounding, and differences over, the status and meaning of sovereignty in post-Soviet, interstate relations. What was, in theory, a five-year disagreement about the division of strategically (and sometimes technologically) obsolete assets which none of the parties could afford to maintain, can be better understood when the implications of some of the points of dispute and the underlying assumptions are considered in the context of these states' post-Soviet sovereignty projects. Although the final settlement was obviously driven by relative economic and political capabilities, the terms of the dispute and its intensity need to be understood as a reflection of the way in which the division of the Black Sea Fleet both touched on fundamental aspects of state sovereignty and exposed radically different understandings of what sovereignty meant in the post-Soviet context.

The ways in which the issue of state sovereignty affected the question of the division of the Black Sea Fleet are, not surprisingly, radically different in the cases of Ukraine and Georgia. One constant in both cases, however, was the approach of the Russian and CIS military (and some sections of the Russian political elite), an approach implying that the sovereignty of these two states in relation to Russia or the CIS could be understood in a similar way as the sovereignty of the union republics in relation to the Soviet federal center. Thus, the location of military assets such as the Black Sea Fleet on Georgian or Ukrainian territory did not imply these states' ownership of such assets, which were assumed to belong to the "center"; on this matter, the perception of Russia's prior claim over assets on other states' territory reflects both the limited sovereignty of the repulics within Soviet federal structure and the essentialist nature of claims founded in nationalist mythology. Equally significant, there was clearly a perception that the CIS JAF and/or Russia could and should determine for these states what their security needs were and allocate them assets on that basis, irrespective of these states' own views of their security needs. Thus, various CIS and Russian actors connected to the dispute expressed the view that both Ukraine and Georgia required only a coastguard capability, and that they should be awarded only as much of the fleet as would be consistent with that function (in practice, less in the case of Georgia). Categorical Ukrainian and Georgian rejection of proposals and claims apparently informed by this Soviet understanding of sovereignty were not surprising given their attempted adoption of a broadly "Western" model of state sovereignty, which the Russian and CIS position radically undermined.

Looked at together, the various aspects of the Russian-Ukrainian dispute over the Black Sea Fleet illustrate a systematic and fundamental linkage of the issue of the fleet to ideas about Ukrainian sovereignty. For Ukraine, the idea of state sovereignty over the territory and assets within its borders underpinned its view of the status of the fleet and the nature of its dispute with Russia. The view that the way in which Russia characterized its claims to the fleet and its bases presented a challenge to Ukrainian sovereignty was expressed to varying degrees by a wide range of military and political actors, including nationalist parties and political movements such as Rukh, the presidents and foreign ministers of Ukraine, the Defense Ministry and senior Ukrainian naval officials, and nationalist military groups such as the Union of Ukrainian Officers. The perception that the Russian government, military officials, and the theoretically nonpartisan officers of the CIS JAF and the Black Sea Fleet all viewed Ukrainian claims to sovereignty over the territory within its borders, the assets on that territory, and its security policy as weaker than the claims of Russia and the rights of a continuing, centralized post-Soviet military was clearly given substance by the actions and comments of these groups. The dispute was ultimately resolved by bargaining the formal recognition of Ukrainian sovereignty and energy debt forgiveness by Russia for the greater part of the Ukrainian share of the fleet. Importantly, however, the final agreement on the fleet upheld the two key principles of Ukrainian sovereignty on this issue: that it owned—at least nominally—50 percent of the Black Sea Fleet; and that it did not have to relinquish de facto sovereignty over part of its territory by agreeing to withdraw from Sevastopol, since the agreement provided for the Sevastopol facilities to be shared with Russia.

In contrast, the resolution of the Black Sea Fleet dispute exposed the failure of sovereignty in the case of Georgia. As noted earlier, Georgia, unlike Belarus on the issue of nuclear weapons, did not voluntarily abandon its claims; instead, its failure of sovereignty in relation to Russia on military questions and the interrelated failure to achieve internal sovereignty left it unable either to present a strong claim in relation to Russia or to prioritize the issue of the fleet's division in the way that Ukraine was able to do. Thus, if sovereignty was perceived to be a fundamental issue for Ukraine's negotiations with Russia, it was, in contrast, the defining issue accounting for the Georgian failure to gain a place at the negotiating table at all.

Although the dispute appeared resolved by the 1997 agreement, the changing nature of the Russian-Ukrainian relationship—and the closely related issue of Ukraine's security reorientation westward—has reopened the problem. It seems possible that the revived dispute may be exacerbated by the increasing global strategic importance of the Black Sea—and thus, to the parties to the dispute, the growing importance of the fleet and its bases—with the increased engagement of the United States since late 2001; NATO and EU membership of a number of littoral states; and the development of energy pipelines in the region. As so often before, it appears that the fate of the Black Sea Fleet has not, after all, been decided, and that this fate is understood by all those involved to be tied to issues of state identity, sovereignty, and the contest over regional security politics.

Notes

1. The fleet's minimal strategic importance is noted, however, by Pavel K. Baev, *The Russian Army in a Time of Troubles* (London: Sage, 1996), p. 96.

2. *Izvestiia*, 5 August 1992, *FBIS-SOV-92-152*, p. 47.

3. *Novoye Vremya*, no. 5, January 1993, *FBIS-SOV-93-026*, pp. 1–3. The same question in relation to Ukraine's claim to the fleet was raised by Radio Moscow World Service (*FBIS-SOV-92-078*, p. 17).

4. *Holos Ukrainy,* 23 January 1993, p. 3, *FBIS-SOV-93-014.*

5. Ustina Markus ("The Ukrainian Navy and the Black Sea Fleet," *RFE/RL Research Report* 3, no. 18 [6 May 1994]: 33) puts the figure at between 300 and 440 vessels. The question of the exact size of the Black Sea Fleet at the point of the breakup of the USSR proved to be surprisingly opaque. One of the conditions stipulated by the Ukrainian side of the negotiations over the fleet was that Russia produce an accurate inventory of the fleet's total assets as of December 1991; this was something that the Russian Ministry of Defense repeatedly refused to do in the 1990s and that it has still failed to do despite renewed requests by the Ukrainian government. In addition, early estimates by analysts of the size of the fleet only included warships and other large vessels. Later estimates, used in negotiations, included the large number of smaller support vessels, roughly doubling its size.

6. Arkady Moshes, "Conflict and Cooperation in Russo-Ukrainian Relations," in Bruno Coppeiters, Alexei Zverev, and Dmitri Trenin, eds., *Commonwealth and Independence in Post-Soviet Eurasia* (London and Portland, OR: Frank Cass, 1998), p. 135.

7. Radio Moscow, 12 May 1994, *FBIS-SOV-94-094,* p. 42.

8. Moshes, "Conflict and Cooperation," p. 52. He also notes that "even the [Ukrainian] Navy's repair facilities are believed to be in a poor state due to lack of money for necessary upkeep" (p. 53).

9. UNIAN, 10 March 1994, *FBIS-SOV-94-049,* p. 45.

10. See, for example, Baltin's assertion that "Ukraine claims for a part of the Black Sea Fleet ships only in order to immediately sell them abroad as scrap." Interfax, 28 April 1994, *FBIS-SOV-94-083,* p. 8.

11. See, for example, Viktor Glebov, "The Black Sea Region, European Security, and Ukraine," in David E. Albright and Semyen J. Appatov, *Ukraine and European Security* (Basingstoke, UK: Macmillan, 1999); and Deborah Sanders, "The Black Sea Fleet," in *Security Cooperation Between Russia and Ukraine in the Post-Soviet Era* (Basingstoke, UK: Palgrave, 2001).

12. *FBIS-SOV-92-007,* p. 6.

13. Interfax, 4 April 1992, *FBIS-SOV-92-066,* pp. 52–53.

14. Ukrinform, 9 April 1992, *FBIS-SOV-92-069,* p. 46.

15. *Krasnaia Zvezda,* 28 May 1992.

16. ITAR-TASS, 19 June 1992, *FBIS-SOV-92-119,* p. 10.

17. In November 1992, for example, there were reports in the Ukrainian press that the Ukrainian Foreign Ministry had sent a note of protest to the Russian Foreign Ministry over the alleged embezzlement of fleet property with the collusion of the Russian Ministry of Defense.

18. Ben Lombardi, "Ukrainian Armed Forces: Defence Expenditure and Military Reform," *The Journal of Slavic Military Studies* 14, no. 3 (September 2001): 52; *RFE/RL Newsline,* 30 May 1997.

19. See, for example, Taras Kuzio, "Is Ukraine Part of Europe's Future?" *Washington Quarterly* 29, no. 3 (Summer 2006): 89–108.

20. "When Will the Russian Fleet Pull out of Ukraine?" RIA Novosti, 1 June 2005, *Johnson's Russia List,* 2 June 2005.

21. "Ukraina ne namerena peresmatrivat' solglasheniya s Rossei po [Chernomorskii Flot]—Yushchenko," RIA Novosti, 9 March 2006.

22. "Ivanov: RF ne blokiruet vypolnenie soglashenii po Chernomorskomu Flotu," RIA Novosti, 31 May 2006.

23. "Ukraine-NATO Exercises to Proceed Despite Protests," *RFE/RL Newsline,* 4 June 2006.

24. "Luzhkov riskuet popast' b odnu kompaniiu c Zhirinovskim," RIA Novosti, 23 February 2007.

25. "Yushchenko Tells Putin Ukraine Can Defend Itself," RFE/RL, 20 October 2006; Vladimir Socor, "Putin Testing Ukraine's Political System with His Black Sea Fleet Proposal," Jamestown Foundation, *Eurasia Daily Monitor,* 1 November 2006.

26. "Kiev Urges Moscow to Obey Court Order on Return of Naval Sites," RIA Novosti, 25 January 2007.

27. Vladimir Socor, "Political Battle in Ukraine over the Conduct of Foreign Policy," Jamestown Foundation, *Eurasia Daily Monitor,* 6 November 2006.

28. *FBIS-SOV-92-083,* pp. 47–48.

29. ITAR-TASS World Service, *FBIS-SOV-92-066,* p. 54.

30. *FBIS-SOV-92-009,* p. 15.

31. *Krasnaia Zvezda,* 7 January 1992, p. 2.

32. See, for example, the statement by Stanislau Shushkevich in response to the Yalta agreement, ITAR-TASS, 6 August 1992, *FBIS-SOV-92-153,* p. 70.

33. Vladimir Chernavin, interviewed on Russian television, 6 January 1992, *FBIS-SOV-92-004;* Deputy Commander in Chief of CIS JAF, Boris Pyankov, interviewed in *Trud,* 9 January 1992, *FBIS-SOV-92-006,* pp. 9–10.

34. *Rossiiskaia Gazeta,* 8 May 1992, *FBIS-SOV-92-091.*

35. ITAR-TASS, 18 April 1992, *FBIS-SOV-92-076,* p. 17.

36. *Krasnaia Zvezda,* 7 January 1992, p. 2.

37. *Krasnaia Zvezda,* 4 March 1992, p. 2.

38. TASS, 9 January 1992, *FBIS-SOV-92-006,* p. 12; TASS, 30 May 1992, *FBIS-SOV-92-105,* p. 6.

39. *Holos Ukrainy,* 9 February 1994, *FBIS-SOV-94-030,* p. 43.

40. ITAR-TASS, 21 May 1994, *FBIS-SOV-94-099,* p. 1.

41. 10 January 1992, *FBIS-SOV-92-007,* pp. 9–10.

42. *Rossiiskaia Gazeta,* 9 January 1992, *FBIS-SOV-92-006,* p. 40.

43. Presidential Decree no. 375, "On the Transfer of the BSF to the Russian Federation's Jurisdiction," *Rossiiskaia Gazeta,* 8 April 1992, p. 1, *FBIS-SOV-92-068,* p. 23.

44. Interfax, 13 April 1992, *FBIS-SOV-92-071,* p. 42.

45. *Krasnaia Zvezda,* 22 April 1992, p. 1.

46. *FBIS-SOV-92-083,* pp. 47–48.

47. Postfactum, 12 January 1992, *FBIS-SOV-92-008,* p. 48.

48. *Krasnaia Zvezda,* 21 April 1992, p. 1.

49. *Rossiiskaia Gazeta,* 8 April 1992, *FBIS-SOV-92-068,* p. 23.

50. *Rossiiskaia Vesti,* 5 May 1993, *FBIS-SOV-93-086,* p. 14.

51. Radio Ukraine World Service, 11 June 1993, *FBIS-SOV-93-112,* pp. 52–53.

52. Zenon E. Kohut, "Making the Ukrainian Armed Forces Ukrainian," in *The Military Tradition in Ukrainian History: Its Role in the Construction of Ukraine's Armed Forces* (Cambridge, MA: Ukrainian Research Institute, 1995; distributed by Harvard University Press), p. 11.

53. *Svobodnaia Gruziia,* 23 July 1992, p. 2.

54. Historical note, at www.ukr-navy.iuf.net/english/. Accessed 14 June 2002.

55. In January 1992, for example, senior naval officers wrote to Kravchuk, stating that "Crimea is historically the territory of Russia and the Russian people" and that when it was transferred in 1954 "Russia lost an inalienable, truly Russian part of its territory." *Rossiiskaia Gazeta,* 15 January 1992, *FBIS-SOV-92-010,* p. 10.

56. *Sovetskaia Rossiia,* 9 January 1992, *FBIS-SOV-92-006.*

57. *Krasnaia Zvezda,* 17 October 1992, pp. 1–2.

58. Interfax, 4 April 1992, *FBIS-SOV-92-066,* pp. 52–53.

59. N. A. Kryukov, "Evolution of Russian-Ukrainian Relations: The Legal Status of the Black Sea Fleet," *Military Thought* 15, no. 2 (April 2006): 131.

60. John W. R. Lepingwell ("The Black Sea Fleet Agreement: Progress or Empty Promises?" *RFE/RL Research Report* 2, no. 28 [9 July 1993]: 49) comments that in spring 1992, "the Russian position emphasised the subordination of the bulk of the fleet to the CIS Joint Forces command, rather than openly calling for the creation of a Russian Black Sea Fleet. Given the predominant role played in the CIS command by officers with strong ties to the Russian leadership and Defence Ministry, the distinction may have been moot."

61. *Nezavisimaia Gazeta,* 30 January 1992. In the same interview he commented that Russians had become used to everything else being part of Russia and that they were unable to abandon this assumption.

62. TASS, 16 January 1992, *FBIS-SOV-92-011,* p. 57.

63. Ibid.

64. Postfactum, 6 February 1992, *FBIS-SOV-92-026,* p. 66. At the same time, it also decided to form a commission to investigate the legitimacy of the 1954 transfer of Crimea.

65. UNIAN, 16 June 1993, *FBIS-SOV-93-115,* p. 55.

66. TASS, 26 February 1992, *FBIS-SOV-92-039,* p. 18. Also in February, the Black Sea Fleet staff report was published, describing the fleet as an integral part of the CIS forces.

67. *Rossiiskaia Gazeta,* 15 January 1992, *FBIS-SOV-92-010.*

68. *Rabochaia Tribuna,* 7 January 1992, FBIS-*SOV-92-004,* p. 15; "Eshchë odna popytka razdela Chernomorskogo Flota," *Krasnaia Zvezda,* 8 April 1992, available from http://dlib.eastview.com/sources/ article.jsp?id=3361180.

69. Interfax, 24 January 1992, *FBIS-SOV-92-017,* p. 57.

70. Interfax, 3 August 1992, *FBIS-SOV-92-150,* p. 7.

71. *Sovetskaia Rossiia,* 9 January 1992, *FBIS-SOV-92-006,* p. 7.

72. *Trud,* 9 January 1992, *FBIS-SOV-92-006,* p. 10.

73. *Rabochaia Tribuna,* 6 January 1992, *FBIS-SOV-92-004,* p. 15.

74. *La Repubblica,* 23 April 1992, *FBIS-SOV-92-081,* p. 12; Interfax, 24 January 1992, *FBIS-SOV-92-017,* p. 57.

75. 22 April 1992, *FBIS-SOV-92-082,* p. 7.

76. *Rossiiskaia Vesti,* no. 6, 13 February, *FBIS-SOV-92-036,* p. 18.

77. *Krasnaia Zvezda,* 4 March 1992, p. 2.

78. *Rossiia,* 12–18 May 1993, *FBIS-SOV-93-091,* pp. 10–11.

79. *FBIS-SOV-92-149,* p. 7.

80. "Black Sea Fleet Developments," *OMRI Daily Digest,* 9 January 1995.

81. *FBIS-SOV-93-070,* pp. 61–62.

82. Interfax, 30 April 1992, *FBIS-SOV-92-117,* pp. 7–8.

83. *Nezavisimaia Gazeta,* 19 June 1993, p. 1.

84. *Krasnaia Zvezda,* 11 March 1993, p. 1.

85. "Duma Warns Ukraine on Sevastopol," *OMRI Daily Digest,* 25 October 1996.

86. *OMRI Daily Digest,* 18 April 1997.

87. ITAR-TASS World Service, 21 January 1993, *FBIS-SOV-93-014,* p. 16.

88. Interfax, 24 May 1994, FBIS-SOV-94-101, p. 4. A variant of these formulations is given by UNIAN, translated in *FBIS-SOV-94-111,* p. 49, in which the Ukrainian proposal is given as "the main base of the Black Sea Fleet is in the city of Sevastopol" and the Russian version as "the main base of the Black Sea Fleet is the city of Sevastopol."

89. *Holos Ukrainy,* 8 June 1993, *FBIS-SOV-93-110,* p. 43.

90. Interfax, 24 May 1994, *FBIS-SOV-94-101,* p. 4.

91. UNIAR, 17 February 1994, *FBIS-SOV-94-034,* p. 28.

92. Interfax and UNIAN, 19 April 1994, *FBIS-SOV-94-076,* p. 50; ITAR-TASS World Service, 20 April 1994, *FBIS-SOV-94-076,* p. 51.

93. *Rossiiskaia Gazeta,* 20 April 1994, *FBIS-SOV-94-077,* p. 16.

94. Ihor Smeshko appears to suggest an explanation for this when he notes that "The Ministry of Defence was the only ministry that truly was born of the independent Ukraine. The Ministry of Foreign Affairs existed already in the Soviet period—it was artificial and small, but it did exist before independence. The other ministries were the same and were occupied by the apparatchiks of the old system." *The Military Tradition in Ukrainian History,* p. 60.

95. *Pravda,* 19 May 1993, *FBIS-SOV-93-096,* p. 52.

96. *Krasnaia Zvezda,* 13 April 1993, p. 3.

97. Radio Ukraine World Service, 26 April 1994, *FBIS-SOV-94-082,* p. 54.

98. *La Libre Belgique,* 26 April 1994, *FBIS-SOV-94-082,* p. 52.

99. ITAR-TASS, 23 April 1994, *FBIS-SOV-94-079,* p. 63.

100. In October 1997, Georgia did receive more ships from Russia, which now form the basis of the Georgian navy. See *Svobodnaia Gruziia,* 23 October 1997, p. 2.

101. *FBIS-SOV-92-076,* pp. 63–64.

102. *Svobodnaia Gruziia,* 7 May 1992, *FBIS-SOV-92-094,* pp. 71–72.

103. *FBIS-SOV-92-100,* p. 62.

104. "Foreign Relations," *The Georgian Chronicle,* September 1993, available from www.cipdd.org/cipdd/prod04.htm.

105. *Nezavisimaia Gazeta,* 23 January 1993, p. 1.

106. Interfax, 1 March 1996, *FBIS-SOV-96-043,* pp. 64–65.

107. *Nezavisimaia Gazeta,* 26 March 1996, p. 2.

108. The figure of twenty vessels was given by RFE/RL on 7 May 1997; the figure of thirty-two by *RFE/RL Newsline* on 30 May 1997. On presummit expectations, see *Svobodnaia Gruziia,* 8 May 1997, p. 1.

109. "Georgia: Shevardnadze Assails Moscow Over Black Sea Fleet," *RFE/RL Newsline,* 9 June 1997.

110. "Georgia Loses Out Over Black Sea Fleet Division," *RFE/RL Newsline,* 30 May 1997.

111. *RFE/RL Newsline,* 3 July 1997.

112. *RFE/RL Newsline,* 3 September 1997.

113. Talks on this were held, for example, in January 1998. See "Russian Defence Ministry Delegation in Georgia," *RFE/RL Newsline,* 8 January 1998.

114. *Nepszabadsag,* January 1993, *FBIS-SOV-93-009,* p. 71.

115. Interfax, 12 November 1992, *FBIS-SOV-92-220,* p. 83.

116. For a discussion of these problems, see Chapter 5.

117. *Iberia-Spektr,* 11–17 June 1992, *FBIS-SOV-92-126,* p. 56.

118. *Krasnaia Zvezda,* 19 January 1993, p. 1.

119. A point made by *The Georgian Chronicle* in numerous editions, including July and November 1993, and July and August 1994.

120. See reports of the meetings in *The Georgian Chronicle,* May 1993 and February 1994.

121. On this bargaining of military bases for a settlement in Abkhazia, see, for example, *The Georgian Chronicle* in June 1993 and August 1994.

5

Military Facilities: Russia, Georgia, and Belarus

The disputes over the ownership of and control over the nuclear weapons of the former Soviet Union and the Black Sea Fleet and its infrastructure appeared effectively resolved by the mid-1990s, with the removal of nuclear weapons from Ukraine and Belarus by 1996 and the signing of a (supposedly) definitive agreement on the fleet by mid-1997. This was not, however, the case with all the disputes around the assets of the former Soviet armed forces. One of the most significant problems to remain unresolved into the twenty-first century is use of CIS states' military bases and other military facilities by Russian troops. This is a key issue for the interrelationship between post-Soviet ideas about state sovereignty and security because of what it demonstrates about the structure of Russian political and military attitudes toward claims on other CIS states, both in relation to its continued use of military assets on other states' territory (even where such use was opposed by the host state) and its willingness to manipulate negotiations around the use of these assets as part of a wider strategy relating to security interests in these states. It is equally important for what it reveals about the host states' attitudes toward, and capacity to exercise, sovereignty in relation to Russia.

To a greater extent than in the cases of nuclear weapons or the Black Sea Fleet, the Russian leasing of Belarusian and Georgian military facilities raises fundamental questions of sovereignty. The issue of the ownership of military assets clearly functions, as previously argued, as a marker both of state sovereignty and of the capability and willingness of a state to assert that sovereignty. In particular, the use of one state's military bases by another state raises questions of territorial control—not only over the specific regions in which the military facilities are located, but also over the territory of the state as a whole when the troops of an economically and militarily more powerful state are stationed on its territory. The question of whether a state in this position can not only assert sovereignty in its security decisionmaking but also, more fundamentally, over its own territory and state structures has proved to be a critical one for Georgia, which has been attempting to remove Russian troops from the bases on its territory since independence. Significantly, it has been of less interest to Belarus, where the issue of the Russian use of military facilities became subsumed into the wider question of the future of Belarusian sovereignty within a Russia-Belarus Union. Indeed, the Belarusian attitude toward military integration with Russia—of which a Russian military presence on Belarusian territory was a key part—reflects a significant turn back to the Soviet model of sovereignty.

A central factor in the issue of the Russian use of military facilities has been the timescale for Russian occupation. Although the question of ownership and control of nuclear weapons indicated the capability and willingness of states to use security questions to assert state sovereignty in relation to Russia, the issue of the weapons was limited to the period prior to their removal and destruction, to which both Belarus and Ukraine had agreed. The issue of sovereignty in relation to nuclear weapons was thus a strictly time-limited problem; in contrast, the issue of Russian leasing of bases on the territory of other CIS states has proved to be an open-ended one in practice, if not in theory. The deadlines established by the bilateral agreements on base leasing in Georgia have been unofficially and unilaterally extended by Russia through the use of coercion on other issues, while the original timescale for the Russian use of Belarusian military facilities has been superseded by the integration of security policy and structures under the Russia-Belarus Union.

The basing of Russian troops is an issue that has affected most of the member states of the CIS in various forms and for prolonged periods since the collapse of the USSR. CIS states whose military bases were used by members of the Russian armed forces until the late 1990s or beyond include Armenia, Belarus, Georgia, Tajikistan, Turkmenistan, Ukraine (in the case of the Black Sea Fleet), and Kyrgyzstan, which, since 2003, has hosted the first post-Soviet military base built by Russia outside its borders. Russian forces retained a presence in other states in this period, performing a variety of functions—examples include the leasing of a radar base in northern Azerbaijan and, temporarily, the Skrunda radar base in Latvia; the deployment of border guards on many of the "external" borders of the Caucasus and Central Asia; and the stationing of Russian peacekeepers in Moldova, Georgia, and Tajikistan.[1]

Of all the states required to address the issue of a Russian military presence on their territory, the governments of Belarus and Georgia have perhaps had the most divergent responses and have demonstrated the greatest difference in perception. As this chapter will explore, however, although governmental attitudes toward sovereignty in relation to Russia (on matters of foreign and security policy, and more generally) are radically different in these two states, the outcomes of negotiations around the issue are similar for both—the continued presence of Russian forces on their territory in capacities that promote the interests of Russian foreign and security policy at the expense of the host state's independence. There are also a number of immediate similarities that serve to emphasize the difference in Belarusian and Georgian responses. As late as fall 2007—more than fifteen years after the collapse of the Soviet Union—the Russian armed forces continued to occupy a number of bases in both states, despite varying levels of opposition from sections of both Belarusian and Georgian political and military elites. Although Russian troops were in the process of withdrawing from the two remaining bases in Georgia, the temporary suspension of the process at the height of Russia's dispute with Georgia in late 2006 suggested this could not be taken for granted. In both cases, the retention of military bases was tied, directly and indirectly, to a broader assertion of Russian ownership and control of security policy and assets in these states, and to the advancement of Russian strategic interests in these states' regions (the western former Soviet Union and the Southern Caucasus), both of which the Russian military regard as critical to Russian security interests. This was, in turn, achieved through the linkage of Belarus and Georgia's concessions on the use of bases and related military issues to the provision (or promise of provision) of essential goods of various kinds (energy resources, military training, territorial integrity, and protection from external threats) by Russia.

Russian Bases and Russian Interests

The retention of military bases on the territory of other CIS states has been a security priority for the Russian Federation since the collapse of the Soviet Union and continued to be one into the twenty-first century, as the opening of a new base in Kyrgyzstan in 2003 and the negotiation of basing arrangements with Tajikistan in 2004 indicated. In some cases—notably the Crimean bases of the Black Sea Fleet—the desire to retain bases on the territory of another CIS state can be linked to the desire to retain ownership and control over a particular military asset (although that case, of course, also has wider implications given the nature of Crimean politics). More generally, however, the determination to retain a military presence outside Russian borders needs to be understood in the wider context of Russian military and political elite perceptions of Russian security needs, and in particular the view that the states of the CIS represent Russia's sphere of interest. Since the establishment of a Russian Defense Ministry and Armed Forces in 1992, Russian troops have been stationed outside the borders of the Russian Federation and across the CIS as peacekeeping troops, border guards, or in facilities leased from the host state—or in the case of Georgia, in all three capacities. The need for bases in the "near abroad" was repeatedly asserted by both senior military and political figures and has often been closely connected to the issue of peacekeeping and to what Dov Lynch characterizes as the Russian policy of "suasion."[2] In recent years it has increasingly been linked to Russian attempts to limit, or counter, the growing US presence in the space of the former Soviet Union.

The issue of military bases abroad gathered momentum as an issue during the 1990s, with the reorientation of Russian foreign policy toward a more explicit assertion of Russian security interests, often defined in opposition to the West in general and NATO in particular. This included an increased focus on the rest of the former Soviet Union as a zone of Russian political and security interests and was clearly reflected in the stated desire of the Russian government to retain a military presence in the near abroad. This policy was formalized in the 1993 Russian Military Doctrine (and in later versions), which included wording on the deployment of Russian troops outside Russia to ensure Russian (and CIS) security interests.[3] In January 1994, Andrei Kozyrev—widely regarded as pro-Western and as having little interest in an assertive policy toward the CIS states—claimed that the total withdrawal of Russian troops from the other CIS states would be an "extreme approach." Speaking to the Russian ambassadors to the CIS and Baltic states, he argued that "we should not withdraw from those regions which have been the sphere of Russian interests for centuries and we should not fear these words about military presence" because "as soon as we leave these areas, the ensuing vacuum will immediately be filled by other forces, possibly not always friendly and perhaps even hostile to Russian interests." He described the CIS and Baltic states as a region of "priority vital interests for Russia which also poses the major threat to [those] interests."[4] The following year, Kozyrev told the Russian Federation Council that Russia needed to establish military bases in CIS countries and develop military cooperation with them, in the interests both of Russia and of these other states, which, he said, wanted Russian bases to counter external threats. This was, he stressed, not evidence of Russian imperialist ambition but was normal international practice.[5]

Of all the statements made by senior Russian military and political figures on the issue, none was as high-profile and controversial as Yeltsin's April 1994 decree on bases. Yeltsin caused a serious diplomatic row by issuing an order on the establishment of military bases on the territory of member states of the CIS and in Latvia "to ensure the security of the Russian Federation and the aforementioned states."[6] Despite the controversy generated by this order, however, and although public Russian clarification on the Latvian base was necessary, the directive was in large part simply a statement of an existing position, since agreements or understandings with a number of other

CIS states on the Russian use of military facilities had already been reached.[7] In 1995, in another confirmation of the importance to Russia of a military presence in the rest of the former Soviet Union, another order by Yeltsin, on Russia's strategic course toward the CIS, identified one of the main military goals as the creation of a legal basis for the continued presence of Russian border troops in CIS states.[8]

Although the statements on the need for military bases in the CIS were part of a wider shift in the approach of the Russian military and foreign policy elites, there were also specific issues driving basing policy in respect to some of the CIS states. In the 1990s, the Southern Caucasus states, especially Georgia, remained a strategically key region for Russia; as a result, the retention of a military presence in the region became critical. Concerns about NATO expansion up to, and then inside, the former Soviet borders increased Russia's need for access to military facilities in the western areas of the former Soviet Union, such as Belarus. In the opening years of the twenty-first century, the issue of bases has taken on a new immediacy for Russia and a number of other CIS states. There are two principal, interrelated reasons for this—the increase in US military activity on the territory of the former Soviet Union since 11 September 2001, and the pro–United States orientation of states such as Georgia and Ukraine following the so-called Color Revolutions. In particular, the creation of US military bases in Central Asia, the considerable degree of US security cooperation with Azerbaijan and Georgia in the Caucasus, and the stated aim of the Georgian and Ukrainian governments to seek NATO membership are all sources of concern for Russian policymakers and commentators focused on the growth of US influence and the decline of Russia in the region. Despite the apparent shift away from close security cooperation with the United States in Central Asia in mid-2005 and a strengthening of relations with Russia, Russian concerns remained, and with them a desire to retain military bases in strategically important but less-friendly states, such as Georgia.[9] Nevertheless, the government and parliament of Georgia committed themselves to the closure of all Russian bases in Georgia; to this end, agreement was reached with Russia in May 2005 on the final closure of the bases by the end of 2008.

Thus, the Russian use of military facilities needs to be viewed both as a response to specific security priorities, as in Georgia, and also as part of a wider strategy in relation to the near abroad. The Russian armed forces were based in most of the CIS states in some capacity during the 1990s and are still present in many of them, with their presence increasing in some cases; in this respect, it is arguably one of the most successful Russian security policies in respect to the other CIS states—it has certainly proved to be so in the case of Georgia and Belarus.

Georgia and Russia

The history of the Russian use of Georgian military bases after the collapse of the Soviet Union reflects the shifting and complex relationships between the two states in this period. The retention of bases in Georgia was a security priority for Russia in the 1990s because of the strategic importance of Georgia for Russia; it was equally important for many Georgian politicians that the Russian troops leave Georgian territory.

From the start, the Russian security interest in Georgia was explicit. Speaking in mid-1992, then–defense minister Grachev addressed the Russian Supreme Soviet on the need for a political resolution to the issue of the Russian military presence in Georgia, "especially since, strategically speaking, Georgia's territory is a zone of interest for Russia" and because of the large number of Russian troops on Georgian territory.[10] In 1993, Grachev stated that "the Black Sea coast of the Caucasus . . . is a strategically important area for the Russian army. . . . [Russia] must take every measure to ensure that our troops remain there."[11] A number of factors underpinned Russian interest in Georgia; in particular, the linked issues of energy pipeline routes and fears over the growing influence of both Turkey and the United States (and, to a lesser extent, other NATO states) appear to have been major contributing factors to the determined efforts on the part of Russia to retain a military presence in Georgia. Throughout the 1990s, Russian politicians expressed concerns that withdrawal from Georgia would allow an unacceptable growth in influence on the part of these other states. The rise in Georgian-Turkish military cooperation and the military development assistance given by the United States and a number of Western European states certainly appeared to point to a degree of interest in Georgia that much of the Russian political and security elites considered unwelcome.[12] In order to prevent further erosion of Russian influence, Russian Duma Defense Committee chairman Andrei Nikolaev commented in early 2001, Russia needed to recognize and treat the Northern and Southern Caucasus as a single security region—a proposal that, of course, entirely disregarded the international borders between Russia and the Southern Caucasus states.[13] Thus, the Russian commitment to bases in Georgia needs to be understood as a function of geopolitical concerns about energy, fears about increasing "external" influence, and concerns about activity across the Georgia-Chechnya border. These security problems and the Russian political and military elites' views of possible solutions to them can, in turn, only be understood in the context of their understandings about the nature of other CIS states' sovereignty.

If Russian decisionmakers appeared to be agreed on the importance of maintaining a presence in Georgia, those within Georgia's borders were far from united in their view of the Russian bases. Not surprisingly, leaderships in secessionist regions such as Abkhazia and de facto or de jure autonomous regions such as Javakheti welcomed the Russian military presence. More surprising, perhaps, is that for much of the 1990s, the Georgian political and military establishment was divided on both the desirability and the feasibility of removing the large Russian military presence from its territory. A key factor in this respect was the close linkage of the issue of bases to various other military and security issues such as the establishment and training of the Georgian army; the guarding of the "external" Georgian border; and, in particular, the resolution of the Abkhaz and South Ossetian conflicts and the role played in this by Russian peacekeepers.

The Russian Use of Georgian Military Bases: History and Politics

As with the process of agreement on other issues of dispute between post-Soviet states, the process of agreement on the Russian military presence in Georgia was slow—with events such as treaty signings repeated and ratification delayed—and only partially related to events on the ground. What follows will consider the way in which the issue of Russian military bases on Georgian territory has been negotiated and the way in which this issue should be understood—and has been understood by the main actors—as an issue with profound implications for Georgian state sovereignty, both because of the sovereignty implications of the issues involved (the basing of foreign troops, territorial integrity, and other factors) and because of the way in which the parallel processes of formal negotiation and unofficial coercion demonstrated the relative weakness of Georgian sovereignty in relation to Russia, particularly before the "Rose Revolution." In the period since January 2004, Georgian weakness relative to Russia has been counterbalanced by the emergent security (and political) alliance with the United States; thus, although moves to establish the fundamental elements of internal sovereignty have gathered pace, it is only through the external assistance of a state more powerful than Russia that this has become possible—a fact that underscores the weakness of Georgian sovereignty.

In September 1995, Russia and Georgia signed an agreement that leased four bases on Georgian territory to the Russian armed forces; all occupied positions of strategic importance for Russia—and for Georgia. The four bases were (1) a military airfield at Vaziani, close to Tbilisi, which one article in the Georgian press described as the main base linking the Russian military in the Transcaucasus with Russia (and as a key transit point for "large scale commercial activities" including smuggling and the removal of military equipment); (2) Akhalkalaki, in the predominantly Armenian Javakheti region of southern Georgia, a base of strategic importance because of its proximity to the "external" border with Turkey; (3) Batumi, in the autonomous region of

Adjaria, also close to the Turkish border and on the Black Sea coast; and (4) the military airfield at Gudauta in Abkhazia (which was described by the same Georgian article as playing "a key role in the defeat of the Georgian Armed Forces in Abkhazia").[14] The Akhalkalaki and Batumi bases were occupied by motorized infantry divisions; as with the base at Gudauta, they are situated in areas where the Tbilisi government has exercised little or no influence for most of the post-Soviet period. Following further negotiations and the signing of an agreement in November 1999, the bases at Vaziani and Gudauta were closed in 2001; the Russian leasing of the other two bases, however, was extended with no clear, fixed date for their closure, despite Georgian efforts to end the stationing of Russian troops on Georgian territory. The incentive, and the ability, to exert pressure on Russia to withdraw its troops from the two remaining bases came with the westward reorientation of Georgian foreign and security policy and the increase in US engagement with Georgia in the first years of the twenty-first century. An agreement setting a deadline for the withdrawal of Russian troops from Batumi and Akhalkalaki was finally signed by Russia and Georgia in May 2005; the agreement provided for the last Russian troops to leave Akhalkalaki by the end of 2007 and Batumi by the end of 2008.[15] Unlike numerous other security agreements between Russia and other post-Soviet states, both states appeared to be committed to timely implementation; during the first half of 2006, substantial quantities of hardware left the Akhalkalaki base, as scheduled, and a number of smaller military facilities had been handed over to Georgia by the Russian Group of Forces in the Transcaucasus (RGFT).[16] There were, however, some concerns that loopholes in this and prior treaties might allow a continued Russian military presence in Georgia.[17] Fears that the Russian government would seek to find reasons to halt withdrawal from the bases were given some substance in late 2006, when the sharp deterioration in Russian-Georgian relations, following the arrest of four Russian officers by Georgia on spying charges, led to the temporary suspension of the withdrawal process. Although the process rapidly resumed, the decision to suspend it at all reinforced the impression that Russia regarded its withdrawal commitment as, at best, conditional.

Moscow's military presence in Georgia was problematic even before the definitive breakup of the USSR and continues to be so (it is highlighted as a key security threat to Georgia in the Georgian Strategic Defense Review Progress Review of May 2006).[18] During the Gamsakhurdia presidency, Georgian governmental attitudes toward the troops of the RGFT were hostile, regarding them as an occupation force.[19] In early 1991, the government established the National Guard; in November 1991, parliament demanded the withdrawal of Soviet forces.[20] Following the removal of Gamsakhurdia, the position of the government softened in relation to the Russian military presence; in January 1992, the acting Georgian defense minister Levan Sharishadze (an ex-Soviet officer) described any immediate withdrawal of troops from Georgia as "premature," a view echoed by Shevardnadze later that year when he commented that it was in Georgia's interest for Russian troops to remain in Georgia for "a while."[21] This was not a view shared by all, however; there were calls for both the initiation of negotiations with Russia over the status of the "Russian occupation army" and its removal from Georgian territory, and for the start of negotiations over NATO membership.[22] In early April 1992, the Georgian leadership repealed the decree that described former Soviet troops on Georgian territory as "occupying," and Shevardnadze announced that the issue of the status and future of troops in Georgia would be resolved as part of a wider treaty establishing the legal basis of Russian-Georgian relations, which would be ready for signing that autumn.[23]

In November 1992, the first round of Russian-Georgian negotiations took place, focusing on a proposed friendship and cooperation treaty, the legal status of Russian troops in Georgia, the presence of Russian border troops, and the creation of a Russian-Georgian joint commission on the transfer of "Russian" military property in Georgia to the Georgian state. Agreement was reportedly reached on the preservation of a single system of air defense and on the outlines of an agreement on Russian training of Georgian officers. In this period, Shevardnadze is reported to have taken the view that all Russian troops should be withdrawn from Abkhazia immediately but that some Russian border, air defense, and army units should remain on Georgian territory until equivalent Georgian units had been formed.[24] This was an early statement of a position that was repeated by Shevardnadze and other Georgian politicians throughout the 1990s—that the issue of Russian troops in Abkhazia was to be regarded as a separate problem to the issue of Russian troops based elsewhere in Georgia; as discussed below, this was complicated by the fact that Georgian politicians, including Shevardnadze, also sought to link a resolution of the Abkhazia problem to the basing issue.

Bilateral meetings on the proposed friendship and cooperation treaty and the issue of Russian troops continued to be held regularly. The meeting in February 1993 produced agreement, according to the Georgian foreign minister Aleksandr Chikvaidze, that Russian forces were to remain on Georgian territory until the end of 1995, broadly the timescale that figures in both governments had previously mentioned.[25] According to Feliks Kovalev, the head of the Russian delegation, the draft agreement on troop withdrawals contained the provision that the deadline of the end of 1995 could be extended if both sides agreed on the desirability of keeping Russian troops in Georgia for longer.[26]

In May 1993, Russia and Georgia held the first meeting of their commission on Russian troop withdrawal; meetings continued regularly throughout

1993, but despite regular statements that the Russian and Georgian governments had reached agreement, no treaty was signed by the heads of state. One Russian paper reported in June that the main factor preventing the signing of a treaty between Russia and Georgia was that of Russian troop withdrawal, because the Russian government was unwilling to remove its troops from Georgia in the absence of a clearly framed concept of Russia's political interests in the Transcaucasus.[27] Another report claimed that the failure to reach a final agreement was the result of a Russian desire to restrict any agreement to the issue of the status of its troops in Georgia, rather than linking it to a wider set of agreements.[28]

By mid-1993, the issue of Russian troop withdrawals was becoming increasingly implicated in the Russian-Georgian dispute over the situation in Abkhazia. The Georgian parliament linked these issues explicitly in a resolution, a copy of which was given to Kozyrev, which stated that because of events in Abkhazia it had become impossible to sign the proposed package of Russian-Georgian agreements as a whole and that therefore Russian troops must withdraw as soon as possible from the entire territory of Georgia.[29] The linkage between these two issues did not, ultimately, work to the advantage of those Georgian politicians who wished to remove Russian troops from Georgia. Instead, the escalation of the Abkhaz conflict led to a general weakening of the Georgian government's negotiating position in relation to Russia over a range of military and security issues, leading to Georgian membership of the CIS and the introduction of Russian peacekeepers into Abkhazia. Within days of the announcement of Georgian membership of the CIS, Russian television was reporting that agreement had been reached on the legal status of the Russian troops on Georgian territory, together with a package of eighteen other agreements, and that, in contrast to previous bilateral meetings, no discussion was held of the possible transfer of military hardware on Georgian territory to the Georgian government.[30]

In early February 1994, Yeltsin made his first visit to Georgia, to sign the treaty on "Friendship, Good-Neighborliness, and Cooperation." This treaty, which was strongly opposed by nationalist politicians in both Russia and Georgia, set out a framework for Russian-Georgian cooperation in a number of areas, most prominently security. As in CIS treaties, Article 1 commits the signatory states to

> principles of mutual respect for state sovereignty, territorial integrity and the inviolability of borders, the equality and rights of peoples, the right to decide their own fate, the non-interference in one another's internal affairs, the non-use of force or threat of force, including economic and other methods of pressure.[31]

Having established these commitments, the treaty then proceeded—again, echoing many of the key CIS agreements—to undermine the agreement on noninterference and the right of the signatory states to decide their own fate by committing them to "not participate in any kind of alliances or blocs that are directed against either of them" (Article 4) and, in Article 3, to joint guarding of borders. Although the borders in question are not specified in the treaty, later comments and agreements showed that they included the "external" border between Georgia and Turkey—a border not shared by Russia. Article 3, which attracted most of the opposition to the treaty in both states, set out the agreement in principle that "independently resolving questions of national security and the organisation of defence, will, to this end, engage in close cooperation and practical interaction."[32] One of the key forms of this military cooperation, as set out in Article 3, was the establishment, equipping, and training of a Georgian army with Russian assistance; the other was an agreement on "the temporary presence of Russian Federation military units on the territory of the Republic of Georgia," which was universally taken to refer to the leasing by the Russian armed forces of military bases in Georgia.[33] The treaty did not in itself constitute an agreement on these issues, and although it provided a resolution in principle, an agreement on the detail of basing and Georgian army issues remained unsigned until September 1995.

Despite the 1995 agreement several issues remained unresolved and a number of Georgian political figures (particularly those in the parliamentary opposition factions) continued to express discontent over the continued Russian presence at the four bases. This was in large part a function of the fact that despite the agreement by the two governments on the main terms of the leasing arrangements for the bases, key aspects remained unimplemented. In particular, the agreement that bases would be leased in exchange for Russian assistance in the (re)establishment of Georgian territorial integrity was never upheld—a fact that was repeatedly cited as the reason for the failure of the Georgian parliament to ratify either the friendship and cooperation treaty or the agreement on bases. Members of the Georgian government and parliament continued to draw attention to the Russian failure to uphold their commitments in relation to the basing agreements and to link it to other security issues, including the withdrawal of Georgia from the CIS Collective Security Treaty.[34]

In November 1999, after a long period characterized by intermittent attempts to resolve this problem, Russia and Georgia reached agreement on the closure of the two largest bases, Vaziani and Gudauta.[35] Under the terms of the agreement, Russian troops were scheduled to leave the two bases by early 2001 and the bases themselves were to close by July 2001; it also committed the two states to resolve the future of the other two bases during 2000.[36] This agreement was reached in the context of wider negotiations over rights relating to military equipment in Georgia limited under the Conventional Forces in Europe (CFE) Treaty, with Georgia effectively trading a share of its CFE quota for the closure of the two bases.[37] Prior to this agreement, Georgian politicians had been calling for a reduction of Russian troops and equipment in Georgia in accordance with the CFE Treaty limits and had appeared to be unwilling to donate any of the Georgian quota of treaty-limited equipment to Russia.[38] It appears, however, the failure of Georgia to enforce any of the previous agreements linking the use of Russian bases to concrete gains for Georgia, and the prospect of finally obtaining at least a partial resolution of the basing issue, encouraged the Georgian government to rethink this question. Even this, however, might suggest a greater degree of Georgian success than there was, since the extent to which the closure of Vaziani can be regarded as a diplomatic achievement by the Georgian government is limited by the announcement the previous year that the Vaziani base was due to close as the result of Russian army reforms.

The history of the negotiations over Russian military bases in Georgia in the 1990s demonstrates the close linkages between security and sovereignty issues for the post-Soviet states and the degree to which both security and sovereignty have been conceived of by these states in relation to one another. In the case of Georgia, it is possible to consider the various interconnections between sovereignty and security as divided into two categories of positive and negative linkage—those areas where the linkage was explicitly acknowledged and presented as beneficial to the establishment of de facto Georgian sovereignty by those members of the Georgian and Russian political and military elites engaged in negotiating the leasing of the bases, and those areas where a link was not acknowledged by these groups but was clearly at work as a mechanism to restrict the extent of Georgian sovereignty over its territory, borders, and security policy. The bases issue was directly and explicitly linked to both the problem of Georgian territorial integrity and the formation of the Georgian armed forces; in contrast, the linkage between the location of bases and the possibilities for Georgian sovereignty, or between the bases and Georgian control of its northern border with Russia, were never explicitly acknowledged but clearly drove negotiations and, at least in the cases of negative linkage, appear to have been influential in determining outcomes.

Bases and Territorial Integrity

The issue of the basing of Russian troops in Georgia clearly raised fundamental issues of territorial integrity for Georgia, both because of the implications of having a large foreign troop presence on its territory and because of the explicit positive and negative linkage made between the bases and the future restoration of separatist regions to Georgian governmental control. Members of the Georgian government repeatedly stressed that the Russian use of the bases on Georgian territory was conditional on Russian assistance with the (re)establishment of Georgian territorial integrity, in particular with the restoration of Georgian control over Abkhazia and Russian assistance in reasserting control over western Georgia in 1993; failure to provide such assistance would thus lead to demands for complete Russian military withdrawal.[39] In June 1993, for example, the Georgian foreign minister informed the Russian ambassador to Georgia that as a result of the situation in Abkhazia, and instead of the proposed bilateral agreements on the Russian use of Georgian bases and other issues, the Georgian government demanded the immediate withdrawal of all Russian troops from Georgian territory.[40] The issue appeared at other points as well; in March 1995, Interfax reported that a central problem in the negotiations over the bases treaty was the insistence by the Georgian negotiators that the agreement on bases was conditional on the resolution of the Abkhaz and South Ossetian conflicts.[41]

In addition, as discussed below, the specific location of the four main bases had clear implications for the ability of the Georgian government to assert control within Georgia's borders. While the presence of the Russian bases was not consistently regarded as a negative factor in this respect (for example, in relation to the region of Javakheti), the nonpeacekeeping Russian troop presence in Georgia was overwhelmingly regarded by members of the Georgian political and military elites as an obstacle to the reassertion of control over these areas, which had, to varying degrees, detached themselves from Tbilisi during the 1990s.

The agreement on the bases was consistently presented by Shevardnadze as regrettable but essential both for Georgian security and for the assertion of state sovereignty. Speaking shortly after the basing agreement was reached in 1995, he said:

> The presence of foreign troops on one's own territory would not be welcome in any country . . . on the other hand, we must comprehend why it is necessary today and why it will be necessary tomorrow. I could not see another solution earlier and I cannot see a solution today either for setting up our own armed forces, or owning relevant equipment and arms; or having guarantees for our country's independence and territorial integrity.[42]

This message was repeated still more bluntly a few days later, when he told Georgian radio:

> The question now is whether or not Georgia will become a sovereign state. . . . The decision concerning the bases has been prompted by the harsh reality . . . that without Russia it will now be impossible to unite the country. . . . Is it in Russia's interests that its armed forces remain in Georgia? Of course, it is. But if Russian armed bases are a guarantee for Georgia becoming a single state, will it not be in our interests as well? . . . I

repeat that this is the last chance to save the country and restore its integrity . . . and I repeat that at this stage that it is unrealistic to speak of restoring Georgian integrity without a decisive role played by Russia.[43]

The question of the use of bases was consistently presented by Shevardnadze and the government as inextricably linked to the question of territorial integrity. From an early point in the negotiations over the future of the Russian troops in Georgia a link was made between the resolution of the issue and a settlement of the situation in Abkhazia.[44] Although a treaty on friendship and cooperation with Russia had been signed in 1994 and an agreement on bases in 1995, by 1997 neither had been ratified by the Georgian parliament, and any future ratification was described as contingent on the restoration of Georgian territorial integrity by Russia, as well as on Russian assistance with the development of the Georgian armed forces.[45] In an interview shortly after the signing of the 1995 agreement, Shevardnadze explained this trade-off:

> At the moment two topical problems are on the agenda that we must solve with Russia's help. First, we must establish Georgian armed forces, which is not possible without Russia's help because we lack our own weapons and weapons technology. There is no other partner for this in the world. The second problem is regaining Abkhazia and settling the Georgian-Ossetian conflict. Here, too, Russia will give the decisive word. At the same time, Russia is interested in having its armed forces stay in Georgia and in the Caucasus as a whole. Thus, our interests coincide.[46]

As this suggests, the linkage of these two issues was both positive and negative for Georgia. On the one hand, members of the Georgian political elite, especially in parliament, insisted on the linkage of Russian bases to the restoration of Georgian territorial integrity, attempting to instrumentalize the bases for the purposes of negotiation with a more powerful state. This however, required a degree of control that Georgia simply did not possess in the 1990s; it was unable to effectively instrumentalize assets over which it had no control. On the other hand, therefore, Georgia experienced a negative linkage of the two issues, in which attempts to assert sovereignty over separatist regions was counterbalanced by the limitations placed on independence by the presence of Russian forces, a presence that was the precondition for Russian assistance with Georgian attempts to maintain de jure territorial integrity. Describing the political/security relationship between Georgia and Russia, one Georgian analyst has commented:

> It appears that Georgia has got into a vicious geo-political circle: it cannot get away from Russia. It is not only the "Abkhaz hook" which holds Georgia. If Georgia . . . insist[s] upon the removal of the Russian military bases and will start to carry out a completely independent policy, there are

other "hooks"—actual separatism in South Ossetia and potential separatism in Southern Georgia, or the threat of the splitting up of the nation.[47]

The 1995 agreement on the stationing of Russian troops in Georgia was one of the clearest instances where the problems of establishing sovereignty and security policy intersected, and where, although mutually interdependent, they also proved to be mutually exclusive as realizable political objectives for Georgia. At the center of the Russian-Georgian agreement on bases is a paradox that has undermined the possibility for resolution of some of Georgia's fundamental problems in its relationship with Russia. On the one hand, the agreement on bases appears to be a simple trade of a military asset (the use of the bases) for the (re)acquisition of a key attribute of state sovereignty—territorial integrity. However, this trade-off was necessarily unworkable because of the impossibility of resolving the fact that the trading of this particular asset for assistance in consolidating state sovereignty (the use of military bases on Georgia's territory by another state) posed a fundamental challenge to several aspects of sovereignty on both a theoretical and a practical level. In particular, the agreed presence of a foreign army undermined the principle of the state's monopoly on the legitimate use of force within its territory, a principle that the Georgian government was attempting to establish through the development of the Georgian armed forces. On a practical level, such a presence posed a threat to the ability of a state to assert a foreign or military policy in contradiction to the interests of the state using the military bases, a threat significantly enhanced by the location of the bases near the capital and in separatist or autonomous regions.

In addition, the unworkable nature of the agreement also derived from the fact that the two assets being traded were interdependent in a way that challenged the nature of the linkage established in the agreement. The reason given by key Georgian figures, in particular Shevardnadze, for the acceptance of a continued Russian military presence on Georgian territory was the collapse of internal sovereignty. If, as under the terms of the agreement, Georgia were able to reestablish its territorial integrity with the help of Russia, it would no longer be in a weakened state that required it to make concessions to Russia over the leasing of bases. Thus, the fulfillment of that half of the agreement, which was set as a precondition for the other half, would invalidate the treaty as a whole, since the Georgian state would no longer be in the position that led the government to accept the agreement in the first place. As a result, Russia had a strong disincentive to fulfill its half of the agreement, and this in turn meant that, in its state of extremely reduced sovereignty over its territory and its lack of sovereignty over many of the armed forces within its borders, the Georgian state was unable either to compel Russia to meet its commitments under the agreement or to withdraw its half of the trade, the use of military bases. Only with the changing security politics of the broader region, as the United States increased political and military engagement in the Caucasus after 11 September 2001, did it become possible for Georgia to try to break free from this vicious cycle of insecurity.

The signing of the treaty in 1995 did not put an end to Georgia's attempts to use the bases as a bargaining chip in discussions about the separatist regions. In May 1996, the then–Georgian foreign minister Irakli Mengarishvili reasserted the link, stating that the existence of Russian military bases in Georgia was conditional on Russian assistance with the (re)establishment of Georgian territorial integrity.[48] In August 1999, Shevardnadze, commenting on Georgia's extension of the Russian peacekeepers' mandate in Abkhazia, made it clear that the resolution of the Abkhaz conflict was linked to the issue of a possible Georgian CFE quota transfer to Russia—on which, in turn, depended the ability of Russian troops to continue to use Georgian bases.[49] The linkage of Russian military bases to the issue of Georgian territorial integrity continued even once agreement had been reached on partial closure, with Russia's continued use of the Batumi and Akhalkalaki bases reportedly made conditional by Georgia, in 2000, on Russia's position in respect to Abkhazia.[50] The same linkage was apparently made again later in the year, when it was reported that Shevardnadze had offered to allow the bases at Akhalkalaki and Batumi to remain open for an additional fifteen years if Russia were to assist in finally resolving the issue of Abkhazia. If not, Georgia would demand the immediate closure of the bases. This was not a linkage that Russia was prepared to acknowledge (the Foreign Ministry pointed out that such a link was not incorporated into the 1999 agreement on the base closures); Russian deputy prime minister Ilya Klebanov commented that Russia did not link the two issues, although Russia was interested in restoring Georgian territorial integrity.[51]

The Location of the Bases

One of the most serious problems for the establishment of de facto Georgian internal sovereignty was the location of the bases leased to the Russian armed forces. Three of the bases were located in areas that were either engaged in a secessionist conflict with Tbilisi or, although not attempting to formally secede from Georgia, have had a high degree of official or unofficial autonomy (the Gudauta base was located in Abkhazia, while the Batumi and Akhalkalaki bases were in Adjaria and the predominantly ethnic Armenian region of Javakheti, respectively). During the 1990s, all of these regions successfully sought to minimize Tbilisi's control over them; the presence of the Russian 145th and 147th Motorized Rifle Divisions appeared to be regarded as a key component of their success. The weakness of the Georgian governmental hold over Jakhvetia was evident when, faced with the possible closure of the Akhalkalaki base in the late 1990s, the local government managed to extract a promise from the Georgian government that Georgian troops would not be based there after the Russian troops withdrew.[52] The Russian military presence in these regions has thus been a cause, a marker, and a guarantor of the failure of the Georgian state to extend control to these regions, as some members of the Georgian political and security structures have made clear.

However, although the location of the four bases leased to Russia under the 1995 agreement raised concerns about attempts to place regions of Georgia more firmly outside the control of Tbilisi, it is also clear that the location of two of these bases provided stability benefits, at least in the short term. During negotiations over the closure of the Gudauta and Vaziani bases, it was reported that the Russians were threatening an immediate withdrawal from the other two bases as well, as a means of extracting concessions from Georgia.[53] This appears curious given the apparent commitment on the part of the Georgian government to the closure of all four bases at the earliest opportunity. However, the continued existence of the Russian base at Akhalkalaki was clearly helpful to the Georgian government in two ways. First, the largely ethnic Armenian population of the Javakheti region generally opposed any possibility of more direct rule from Tbilisi, and there was clearly a perception that the possibility for this was reduced by the presence of a large Russian military base. While this in itself does not appear to be an obvious benefit for the Georgian government, the perception of relative security generated by the Russian military presence appeared to reduce the threat of a more formal break by the region from the center, a possible response to the fears about political and economic security that closure of the Russian base would raise.[54] The reduction of sovereignty caused by a foreign military presence in a region over which the Georgian government had little direct control was in fact far more limited than the potential threat to Georgian sovereignty resulting from increased regional insecurity driven by the removal of the Russian military presence. Thus, in March 1999, for example, Revaz Adamia, the chair of the Parliamentary Defense and Security Committee, who had previously been very critical of the continued Russian presence in Georgia, commented that Georgia should not insist on the removal of the Akhalkalaki and Adjaria military bases because of the risk of destabilization.[55]

A second, perhaps more immediate, reason for Georgian reluctance to insist on the removal of the Russian base at Akhalkalaki was economic. Located in the poorest region of Georgia, the base was the largest employer in Akhalkalaki, employing both civilians and, apparently, around 1,500 local people as servicemen (around 50 percent of the total at the base), on wages higher than average for the region.[56] There were concerns in the late 1990s that its closure would mean the removal of an income source that the Georgian government would not be able to replace.[57] This clearly raised problems for the Georgian government, since an achievement of the security goal of base closure would increase the severe economic problems in the area and risk threatening the stability of the region still further. As one analyst noted, the population in this region viewed "the Russian military machine as their most essential source of income . . . [and] have historically regarded the Russian army as the guarantee of stability. . . . Until Tbilisi creates economic alternatives in the region, any actions against the Russian base will prove disadvantageous."[58] When agreement was finally reached on the closure of the base, there were rallies in the region, demanding the retention of the base for economic and security reasons (in addition to the other reasons for support for the continuation of the base, the region's Armenian population reportedly viewed it as a guarantor that Turkish troops would not be based there instead). In an attempt to limit discontent in the region, the Georgian government committed itself to the reemployment of the local base personnel and (in a shift from the commitment made several years earlier) to the replacement of Russian troops with Georgian (not Turkish) troops.[59] Further protests occurred as the Russian withdrawal began; the Georgian Foreign Ministry alleged that certain, unnamed forces were attempting to halt the withdrawal by using the excuse of deteriorating regional conditions.[60]

Other Military Assets

In addition to the issue of territorial integrity, the negotiations around the future of Russian troops in Georgia had implications for other aspects of Georgian security and military development, which linked fundamentally to the failed attempt to establish a Western model of sovereign statehood in Georgia in the 1990s. Some of the most notable of these were the linkage of Russian bases to the development of the Georgian army, the ownership of military assets on Georgian territory, the use of the numerous minor military facilities on Georgian territory, CFE Treaty quotas, control over borders, and the movement of Georgian citizens across the border with Russia. In all cases, Georgia failed either to ensure that agreements on this linkage were adhered to or, in other cases, to prevent such a linkage being made to Russian advantage. In the cases of the issues of borders and Georgian citizens' movement across them, no link was ever made explicitly; however, the timing of Russian actions on these questions can be regarded as at least suggestive of such a link. In most of these cases, however, the increased engagement of the United States and the reorientation of Georgian foreign and security policy by the Saakashvili administration have resulted in a clear shift in the relative ability of Russia and Georgia to instrumentalize these security assets to achieve wider security or sovereignty gains. Whether this shift is sustainable in the longer term is an open question.

In addition to the issue of the four main military bases leased to Russia in the second half of the 1990s, Russia and Georgia also had to address the issue of the other military facilities in Georgia, and the equipment located at these facilities. Although the four bases and the agreements on them dominated discussions and media debate, the issue of the numerous other military sites on Georgian territory, closely linked to discussions about the future of the four main Russian bases in Georgia, were also of key importance both for the security relationship between the two states and for what they indicated about Georgian inability to exercise control over its territory or to negotiate effectively with a stronger state. As with other post-Soviet military issues (notably the division of the Black Sea Fleet), one of the problems surrounding the military assets on Georgian territory was the apparent lack of clarity about the exact number and nature of military assets.[61] Reportedly, no accurate inventory was available to the Georgian government, clearly in part because of the large-scale, illegal sale of weapons.

In December 1997, the Georgian defense minister announced that Georgia would be seeking the transfer of around fifty military facilities to Georgian control and indicated that Russia was prepared to do this in exchange for the Georgian ratification of the agreement on bases.[62] In January 1998, Russian and Georgian defense officials met to discuss the issue of the transfer of former Soviet military property to Georgia, to sign an agreement on Russian-Georgian military cooperation, and to resolve the issues of compensation claims for the military equipment removed from Georgia since 1991 and of rent payable by Russia for the Georgian bases.[63] The Russian delegation rejected Georgian claims to compensation, calling such claims "unreasonable." Russia did, however, agree to begin the process of transfer of ten Russian military facilities on Georgian territory to Georgian control.[64] This was confirmed by the Russian government in late March 1998. The Russian Duma voted overwhelmingly to call on Yeltsin to ban this transfer on the grounds that NATO troops could be deployed at these bases once they were handed over to Georgia—a vote criticized in advance by the Georgian Foreign Ministry on the grounds that the facilities were Georgian state property, and because Russia had neither paid any rent for the use of facilities on Georgian territory at any point since 1991 nor compensated Georgia for the military equipment it had removed from Georgian territory.[65] The possibility of compensation for military equipment removed from Georgia was again rejected by Russia at talks between the Russian and Georgian defense ministers in late August 1998.[66] This was a reflection of a more fundamental disagreement that was, again, founded in a clash between the Georgian attempt to adopt a Western model of sovereignty and the Russian approach derived from the Soviet model of differentiated and limited sovereignty; Georgian claims to facilities and assets on its territory, and to compensation and rent, were at odds with the perception that these facilities and assets were Russian, not Georgian, property. As on other issues, this dispute based on difference of perception was resolved on a much more material basis—Georgia lacked the capabilities to compel a much more powerful state to meet its demands.

In 1992 the Russian Duma passed a resolution that no military assistance could be given by Russia to Georgia until a final settlement had been reached over Abkhazia. Despite this, the issue of military assistance was frequently linked in negotiations to the issue of bases. The relationship between the issues of military bases and the training and equipment of the Georgian army reflected the same weaknesses on the part of Georgia as the other security linkages had done. A reflection of the multiple weaknesses of the Georgian state, the Georgian armed forces lacked the capability required to perform an effective role as an arm of the Georgian state; as one Russian analyst observed bluntly, "If Georgia wants to be sovereign, it needs to strengthen its own armed forces."[67] The essential training and equipment of the Georgian armed forces was only possible with external assistance; in a period of limited engagement on the part of Western European or North American states, Georgia relied on Russia. Interviewed in late 1995, Shevardnadze observed that "Russia helps us build our army, security forces, and the police. Where else could I obtain money for arms or even uniforms for my people? The West will not send it to me."[68] As a result, Russian assistance in the development of the Georgian armed forces was a key condition for the Russian use of military bases on Georgian territory.[69] In early 1994, after the signing of the friendship and cooperation treaty, Shevardnadze commented:

> No country can be happy at allowing another country's troops to enter its territory. But we can see Russia's interest on the one hand and, on the other hand, we have to create an army. . . . If a country can exist without an army we would not make that decision . . . we would ask the Russians to quit and no talks about any bases would take place.[70]

This emphasis on the linkage between the bases and Russian assistance in the formation of the Georgian army, and the necessity of that assistance, was repeated by Shevardnadze throughout the treaty negotiation and ratification processes. In September 1995, for example, he asserted that "without Russia's active participation it is impossible to restore the territorial integrity of Georgia . . . and it is impossible to set up Georgia's armed forces."[71]

Despite agreements linking the basing of Russian troops to assistance with Georgian army building, Russia failed to provide any substantial help with the development of the army, apart from some officer training. As on the other issues, Georgia was unable to enforce the agreement on bases and training because it was in a position of extreme weakness in relation to Russia. Once again, however, the nature of Russia and Georgia's security-sovereignty relationship was fundamentally altered in the early twenty-first century by the greatly increased security and political engagement of the United States after 2001. The United States' Georgia Train and Equip Program (GTEP) was launched in May 2002 and has, according to the US State Department, "creat[ed] four Coalition/NATO interoperable, light infantry battalions and a mechanized armor company that have served the Global War On Terrorism in Georgia and abroad."[72] A program of equal concern for Russia was the International Military Education and Training Program launched the following year to improve the Georgian armed forces' interoperability with NATO. The US government recorded its financial assistance to Georgia for security programs in fiscal years 2002–2006 as over $210 million; clearly, the scale of financial assistance, together with the focus on English-language training and interoperability with NATO, dramatically altered Russia's ability to achieve security objectives in Georgia by offering limited military assistance. It would appear that this development definitively decoupled the issue of Georgian army development from the issue of bases.

The issue of border control and visas—highly contentious issues in themselves—were also linked to the negotiations over bases at various points. As the deadline to resolve the issue of the two remaining Russian bases approached, it became clear that the question of borders was also at issue. By late 1999, Georgia had formally assumed control over the guarding of its borders, with Russian border guards due to withdraw from their last areas of control, in Abkhazia and Adjaria, by the start of November. As the Russian border troops withdrew, however, Russian politicians were engaged in moves to control the Georgian-Russian border. In mid-September, then–prime minister Putin lifted restrictions on Russian-Georgian border crossings, most significantly removing border restrictions between Russia and Abkhazia, which was described by the Abkhaz president as an end to the economic blockade of the region. This easing of the restrictions imposed on Abkhazia was strongly criticized by Georgia. The Georgian State Frontier Department described the decision as an aid to Abkhaz separatism and an infringement of Georgian sovereignty and called, in response, for the closure of all Russian military bases in Georgia.[73]

In addition to the issue of the physical borders between Russia and Georgia, the issue of free movement by Georgians into Russia also became implicated in the debate over the future of Russian bases in Georgia. In late 2000, as the fate of the two remaining bases was still being negotiated, the Georgian foreign minister reported that Russia would introduce a visa requirement for Georgians wishing to enter Russia, with potentially very serious consequences for many Georgians working or trading within Russia, unless Georgia complied with a number of Russian demands, including a more favorable approach to Russian interests in oil and gas exports from the Caspian region and a more moderate stance on the future of the Russian bases. This was not an isolated incident; visa restrictions have also been used more recently by Russia to attempt to coerce revisions to Georgian policy regarding bases. In February 2006, the Russian government imposed a visa ban on Georgians in response to Georgia's imposition of restrictions on the movement of Russian military personnel from the two remaining bases.[74]

Conclusion: Georgia and Russia

The issue of the Russian use of military bases illustrates the multiple failures of Georgia's attempt to establish a Western model of state sovereignty—sovereignty failure over security; over key aspects of policymaking; over relations with Russia; over its breakaway regions; and over those regions, such as Adjaria and Javakheti, that had not declared independence from Georgia but that were almost entirely detached from the rest of the state. In particular, the negotiations around the Russian use of military bases in Georgia are a clear indicator of the way in which Georgia tried and failed to assert its sovereignty over security problems in relation to Russia during the 1990s. In relations between states, there is no clearer example of the failure of state sovereignty than the inability of a state to prevent unwelcome foreign troop deployments on its territory. At a practical level, Georgian failure to achieve its objectives of full withdrawal of Russian troops; ownership of and control over military assets on its territory (and compensation for the removal of any such assets); development of the Georgian armed forces; and, most important, the restoration of territorial integrity, can be understood to derive from the linked factors of weak Georgian internal sovereignty; weak external sovereignty with respect to Russia; and the fact that it was attempting to instrumentalize a single asset—the leasing of bases on its territory—to achieve multiple security objectives. Although agreements had implicitly or explicitly granted the use of bases for Russian fulfillment of all of the above demands at various points, the only trade that appears to have been successful was that of the closure of two bases for CFE quotas in November 1999. This was clearly the Georgian government's strongest negotiating advantage—all other agreements were based on the continued presence of Russian troops (an advantage Russia already had) being exchanged for the benefits to Georgia that Russia could provide. Negotiations only appear to have been successful in the 1990s when this formula was reversed and Russia was asked to renounce something it already had (two of the bases) in exchange for something it wanted (CFE quotas). However, a final resolution of the bases problem only came in the wider context of assistance on security issues from an external actor, the United States, following Georgia's change of approach to relations with Russia in the period after the "Rose Revolution." That it has only been able to develop its security structures and begin to counteract Russian influence on security problems with the assistance of a state more powerful than Russia suggests that the exercise of Georgian sovereignty in key areas is still dependent, to a significant extent, on the political will and capabilities of another state.

Belarus and Russia

The issue of Russia's use of military bases in Georgia highlighted Georgia's failure to consolidate itself as an independent state conforming to the Western model of sovereignty during the 1990s; in the early twenty-first century, with external assistance, it has taken steps toward this model and has become more effective in asserting sovereignty over security issues in relation to Russia. Belarus, in contrast, has taken the opposite path, moving firmly away from the Western model of sovereignty and toward a revised version of the Soviet model. The issue of the way in which Belarus and Russia negotiated the leasing of two military facilities, at Baranovichi and Vileika, and the wider context of military integration within which this took place, indicates what could be termed a Belarusian loss of appetite for sovereignty in relation to Russia. Although the military and security policy of Belarus in relation to Russia was initially more successful than that of Georgia, any independence in security matters had disappeared by the mid-1990s, under the presidency of Alyaksandr Lukashenka (although his pro-unification rhetoric and actions were arguably a continuation and strengthening of already emerging tendencies in Belarusian governmental policy). This apparent, progressive renunciation of Belarusian state sovereignty in relation to Russia reached its climax in the late 1990s with the signing of a series of bilateral military agreements within the context of their proposed union. Clearly, any putative concerns about the impact of basing arrangements on Belarusian sovereignty were rendered irrelevant by the far more radical rejection of sovereignty in relation to Russia implied in the proposal to (re)create a union.[75]

The Development of Russian-Belarusian Security Cooperation

In contrast to the situation in Georgia immediately after the breakup of the USSR, the presence of former Soviet troops on Belarusian territory does not appear to have been regarded as an urgent security problem by the Belarusian government. There appear to have been two reasons for this— first, many of these troops were incorporated into the new Belarusian armed forces; second, the question of other, Russian, troops was part of the wider issue of continued security cooperation with Russia. Unlike the Georgian government, the new Belarusian government did not appear to envisage an absolute break between the Soviet forces and the new Belarusian forces, or to view the Soviet forces as foreign occupiers. In May 1992, the Soviet Belarusian Military District was formally abolished and all its units were transferred to Belarusian Ministry of Defense command. The Ministry of Defense also took command of those forces previously under central command (and thus not under the command of the Belarusian Military District) that were not part of the CIS strategic forces. A significant part of the issue had thus been resolved within six months of independence.

The military integration of Belarus and Russia (or of Belarus into Russia) predates the decision in the mid-1990s to create a union state; in fact, it has been an almost constant feature of bilateral relations in the postindependence period.[76] Thus, although security integration processes radically developed under Lukashenka, his policies largely continued a process of coordination and integration that had begun before his presidency. In July 1992, little more than six months after the dissolution of the USSR, Russia and Belarus signed a package of military agreements, including an agreement to coordinate defense activities and an agreement on the stationing of strategic forces on Belarusian territory. Mecheslau Hryb, the chairman of the Supreme Soviet, said at the time that approximately 30,000 Russian military personnel would be stationed in Belarus for "about 7 years" and that most of them would constitute strategic forces units; he did not specify what role the nonstrategic Russian troops would have or how many of them there would be.[77] Belarusian politicians repeatedly denied that these agreements constituted a military alliance, which would have been in breach of the constitutional commitments to neutrality.[78] However, the neutrality commitment was undermined further by the Belarusian Supreme Soviet's vote to join the CIS Collective Security Treaty in April 1993. Membership of the treaty was agreed with some provisions, including a ban on the stationing of other states' troops on the territory of Belarus without the approval of the Supreme Soviet.

Although apparently resolved by the agreement signed in July 1992, the question of the future of those troops not incorporated into the Belarusian armed forces but present on Belarusian territory remained unclear. In particular, there appeared to be some confusion over the agreed duration of their stay on Belarusian territory.[79] During a debate on the Collective Security Treaty in the Belarusian Supreme Soviet, for example, one deputy referred to the fact that Russia had seven years to withdraw from Belarus—presumably, therefore, until 2000. This appeared to extend the agreed length of stay for Russian troops, since Hryb had also referred to a seven-year period the year before. However, this was contradicted in mid-July by Kozlovskiy, who commented that the timescale for withdrawal of Russian troops had already been agreed, and that it was to be completed by 1995–1996.[80] In September 1992, the Russian and Belarusian prime ministers signed a treaty on the status of strategic Russian troops in Belarus, and a treaty on procedures for their eventual withdrawal, which was ratified by the Belarusian Supreme Soviet two months later. This formalized the presence of the Russian armed forces on Belarusian territory but also defined an end point for their stay.

As already discussed, Yeltsin's April 1994 decree on the establishment of military bases in other CIS states and Latvia provoked a crisis in Russia's relations with some of the states concerned. Perhaps not surprisingly, given the generally positive character of Russian-Belarusian security relations, the reaction of Belarus was more muted. One Belarusian security official stated that although the Belarusian government had not announced any official position on the Russian proposal on bases, Russian strategic units could not be stationed in Belarus because of Belarus's commitment to nonnuclear and neutral status. However, he also indicated that this was an objection specifically regarding strategic units, but that Russian air or air defense forces would help development and maintenance in the Belarusian armed forces, and that "all options of the presence of foreign military bases in Belarus will be thoroughly studied"; Belarus's commitment to neutrality was not mentioned as a potential obstacle in this context.[81] The controversy over Yeltsin's decree in fact occurred at the same time as the Belarusian defense minister was visiting a number of Russian units stationed in Belarus and negotiating details of their withdrawal, and the following month, Russian and Belarusian military delegations met again to discuss the issue of the Russian military presence on Belarusian territory.[82] The negotiations reportedly produced an agreement that Russia would have use of the Vileika communications center for the Baltic Fleet and the as yet unfinished radar station at Baranovichi (designed to replace the Skrunda radar facility in Latvia) after the withdrawal of Russian strategic troops and after the agreed deadline for full Russian withdrawal from Belarusian territory.[83] This round of negotiations also produced an agreement to allow a Russian air force unit to remain in Belarus until 2000. No explicit link appears to have been made with the response to Yeltsin's April decree, but the timing of the agreement suggests an increased level of urgency about the need to secure a replacement for the Skrunda facility following the negative response of the Latvian government to the decree.

The election of Lukashenka strengthened the favorable tone of Belarusian rhetoric and policy regarding the Russian military presence. In July 1994, Lukashenka announced that one of his aims was to deepen and develop military cooperation with Russia. Other reports suggested that the Belarusian military command was committed to the agreed timetable for Russian strategic troop and missile withdrawals, but that Russia had again asked Belarus to consider whether it could keep some military installations in Belarus because of their strategic importance to Russia, including those at Baranovichi and Vileika.[84] A Belarusian Ministry of Defense spokesman was reported as saying that Belarus was keen to preserve these Russian installations given Belarus's participation in the CIS collective security system and its need for reliable defense, and that, as a result, Russia and Belarus were holding talks to discuss the terms of continued Russian occupation of these installations.[85] The first Yeltsin-Lukashenka summit, held in August, was intended to concentrate on military questions and resulted in agreement on the need for a further package of treaties addressing military cooperation.[86] It was announced after the summit that there had been discussion of the possibility of leasing the two military facilities (and possibly others) because, according to the head of the Belarusian presidential administration, "Belarus has no ambitious geopolitical plans, it does not need these military sites at all because we are unable to maintain them" and "Belarus and Russia have entered a deeper stage of integration compared with other CIS states."[87] Yeltsin and Lukashenka also affirmed their commitment to cooperate on the basis of "state sovereignty, territorial integrity, [and] inviolability of borders."[88] According to the recently appointed defense minister Anatol Kastenka, leasing terms for the basing of Russian troops had been relaxed and "as for the two stations and other Russian installations in our country, it was agreed that these must be part of an overall integration system."[89]

In the period from the election of Lukashenka to January 1995, a comprehensive transformation was effected in Belarusian security structures, including the replacement of the defense minister and most of his deputies, and the creation of a Republican Security Council with four permanent members—Lukashenka, the presidential chief of staff, the prime minister, and the first deputy parliamentary chairman—and the defense, interior, and foreign ministers; the chair of the National Security Committee; and the prosecutor general as nonpermanent members.[90] This reflected the shift in approach in military relations with Russia, which culminated in the signing of a twenty-five-year leasing arrangement (agreed in principle the previous year) of the two facilities at Baranovichi and Vileika in January 1995, as part of a wider package of military and economic agreements with Russia. Many Supreme Soviet members and members of the wider Belarusian opposition attacked the agreements, accusing the government of exceeding its powers, violating the law on the presence of Russian troops in Belarus requiring Russian troops to leave by 1996, and undermining Belarusian state sovereignty. Opposition members were further angered by the signing of the friendship and cooperation treaty and more economic and political agreements the following month, which were described by the leader of the Belarusian Popular Front (BPF) Zenon Poznyak as "the creation of a basis for incorporating Belarus into Russia," and, by one opposition deputy, as providing for the "liquidation of Belarus as a subject of economic management and international law."[91]

The issue of the stationing of Russian troops and the leasing of military facilities in Belarus acquired a different political significance as Russia and Belarus began moves to form a union. As with most features of the integration process between Russia and Belarus, there was considerable uncertainty about the full extent of formal military integration, with the then–Belarusian defense minister Leanid Maltsau detailing aspects of cooperation, including training and the use of Russian test range facilities, and stating that "we will resolve all issues in close interaction with the Russian Army," while asserting that "the treaty does not infringe on our independence."[92] Speaking to the Coordinating Council of Officer Associations of the Belarusian Armed Forces, he asserted that "the Armed Forces of the Republic will remain the armed forces of an independent and sovereign state, under the command of the Commander in Chief, the President. . . . No threats to sovereignty and independence ensue from the Treaty."[93]

The Russian-Belarusian Union Treaty signed on 2 April 1997 and ratified in June 1997 again raised the question of the future of Belarus's military independence, despite Yeltsin's assurances that Russia and Belarus would remain sovereign states. Contrary to expectations, the treaty focused less on commitments to developing a common budget and single currency than on coordinating security policies and border controls. A further move toward the abandonment of independent military structures was signaled in December 1997, with the signing of a bilateral treaty on military cooperation arising from the more general military cooperation commitments signaled in the Union Treaty. The key feature of the treaty, according to reports at the time of the signing, was the establishment of a joint board of the defense ministries of the two countries.[94] Reports at the time of ratification by the Belarusian parliament, however, indicated that the treaty outlined more extensive integration between the military structures of Russia and Belarus, including the formulation of joint defense policies; the unification of military legislation; and the creation of a joint regional group of forces, together with procedures for their command during military actions.[95] Strategic planning and the use of air space and military infrastructure were also mentioned elsewhere as aspects of the coordinated military activity provided for by the December 1997 treaty.[96] Despite this apparent move toward military integration, the Belarusian deputy foreign minister stated shortly after the treaty signing that Belarus did not want Russian troops stationed on its territory, preferring Russia to "make full use of Belarus's military potential" in an unspecified way.[97] This was a view endorsed—at least temporarily—by Lukashenka, who stated in May 1999 that there was no need to build Russian military bases in Belarus because Belarus was a friendly country and its army would also defend Russia if necessary. In late 1998, the head of the Russian Armed Forces General Staff's Tactical Department announced that Russia and Belarus were developing a joint defense system with ten divisions on permanent alert, in response to eastward NATO expansion (although the

Ministry of Defense later claimed that the comments were misinterpreted and that there were only plans for further defense cooperation between Belarus and Russia).[98]

Despite Lukashenka's apparent rejection of the development of Russian military bases in mid-1999 and his threat to improve relations with the West if Russia further delayed the integration process, by December 1999, with the signing of another union treaty (ratified by both states' legislatures by the end of the month) the process of Russian and Belarusian military unification seemed to be gaining momentum. The 1999 treaty stated that Russia and Belarus would develop a joint military doctrine by 2000 (in contrast to the longer timetable envisaged for the economic union sought by Belarus, according to which a single currency would not be introduced until 2005); in addition to the treaty, Yeltsin and Lukashenka agreed on the need for the development of a joint military formation, incorporating the Moscow Military District and the Belarusian armed forces.[99] Despite the cooling of Russian-Belarusian relations under Putin, consolidation of the military integration process continued, although it was not entirely free from disruption (in particular, in the case of the creation of a unified air defense system, which failed to develop for several years).[100] In October 2003, the Belarusian parliament ratified an agreement on joint logistical support for the Russian-Belarusian regional group of forces, which included provisions allowing the Russian use of Belarusian logistical support facilities and the creation of joint medical support.[101] October 2003 also saw a joint exercise, Clear Sky 2003, and an agreement on the leasing of Russian S-300 air defense missile systems to Belarus.[102] The institutionalization of military integration developed in this period, with regular meetings of the joint collegium of Belarusian and Russian ministries of defense. After many delays, the unified air defense system also began to develop, with Union Shield 2006 air defense exercises taking place in June 2006.

Thus, by the early twenty-first century, the issues of sovereignty and independence raised by the Russian use of Belarusian military facilities had been displaced by the more fundamental challenge posed by the union framework to the existence of Belarus as a sovereign state and to its possibilities for autonomous action in the security sphere, given the steps taken to unify military doctrines and formations.

Belarusian Attitudes to the Russian Military Presence

The different aspects of the problem of the status and future of the post-Soviet troops and military facilities on Belarusian territory at the point of independence reflect much less anxiety within the structures of Belarusian government about sovereignty and security threats from Russia than the Georgian political elites exhibited on the same issue. These aspects include the way in which the former Soviet military organizational structure—the Belarusian Military District—was absorbed into post-Soviet security structures; the way in which the issue of military facilities was addressed; the view, arising after the resolution of the issue of the Belarusian Military District, of the other troops on Belarusian territory; and finally, the way in which all these issues were addressed within a wider framework of military relations between Russia and Belarus.

One of the most striking differences between Georgia and Belarus over the issue of former Soviet troops on their territories was the way in which these troops were perceived and redefined in the period immediately following the dissolution of the USSR. As noted earlier, the Gamsakhurdia government categorized the troops of the Transcaucasus Military District (later, the RGFT) as an occupying force that had to be removed from the territory of Georgia at the earliest opportunity. Although this was not a perspective shared by either the Russian government or the military structures of the CIS, it was clear that all three organizations viewed the forces in question as non-Georgian and that, as a consequence, even if they were to remain on the territory of Georgia they would not form part of a Georgian army (as noted above, however, the Georgian government took the view that the military district's equipment *did* belong to the Georgian state). In contrast, the Belarusian government viewed the Belarusian Military District as the foundation for the development of the Belarusian armed forces; this view was not challenged by Russia or the CIS JAF structure, and the troops and equipment of the military district were incorporated into the Belarusian armed forces in March 1992.

As discussed earlier, the location of Soviet, Russian, and CIS troops on Georgian territory was a highly contentious issue even before the collapse of the USSR. In the case of Belarus, the question of Russian military bases did not emerge as an issue either at the interstate level or within Belarusian domestic politics until comparatively late. From the breakup of the Soviet Union onward, Belarusian politicians appeared less concerned than their Georgian counterparts by the interlinked questions of the creation of a Belarusian armed forces and the stationing of Russian troops. In mid-January 1992, Shushkevich told *Krasnaia Zvezda,*

> We are in no hurry to create our own armed forces. We cannot decide in one month, three months, or maybe even in a year or two the fate of officers who wish to serve in other republics. . . . It is possible that Russia's armed forces will also be in Belarus. . . . Such questions must be resolved on the basis of compensation and also, maybe, the organization of another state's units on our territory. Russia's, for example, if such a treaty is concluded.[103]

Elsewhere, he commented that he did not rule out the idea of some Russian troops remaining on Belarusian territory after the formation of the Belarusian armed forces (formally created on 16 January 1992) and that all such issues "should be settled on the basis of good will."[104]

Nevertheless, some opinion within the governmental structures of Belarus was more clearly focused on the resolution of these two interlinked issues—in August 1992 (shortly after the signing of the Russian-Belarusian military agreements), then–defense minister Kozlovskiy described the development of a Belarusian army and the removal of all Russian troops from Belarus as Belarus's main military-political aim, suggesting that the development of a Belarusian army was to some extent dependent on the removal of the Russian troops.[105] Such a position did not, however, imply opposition to multilateral or bilateral cooperation with Russia; in January 1994, in a speech to the Supreme Soviet asking it to ratify the Collective Security Treaty, Kozlovskiy stated: "Close military cooperation with CIS countries will reduce our losses while reforming our Armed Forces, secure the civilised withdrawal of Russian troops from Belarusian territory, . . . and create favourable internal and external conditions for establishing the state."[106] This linkage of armed forces development to CIS cooperation was reiterated later that year by Supreme Soviet chairman Hryb, when he commented that although the deadline for Russian withdrawal had been agreed, the Belarusian army could not exist without the support of other CIS states (clearly, for Belarus, Russia).[107] In contrast to Kozlovskiy's statements, the implication of this claim was clearly that a continued Russian presence was a trade-off for assistance with armed forces development.

Nevertheless, despite this comparatively permissive attitude toward the Russian military presence, it is important to note that proposals for the large-scale deployment of Russian troops in Belarus were publicly rejected by the Belarusian government on at least two occasions in the 1990s, although the different reasons given reflect the change in this period in Belarusian governmental attitudes to, and dependence on, Russia. When members of the Russian general staff suggested in 1995 that a large Russian-Belarusian force be deployed on the Belarusian-Polish and Belarusian-Lithuanian borders in the event of an eastward expansion of NATO, the Belarusian defense minister rejected the plan, noting the legal problems that would be created by a non-Belarusian troop presence on Belarusian territory.[108] In contrast, in 1999 Lukashenka announced that there was no need for the creation of Russian military bases in Belarus because of Belarus's friendly relations with Russia and because the Belarusian army was prepared to defend Russia if necessary.[109] The shift in argument, from illegality under Belarusian law, to unnecessary duplication of military structures defending Russia, makes clear the move away from independence in relation to Russia that has taken place under Lukashenka.

If the integrationist policies of the Lukashenka administration explain why the Russian use of Belarusian military facilities is not a source of dispute between the two states, as it is between Russia and Georgia, the question of prior perception remains—the question of why the former Soviet troops based on Belarusian territory were not seen from the start as an outside presence, as occupiers, in the way that they were in other states, such as Georgia. The difference in response by both the two governments and the military forces themselves on this issue cannot be explained primarily in terms of the national identity of the military personnel concerned, since in Belarus, as in Georgia, the troops stationed on its territory were neither exclusively members of the republic's titular nationality, nor exclusively Russian. In both cases, forces included Russians, titular nationals, and personnel from other areas of the former Soviet Union—for example, the Soviet forces stationed in Georgia included Georgian officers, some of whom (including Vardiko Nadibaidze, the Georgian defense minister from 1994 to 1998) moved directly from Russian military to Georgian defense structures. In the case of Belarus, official attitudes toward the post-Soviet forces in Belarus were clearly not driven by considerations of nationality—indeed, an absence of exclusivity regarding the nationality of military personnel extended to appointments within Belarusian defense structures. Following the transfer of Belarusian Military District units to the Belarusian Ministry of Defense, eight of Defense Minister Kozlovskiy's nine deputies were ethnic Russians and only one—previous acting defense minister Chaus—was ethnically Belarusian; all had previously served in command and staff posts of the Belarusian Military District.[110]

The difference in attitudes toward the post-Soviet forces and broader security relations with Russia cannot satisfactorily be explained, either, as a result of the relative Russian security interests in the two states, and thus as a response to differing levels of Russian engagement and assertiveness. Both the Georgian border with Turkey and its Black Sea coastline and the western border of the former Soviet Union were regarded as strategically sensitive by the Russian military from the early 1990s. Concerns about the development of other Eastern European political, economic, and security groupings that had the potential to counteract Russian interests, such as the Baltic–Black Sea confederation, increased the geopolitical importance of Belarus to Russia in this period.[111] Once the EU and NATO had expanded to include three states on Belarus's western and northern borders (including two former Soviet republics bordering Belarus), and as the prospects for closer integration of Ukraine to Western security structures appeared to increase following the election of Yushchenko in Ukraine, the strategic importance of Belarus increased still further.[112] As one analyst has observed, Belarus is Russia's "cordon sanitaire, a nuclear-free zone and a zone that counters NATO enlargement, or a zone of expanded external pressure and influence . . . Belarus serves as Russia's natural shield."[113]

If Georgia and Belarus's difference in approach to the inheritance of Soviet forces on their territory cannot be explained as a consequence of differences in either the national composition of the forces or Russian security pressures, the explanation must lie elsewhere. The radical difference in attitudes and approach needs, then, to be considered not as a consequence of external pressures but of domestic understandings—of different policies formed by divergent perceptions of Russia, which were, in turn, informed by different views of the constitutive basis of national identity and the nature of state sovereignty. First, the incorporation of the Belarusian Military District, and thus most of the Soviet troops stationed on Belarusian territory, into the Belarusian armed forces ensured that the problem of the presence of large numbers of foreign troops never existed. Since the Belarusian government did not identify most of the troops on its territory as "foreign," there was no problem of a large foreign military presence, as there was in Georgia, where former Soviet forces were seen as foreign and thus as occupiers. The fact that those troops not incorporated into the Belarusian armed forces were members of the strategic rocket forces, stationed on Belarusian territory for a short, treaty-limited period of time, removed another potential source of concern. Thus, the issues of both the open-ended nature of the Russian stay in Georgia and the legal status of their stationing, were resolved almost from the outset in the case of Belarus, undercutting the possibility of the Russian military presence establishing itself as a significant problem in the Russia-Belarus security relationship. The issue of the Russian use of the two stations at Baranovichi and Vileika did not emerge until the mid-1990s, by which time the Belarusian government's view of Belarusian sovereignty in relation to Russia had begun to move away from the moderately independent line of the first two years of independence and toward ideas of reintegration.

This in turn indicates one of the other reasons why the response to Russian military facilities in Belarus was so different from that in Georgia during the first few years of the 1990s—the fact that the Belarusian political elite (with the obvious exception of the BPF) adopted a far less nationalistic position in relation to Russia than their Georgian counterparts, reflecting the widely noted absence of radical nationalism and the positive attitudes toward Russia evident in large sections of the Belarusian population.[114] The radical nationalist politics, founded in conceptions of ethnicity, which dominated Georgia's early postindependence politics was absent from Belarusian decisionmaking structures in the same, critical period. While this was clearly not the case for all members of the Belarusian political elite—since nationalist politicians clearly did regard close cooperation with Russia as a threat to sovereignty—it certainly characterized governmental security relations between the two states in the 1990s and the early twenty-first century.

Indeed, rather than perceive the presence of the Russian armed forces as a threat to Belarusian state sovereignty, senior political and military figures, particularly after the election of Lukashenka, expressed the view that Russian troops provided protection against the threat posed by NATO expansion.[115]

As security integration with Russia has strengthened and relations with Western states has deteriorated, this perspective has become formalized and institutionalized. Although not identified explicitly, NATO is clearly the subject of the Belarusian Military Doctrine's statement that the "expansion of military blocs and alliances to the detriment of the military security of the Republic of Belarus" is one of the main external threats to military security, and that the creation of offensive military potential is leading to "a violation of the balance of power."[116] Belarus thus "gives priority to the formation of a single defense space with the Russian Federation, promotes the development of joint military structure, and takes other measures for the maintenance of the defensive capability of the union state"[117] as one of the primary mechanisms for ensuring Belarusian military security because, as is claimed somewhat optimistically in the doctrine, this framework permits "the maintenance of military parity and geostrategic stability in the region."[118]

The difference in Belarus and Georgia's responses to the Russian presence and to Russian security interests in them needs, then, to be understood as a product of the differing character of broader bilateral relations between Russia and Georgia, and Russia and Belarus, and of the related difference in relations with states outside the post-Soviet space, particularly the EU and NATO states. This difference in relations reflected and affected the twin problems of sovereignty and nationalism in Belarus and Georgia. From independence onward, military relations between Russia and Georgia have been characterized by hostility, suspicion, and elements of coercion on the part of Russia. Russian troops have been viewed as an occupying force; as a threat to the sovereignty of Georgia; as active, if covert, participants in the conflict in Abkhazia; and as a potential contributing factor to centrifugal movements elsewhere within Georgia's borders. In contrast, relations between Russia and Belarus were never hostile, even in the period before the election of Lukashenka, and, critically, there was no sense that Belarus was seeking to establish a security policy that ran counter to Russian security interests. The twin pillars of Belarusian security policy in the early postindependence period were neutrality and nonnuclear status, neither of which presented a threat to Russian interests in the way that, for example, Georgian statements about future NATO membership were perceived to do. When the commitment to neutrality was abandoned, it was abandoned in favor of close military cooperation, and then union, with Russia. As one analyst has noted, "since becoming independent, neither Russia nor Belarus has ever seriously questioned the need for close economic, military and political integration."[119]

Indeed, the extent to which Russia and Belarus have ever had clearly differentiated defense establishments is questionable. The creation of the post-Soviet Belarusian armed forces is both symptomatic of this and a determining factor in this regard. One of the central reasons for the development of the military aspects of the union (arguably a key permissive cause) has been the orientation of the Belarusian defense establishment, which is in turn largely a product of its origins (and, latterly, of Lukashenka's appointments). In contrast to a number of other post-Soviet states, which created new defense structures after independence, the Belarusian armed forces were created on the basis of the previous Soviet military structure in the republic. Whereas other states (the Baltic states, Georgia, and Ukraine, for example) viewed the former Soviet military structures on their territory as alien and potentially or actually hostile, Belarus accepted them as the basis of its armed forces. In terms of institutional origins, then, the personnel and structures of the Belarusian defense establishment were never distinct from either the Soviet-era Belarusian Military District or the Russian defense establishment (itself largely created on the basis of residual Soviet structures) in the way that, for example, the Ukrainian defense establishment was. This has arguably been a factor influencing the approach of the Belarusian Ministry of Defense toward military relations with Russia. To some extent, then, it is perhaps more useful to view the increasingly well-defined Russia-Belarus military union not as the creation of a new supranational structure but as the reinstatement of a structure temporarily suspended by the collapse of the USSR.

Military Cooperation: A Return to Soviet Sovereignty?

The relatively benign approach to Russia exhibited by Belarus reduced the need to assert a military presence on Belarusian territory, contrasting with the way that the Russian defense structures had obviously considered necessary in the case of the much more hostile Georgia. Most important, the closely related questions of the presence of ex-Soviet/Russian troops in Belarus and the leasing of military facilities need to be understood as part of the broader movement toward more general military cooperation. As noted earlier, the agreement on the twenty-five-year leases for Baranovichi and Vileika were part of wider-ranging military agreements, which were themselves part of the complex network of agreements linking Belarusian and Russian policy in a wide range of areas, and ultimately in the union. Given the willingness of the Belarusian government to cooperate ever more closely with Russia on defense issues, it is hardly surprising that the government was not concerned about the implications for sovereignty raised by the leasing of Baranovichi and Vileika.

One of the striking aspects of the way in which the development of Russian-Belarusian integration—primarily, in the 1990s, an integration of military policy—was described by those involved in the process was the way in which it was repeatedly asserted by both Russian and Belarusian officials that such a process posed no threat to Belarusian sovereignty. One early manifestation of this approach was an article written by a Belarusian defense official, who commented that:

> I am surprised when some politicians criticise the [July 1992] Belarusian-Russian treaty on coordination of their military activities, and a number of agreements in the sphere of military and technical cooperation. . . . From the political point of view, the documents that were signed with our neighbour . . . confirm our republic's independent course. . . . This military policy does not threaten our independence and neutrality. Any sovereign state pursues such a policy.[120]

In 1994, Kozyrev commented that the election of President Lukashenka signaled a new approach to Russia in Belarus, which was now beginning "to understand the objective necessity of cooperation with Moscow" but that this was not indicative of a renunciation of sovereignty on their part: "It is rather a stage of better understanding the realities of independence and how to implement one's sovereignty by strengthening integrational links, including links with Russia."[121] On a visit to Minsk to discuss aspects of proposed integration between the two states, then–Russian foreign minister Primakov commented that "Russian-Belarusian integration will in no way undermine the sovereignty of Belarus," despite the fact that, as reported by Russian radio, he also believed that "the Russian and Belarusian nations were linked by their common history and common destiny and that their ties must develop very intensively."[122] Shortly before this visit, the leader of the Belarusian Supreme Soviet bloc "Belarus" stated that the bloc was committed to integration with Russia proceeding from the basis of Belarusian state sovereignty.[123] In May 1996, the Belarusian foreign policy concept identified the main policy priorities as the strengthening of Belarusian sovereignty, independence, and territorial integrity and also highlighted the need to deepen the regional integration process, without explaining how this apparent contradiction was to be resolved.[124]

Such statements of a dual commitment to Belarusian state sovereignty and to integration with Russia (which are also assertions of the compatibility of these two aims) appear profoundly contradictory if viewed through the Western set of understandings about sovereignty. They are, however, entirely consistent with the Soviet model of sovereignty. The language and actions of the Russian and Belarusian governments and military elites suggest that as in the Soviet era, the sovereignty of the states on the territory of the former USSR was not understood as necessarily implying de facto independence or legal-political demarcation from other post-Soviet states, and in particular, that it did not imply sovereignty in relation to the successor state of the former Soviet center, Russia, on critical matters of security and other key policy areas. This was confirmed by the statement of a member of the Belarusian delegation to the January 1996 CIS summit that "the

Belarusian delegation will champion the distinction between the internal and external borders of states within the Commonwealth"—in other words, that it would seek formal recognition of a difference in kind between CIS state/non–CIS state borders (so-called external borders) and borders between states of the CIS.[125] Perhaps inevitably, this reflection of the Soviet model of sovereignty found its most prominent expression in the statements made about the Russia-Belarus Union, which Lukashenka described as compatible with Belarusian state sovereignty.[126] The Union Treaty signed in December 1999 outlined coordinated military and foreign policies and the partial transfer of sovereignty to the suprastate institutions created as part of the union and also declared that Russia and Belarus would both retain "sovereignty, independence, territorial integrity, political systems, constitutions, state symbols and other statehood attributes."[127]

Thus, by the end of the 1990s, the policies and rhetoric around Belarusian security and sovereignty questions had come full circle to reproduce, in key respects, those of the Soviet era. In 1993, Shushkevich commented that "without national concepts there can be no statehood"; by the time of the signing of the Russia-Belarus Union Treaty, it was clear that neither a sense of national identity nor the maintenance of independent statehood were regarded as necessary or desirable by the Lukashenka administration.[128] The issues of the presence of Russian troops and the Russian use of military facilities, never regarded as a fundamental security problem or as a challenge to emergent sovereign statehood by the Belarusian government, had become, by the end of this period, just one detail in the much wider process of military reintegration with Russia. This reintegration was, in turn, envisaged as a single aspect of a wider union between the two states, which signified a return to Soviet models in its proposed structures and conception of sovereignty.

Conclusion

Until December 1991, the USSR had troops stationed in bases across its territory, in all of the constituent republics. With the disintegration of the Soviet Union came the closely linked questions of to which state these troops now belong and what would happen to them. The desire on the part of Russia, particularly evident from the mid-1990s onward, to retain the use of bases and other military facilities outside its own borders, gave greater urgency to the issue of the future of the former Soviet troops. For Russia, both Belarus and Georgia represented (for different reasons) areas of geostrategic interest; its engagement with them on the issue of the use of military facilities on their territory and their approaches to this issue were, however, radically different. The absorption of the Belarusian Military District into the Belarusian armed forces immediately eliminated part of the question about the future of the former Soviet troops in Belarus; agreements with Russia on the withdrawal of strategic and nonstrategic forces and on the use of military facilities on Belarusian territory proved to be unclear at points but essentially unproblematic. The issue of the future of Russian use of Belarusian military facilities became subsumed, from the mid-1990s, into the wider issue of the proposed Russia-Belarus Union, and the numerous agreements on military integration related to it. In this sense, the question of the military facilities needs to be understood simply as a single facet of a far broader process.

Although the Georgian government under Shevardnadze adopted a much less antagonistic attitude toward the presence of former Soviet forces on its territory than that of the previous administration, there seems to have been no doubt on the part of either Russia or Georgia that the troops of the Transcaucasus Military District were to be incorporated into the Russian armed forces. As a result, and unlike Belarus, Georgia was faced with the question of what to do about the roughly 20,000 troops stationed on its territory. During the 1990s as a whole, there was a clear consensus among the members of the Georgian political elite that these troops should be withdrawn from Georgian territory. Despite this consensus, however, by the end of the 1990s, the Georgian government had not succeeded in effecting the withdrawal of Russian troops from all the bases they had occupied on Georgian territory. Agreement on the closure of two of the bases had only been achieved at the cost of a transfer of part of its CFE Treaty quotas to Russia; a transfer that Georgia had previously resisted. Definitive movement on the issue of bases only came with the reorientation of Georgia's security policy following the "Rose Revolution" and with the related increase in security engagement by the United States.

Despite the dramatic differences in the character of Russian negotiations with Georgia and Belarus, in both cases the position of all parties involved, and the resolution of the issue, reflected a failure of the Western model of state sovereignty in relation to Russia. In the case of Belarus, the moves toward military integration and ultimately union with Russia can be seen as a renunciation of sovereignty over military and other issues; this rejection was accompanied by a reversion to Soviet-era understandings of the idea of sovereignty, evident in the comments of key actors in the process and in the formal agreements between the two states. In the case of Georgia, the failure to achieve the withdrawal of troops from all the bases on its territory and the failure to enforce the terms of agreements on leasing facilities (army development assistance, weapons transfer, Russian assistance with the restoration of Georgian territorial integrity) point to a fundamental failure of Georgian sovereignty in relation to Russia over security questions. The closure of the bases and financial and technical assistance with the training and equipment of the Georgian army eventually occurred at the start of the twenty-first century, when assistance from a state more powerful than Russia counteracted Russian resistance on these issues. The exercise of Georgian sovereignty on these security issues was thus still dependent to a significant extent on the political will and capabilites of another state. The issue of bases can thus be seen as one of the clearest indicators of the limits of Georgian internal and external sovereignty.

Notes

1. On the issue of Russia's military bases in the post-Soviet states as an aspect of Russia's broader, "postimperial" security policy, see Pavel K. Baev, *The Russian Army in a Time of Troubles* (London: Sage, 1996), especially chapter 5.

2. Dov Lynch, *Russian Peacekeeping Strategies in the CIS: The Cases of Moldova, Georgia and Tajikistan* (Basingstoke, UK: Macmillan, 2000).

3. For an analysis of this and later versions of the doctrine, see Marcel De Haas, "An Analysis of Soviet, CIS and Russian Military Doctrines 1990–2000," *Journal of Slavic Military Studies* 14, no. 4 (December 2001): 1–34.

4. ITAR-TASS, 18 January 1994, *FBIS-SOV-94-011,* p. 1.

5. Interfax, 6 July 1995, *FBIS-SOV-95-130,* p. 5.

6. *Rossiiskiye vesti,* 7 April 1994, *The Current Digest of the Post-Soviet Press* (CDPSP) 46, no. 14: 1.

7. Baev, *The Russian Army,* p. 109.

8. Hannes Adomeit, "Russian National Security Interests," in Roy Allison and Christopher Bluth, eds., *Security Dilemmas in Russia and Eurasia* (London: Royal Institute of International Affairs, 1998), p. 39.

9. Ruth Deyermond, "Matrioshka Hegemony? Multi-levelled Hegemonic Competition and Security in Post-Soviet Central Asia," Paper, British International Studies Association Conference, 19–21 December 2005. Possible factors contributing to the decline in the United States' political and security relationship with the states of Central Asia include concerns on the part of authoritarian leaderships in the wake of US support (or active promotion) of the "Color Revolutions" and the—coincident—condemnation by the United States of the events in Andijan in May 2005.

10. Mayak Radio Network, 29 May 1992, in *FBIS-SOV-92-105,* p. 36.

11. Quoted in Duygu Buzoglu Sezer, "Balance of Power in the Black Sea in the Post–Cold War Era: Russia, Turkey and Ukraine," in Maria Drohobycky, ed., *Crimea: Dynamics, Challenges and Prospects* (Lanham, MD: Rowman and Littlefield; Washington, DC: American Association for the Advancement of Science, 1995), p. 177.

12. Baev notes that Russian concerns about Turkey as a growing regional power in the South Caucasus region have decreased since their peak in the mid-1990s and that Turkey is now "normally portrayed as [a] weakening competitor, preoccupied by internal political instability and economic troubles" (Pavel K. Baev, "Russia's Policies in the Southern Caucasus and the Caspian Area," *European Security* 10, no. 2 (Summer 2001): 102).

13. "Moscow Mulling 'Greater Caucasus' Strategy," *RFE/RL Security Watch* 2, no. 2 (15 January 2001), available from www.rferl.org/securitywatch/.

14. *FBIS-SOV-95-194,* pp. 73–74.

15. "Sovmestnoe Zayavlenie Ministerov Inostrannykh Del Rossiiskoi Federatsii i Gruzii," 30 May 2005.

16. For details see the Georgian Ministry of Defense news releases in September 2005 and from 15 May 2006 onward, available from www.mod.gov.ge/?l=E&m=13&sm=0&st=115&id=168.

17. The reference in the May 2005 agreement to the development of an antiterrorism center was seen by some Georgian politicians and commentators as a loophole to allow a continued Russian military presence in Georgia after the closure of the bases (Molly Corso, "Some in Georgia Worry That the Russian Base Withdrawal Deal Comes with a Catch," *Eurasia Insight,* 1 June 2005).

18. Available from www.mod.gov.ge/pages/m15_3_1.pdf.

19. Jonathan Aves notes that "the Georgian parliament had declared Georgia an 'occupied country' as early as February 1990" ("The Caucasus States: The Regional Security Complex," in Allison and Bluth, eds., *Security Dilemmas in Russia and Eurasia,* p. 176).

20. Ibid.

21. Interfax, 26 October 1992, *FBIS-SOV-92-207,* p. 79.

22. Interfax, 21 March 1992, *FBIS-SOV-92-057,* p. 78.

23. ITAR-TASS, 2 April 1992, *FBIS-SOV-92-066,* p. 80.

24. 24 November 1992, *FBIS-SOV-92-228,* p. 68.

25. See, for example, the report in *The Georgian Chronicle,* January–February 1993.

26. Interfax, 5 February 1993, *FBIS-SOV-93-024,* p. 53.

27. *Novaia Yezhednevnaia Gazeta,* no. 11, 18–25 June 1993, *FBIS-SOV-93-119,* p. 8.

28. "Foreign Relations," *The Georgian Chronicle,* March 1993.

29. Contact Information Agency, 29 June 1993, *FBIS-SOV-93-124,* p. 71.

30. *FBIS-SOV-93-197,* p. 94.

31. *Svobodnaia Gruziia,* 4 February 1994, pp. 1, 2.

32. Ibid.

33. Ibid.

34. Emil Danielyan, "Georgia: Participation in CIS Defense Pact Less Certain," *RFE/RL,* 22 March 1999.

35. "Miscellany," *The Army and Society in Georgia,* May 1998 and June 1998.

36. For the text of the agreement, see "Joint Statement of the Russian Federation and Georgia," *The Army and Society in Georgia,* November 1999.

37. The CFE Treaty, signed in November 1990, set quotas for different categories of conventional weapons in Europe, based on the NATO and Warsaw Pact blocs. With the collapse of the USSR, its CFE Treaty quotas had to be renegotiated by the successor states. At the CIS Tashkent summit in May 1992, eight of the successor states (Armenia, Azerbaijan, Belarus, Georgia, Kazakhstan, Moldova, Russia, and Ukraine) signed an agreement on the division of the USSR's treaty-limited equipment quotas. For a discussion of the CFE Treaty negotiations between the Soviet successor states, and Russian military dissatisfaction with quota allocations, see Baev, *The Russian Army,* pp. 80–90, and Christopher Bluth, "Arms Control and Proliferation," in Allison and Bluth, eds., *Security Dilemmas in Russia and Eurasia,* pp. 308–311. Despite the signing of the bases agreement, however, there were reports in 2000 that Russia was attempting to keep the Gudauta base open as a CIS peacekeepers' recreation center.

38. See, for example, *RFE/RL Newsline,* 9 September 1999.

39. Baev, *The Russian Army,* p. 120.

40. Contact Information Agency, 29 June 1993, *FBIS-SOV-93-124,* p. 71.

41. Interfax, 20 March 1995, *FBIS-SOV-95-054,* p. 82.

42. Radio Tbilisi, 23 March 1995, *FBIS-SOV-95-057,* p. 65.

43. Radio Tbilisi, 27 March 1995, *FBIS-SOV-95-059,* pp. 39–41.

44. For example, the linkage of this question was acknowledged at the time of the third round of negotiations over the legal status of Russian troops in Georgia, in February 1993. See *Krasnaia Zvezda,* 6 February 1993, p. 2.

45. *RFE/RL Newsline,* 30 May 1997 and 28 December 1998.

46. *Die Tagezeitung,* 3 November 1995, *FBIS-SOV-95-215,* p. 57.

47. Revaz Gachechiladze "The Making of the New Georgia: Development Factors—Pluses and Minuses," *Caucasian Regional Studies* 3, no. 1 (1998), available from http://poli.vub.ac.be/publi/ crs/eng/0301-03.htm.

48. Interfax, 19 May 1996, *FBIS-SOV-96-098,* pp. 74–75. The linkage is discussed in more general terms in *Kommersant,* 21 April 2000, p. 11.

49. *Kommersant,* 31 August 1999, p. 4.

50. *Kommersant,* 26 April 2000, p. 11.

51. "Georgia, Azerbaijan Propose Strategic Quid Pro Quo," *RFE/RL Caucasus Report* 3, no. 50 (29 December 2000).

52. Emil Danielyan, "Georgia's Armenian-Populated Region in Limbo," *RFE/RL Newsline,* 20 September 1999.

53. Liz Fuller, "Mission Impossible?" *RFE/RL Newsline,* 10 September 1999.

54. See, for example, Anatol Lieven, "Imperial Outpost and Social Provider: The Russians and Akhalkalaki," *Eurasia Insight,* 20 February 2001.

55. "Visits, Negotiations, Co-operation," *The Army and Society in Georgia,* March 1999.

56. Troops were paid $100 per month according to David Darchiashvili, "The Army and Society in Djavakheti," *The Army and Society in Georgia,* May 1998.

57. See Danielyan, "Georgia's Armenian-Populated Region," and Emil Danielyan, "Fate of Russia's Akhalkalaki Base Still Unclear," *RFE/RL Caucasus Report* 3, no. 45 (16 November 2000), available from www.rferl.org/caucasus-report.

58. Darchiashvili, "The Army and Society in Djavakheti."

59. Vladimir Socor, "Risks in Georgia's Javakheti Province Can Be Defused," *Eurasia Daily,* 4 April 2005.

60. "Georgian Ministry Comments on Akhalkalaki Base," *UNOMIG Latest Headlines,* 28 April 2006, available from www.unomig.org/media/headlines/?id= 5860&y=2006&m=4&d=28.

61. See, for example, "Army Building," *The Army and Society in Georgia,* March 1999.

62. *RFE/RL Newsline,* 23 December 1997.

63. *Nezavisimaia Gazeta,* 13 January 1998, p. 5.

64. *RFE/RL Newsline,* 8 and 13 January 1998.

65. *RFE/RL Newsline,* 8 and 9 April 1998.

66. *RFE/RL Newsline,* 31 August 1998.

67. *Nezavisimaia Gazeta,* 13 January 1998, p. 5.

68. Interview with *Gazeta Wyborcza,* 19 October 1995, p. 11, *FBIS-SOV-95-207,* pp. 72–73.

69. See, for example, comments in early 1994 by the chief negotiator of the Russian delegation (Interfax, 4 February 1994, *FBIS-SOV-94-025,* p. 17) and a Georgian government official in *Svobodnaia Gruzia,* 13 January 1994, p. 1.

70. Radio Tbilisi, 7 February 1994, *FBIS-SOV-94-025,* p. 65.

71. ITAR-TASS World Service, 29 September 1995, *FBIS-SOV-95-190,* p. 69.

72. Available from www.state.gov/p/eur/rls/fs/66198.htm.

73. *RFE/RL Newsline,* 20 September 1999. Russia's issuing of citizenship and its favorable visa policy toward the populations of Abkhazia and South Ossetia continued to provoke Georgia. See, for example, "The Resolution of the Parliament of

Georgia Regarding the Current Situation in the Conflict Regions on the Territory of Georgia and Ongoing Peace Operations," 11 November 2005.

74. "Russia Partially Lifts Visa Ban on Georgians," *RFE/RL Newsline,* 10 March 2006.

75. On the military aspects of the Russia-Belarus Union project see Ruth Deyermond, "The State of the Union: Military Success, Economic and Political Failure in the Russia-Belarus Union," *Europe-Asia Studies* 56, no. 8 (December 2004): 1191–1205.

76. In contrast, single currency plans, which also predate the union agreements, were advanced much more sporadically. Agreement on monetary union was signed in 1993; by the following year, however, the plans had been abandoned.

77. Interfax, *FBIS-SOV-92-137,* p. 63. This timescale was repeated by Shushkevich the following month.

78. See, for example, Minister of Defense Pavel Kozlovskiy, in *Izvestiia,* 17 September 1992, *FBIS-SOV-92-183,* p. 47.

79. This confusion appears to have been, in part, the result of the distinction made between Russian strategic forces, which were required to withdraw from Belarus by 1997 under the 1992 agreements, and other Russian troops stationed in Belarus.

80. Radio Rossii, 12 July 1993, *FBIS-SOV-93-132,* p. 64. Kozlovskiy noted that a more definite date would be fixed after the signing of a proposed bilateral Russian-Belarusian agreement.

81. Interfax, 7 April 1994, *FBIS-SOV-94-068,* p. 48, also reported by Interfax on 10 April, *FBIS-SOV-94-069,* p. 45.

82. Radio Minsk, 8 April 1994, *FBIS-SOV-94-069,* p. 45.

83. Radio Minsk, 25 May 1994, *FBIS-SOV-94-102,* p. 30.

84. Belarusian Defense Ministry spokesman cited by Interfax, 28 July 1994, *FBIS-SOV-94-146,* p. 30.

85. Ibid.

86. *Krasnaia Zvezda,* 29 July 1994.

87. Interfax, 5 August 1994, *FBIS-SOV-94-152,* pp. 45–46.

88. Summit Communique, *Sovetskaia Belorussiia,* 5 August 1994, p. 1.

89. Interfax, 5 August 1994, *FBIS-SOV-94-152,* p. 46.

90. Interfax, *FBIS-SOV-94-176,* p. 60. The replacement of virtually all the Belarusian deputy defense ministers took place immediately after the first Yeltsin-Lukashenka summit; it is unclear whether these two events were connected, but the timing of the sackings is at least suggestive of a link.

91. Interfax, *FBIS-SOV-95-037,* p. 52.

92. Interview on Radio Minsk, 3 April 1996, *FBIS-SOV-96-066,* pp. 42–43.

93. Belaplan, 11 April 1996, *FBIS-SOV-96-071,* p. 46.

94. *RFE/RL Newsline,* 19 December 1997.

95. *RFE/RL Newsline,* 10 April 1998.

96. *RFE/RL Newsline,* 16 October 1998.

97. *RFE/RL Newsline,* 8 January 1998.

98. *RFE/RL Newsline,* 5 November 1998.

99. *RFE/RL Newsline,* 8 and 9 December 1999.

100. Deyermond, "The State of the Union."

101. Belapan, 17 October 2003, *FBIS-SOV-2003-1017.*

102. ITAR-TASS, 31 October 2003, *FBIS-SOV-2003-1031.*

103. *Krasnaia Zvezda,* 17 January 1992, *FBIS-SOV-92-014,* p. 78.

104. Postfactum, 17 January 1992, *FBIS-SOV-92-013,* p. 82.

105. Interfax, 20 August 1992, *FBIS-SOV-92-163,* p. 60.

106. *Vo Slavu Rodiny,* 21 January 1994, *FBIS-SOV-94-016,* p. 53.

107. *Narodnaia Gazeta,* 6 May 1994, *FBIS-SOV-94-090,* p. 22.

108. Cited in Vyachaslau Paznyak, "Belarus: In Search of a Security Identity," in Allison and Bluth, eds., *Security Dilemmas in Russia and Eurasia,* p. 166.

109. *RFE/RL Newsline,* 7 May 1999.

110. *FBIS-SOV-92-091,* p. 52.

111. Nadezhda Pastukhova, "The Union Between Russia and Belarus," *International Affairs* (Moscow) 46, no. 4 (April 2000): 131.

112. Andrei Sannikov, "Russia's Varied Roles in Belarus," in Margarita M. Balmaceda, James I. Clem, and Lisbeth Tarlow, eds., *Independent Belarus: Domestic Determinants, Regional Dynamics, and Implications for the West* (Cambridge, MA: Ukrainian Research Institute and David Centre for Russian Studies, 2002), pp. 197–231; Deyermond, "The State of the Union."

113. Hrihory Perepelitsa, "Belarusian-Russian Integration and Its Impact on the Security of Ukraine," in Sherman W. Garnett and Robert Legvold, eds., *Belarus at the Crossroads* (Washington, DC: Carnegie Endowment for International Peace, 1999), pp. 82–83.

114. Steven M. Eke and Taras Kuzio, "Sultanism in Eastern Europe: The Socio-Political Roots of Authoritarian Populism in Belarus," *Europe-Asia Studies* 52, no. 3 (May 2000): 523–547; David Marples, *Belarus: From Soviet Rule to Nuclear Catastrophe* (Basingstoke, UK: Macmillan, 1996); Timothy J. Colton, "Belarusian Popular Opinion and the Union with Russia," in Balmaceda, Clem, and Tarlow, *Independent Belarus,* pp. 21–54.; Marek J. Karp, "Escape from Freedom," *The Journal of Slavic Military Studies* 11, no. 4 (December 1998): 146–163.

115. For discussions of the Belarusian governmental perceptions of a NATO threat see, for example, John Löwenhardt, Ronald J. Hill, and Margot Light, "A Wider Europe: The View from Minsk and Chisinau," *International Affairs* 77, no. 3 (July 2001): 609–611; and chapters by Rainer Lindner, John C. Reppert, and Andrei Sannikov in Balmaceda, Clem, and Tarlow, *Independent Belarus.*

116. *Voennaia doktrina Respubliki Belarus,* chapter 1, clause 7, available from www.mod.mil.by/doktrina.html.

117. *Voennaia doktrina,* chapter 1, clause 10.

118. *Voennaia doktrina,* chapter 2, clause 3.

119. Vyacheslav Nikonov, "The Place of Belarus on Russia's Foreign Policy Agenda," in Garnett and Robert, *Belarus at the Crossroads,* p. 119.

120. Gennadiy Danilov, Chief of the Security and Defense Department at the Administration Office of the Belarusian Council of Ministers, *Vo Slavu Rodiny,* 1 October 1992, *FBIS-SOV-92-213,* pp. 59–60.

121. Russian television interview, 20 July 1994, *FBIS-SOV-94-140,* p. 8.

122. Interfax, 31 January 1996, *FBIS-SOV-96-021,* p. 58; Radio Rossii Network, 30 January 1996, *FBIS-SOV-96-021,* p. 58.

123. Radio Minsk, 7 January 1994, *FBIS-SOV-94-005,* p. 48.

124. *Belorusskaia Delovaia Gazeta,* 20 May 1995, p. 5, *FBIS-SOV-96-102,* pp. 46–48.

125. *Pravda,* 18 January 1996, *FBIS-SOV-96-013,* p. 60.

126. Jan Maksymiuk, "Gambling with Belarus's Sovereignty," *RFE/RL Newsline,* 30 December 1998.

127. Jan Maksymiuk, "An Epoch Making Treaty for Half a Year?" *RFE/RL Newsline,* 21 December 1999.

128. Interview in *Sovetskaia Belorussiia,* 9 September 1993, p. 2.

6

Sovereignty and Security in the Twenty-First Century

In the period following the collapse of the USSR, the Soviet successor states were confronted with a number of urgent and apparently intractable problems arising out of their shared inheritance. One, which was a subject of particular concern both to the states involved and to the wider international community, was the question of the future of the former Soviet armed forces. Perhaps inevitably, the primary focus of international attention was on the fate of the former Soviet nuclear arsenal; for the former Soviet states themselves, other issues including the division of military assets (such as the Black Sea Fleet) and the transformation of a Soviet military presence to a Russian—and hence for the non-Russian states, foreign—presence on their territory, were equally pressing. By the end of the 1990s, the three disputes that form the subject of this book appeared to have been resolved. The mechanisms by which this was achieved and the result in each case revealed fundamental differences in both the attitudes toward statehood and toward one another, and in the capabilities of the states concerned.

In the dispute over nuclear weapons and the Black Sea Fleet, Ukraine asserted a commitment both to the idea of an independent security policy and, through it, to a wider idea of state sovereignty consistent with the Western model. Its repeated assertions of claims to own and control the nuclear weapons on its territory were a clear indication of this, as was its claim to ownership of some (occasionally all) of the Black Sea Fleet. In both cases, although the Ukrainian government did not achieve all its stated objectives (over control of nuclear weapons on Ukrainian territory, for example), it was successful in its attempt to achieve formal recognition of Ukrainian claims in these areas and hence recognition, to some degree, of Ukrainian independence on issues of foreign and security policy.

This recognition of claims to assets and claims to sovereignty depended not only on the willingness of Ukraine to assert them, but also, of course, on

185

its ability to do so and thus on its political and other capabilities in relation to Russia. Ukraine's position as the largest of the successor states after Russia; its location on the Black Sea and in the west of the former Soviet Union, and thus within Europe; and its relative internal stability (compared with states such as Georgia, Azerbaijan, and Moldova, which faced armed challenges to their territorial integrity) placed it in a stronger initial position in its relations with Russia than was the case for smaller, weaker states. At least three additional factors also helped to strengthen Ukraine's bargaining position over the Soviet military inheritance. The first of these was the fact that the success of the CIS project was regarded by many of those involved, in particular Russian political and military elites, as dependent on the membership of Ukraine. To this extent, and given the relative material capabilities of Ukraine, the Russian government was limited in its ability to coerce Ukraine, had it wished to do so. The second factor was the presence of nuclear weapons on Ukrainian territory at the point of independence. The interest in Ukraine on the part of NATO states, and above all of the United States (by this point the world's only remaining superpower) was understood by all actors to have been greatly increased by the fact that Ukraine had inherited a nuclear arsenal. This US and Western European interest in Ukraine in turn greatly strengthened its negotiating position in relation to Russia on the issue of nuclear weapons. The third factor that strengthened the Ukrainian position was Ukraine's ability and willingness to instrumentalize precisely those assets under dispute. The use of nuclear weapons to focus international attention and obtain financial assistance; the linkage of nuclear weapons to the Black Sea Fleet in negotiations; and the willingness to trade part of the fleet for debt write-off all contributed to the comparatively successful resolution of these disputes for Ukraine. Despite the many weaknesses of the Ukrainian state in the 1990s, and the divisions within its political and military elites about how to resolve these problems, the Ukrainian approach, which clearly took the Western conception of sovereignty-as-independence as the constituting principle of relations with Russia, enabled it to utilize its considerable relative material and political capabilities to improve the outcome of these disputes over assets.

Like Ukraine, Georgia attempted to clearly demarcate its sovereignty in relation to Russia. However, the failure of Georgian sovereignty within its borders on almost all the indicators generally understood to constitute sovereignty (most notably territorial control, the monopoly on the legitimate use of force, and the control of state borders) meant that it was unable to successfully pursue its policies in respect to the Black Sea Fleet or the Russian military presence. Georgia was unable to assert any meaningful claim to a share of the Black Sea Fleet for three related reasons. First, the issue of the fleet occupied an inevitably low place on the Georgian security agenda during the early and mid-1990s when the Georgian government was engaged in two separatist conflicts and in the attempt to suppress the antigovernment uprising in the west of the country. Second, the location of the fleet's bases in areas effectively outside Georgian state control for some or all of this period meant that it was unable to assert any form of control on the ground; as a result, one base in Abkhazia was nominally ceded to Georgia but has remained inaccessible to the Georgian navy, while the other main base was seriously damaged and looted during fighting. This breakdown of territorial integrity and the consequent inability to exercise any control over the fleet's assets were both the cause and to an extent the result of Georgian weakness in relation to Russia.

A similar set of difficulties accounted for the parallel failure of Georgia to achieve a satisfactory resolution of the question of the Russian use of military facilities during the 1990s. Despite agreement on withdrawal in 1999, Georgia's failure to achieve its goal of the withdrawal of Russian troops from all the bases on its territory for more than fifteen years after independence and the failure of its more immediate goal of enforcing the terms of agreements on leasing facilities (army development assistance, weapons transfer, Russian assistance with the restoration of Georgian territorial integrity) point to a failure of Georgian sovereignty in relation to Russia over security questions, in turn a consequence of the fundamental failure of Georgian internal and external sovereignty.

In contrast to Ukraine and Georgia, which both attempted to establish sovereignty over military and other issues, Belarus, in its bilateral relations with Russia over the issues of nuclear weapons and the Russian use of military facilities, demonstrated a limited interest in establishing its sovereignty, as understood in the Western tradition. In contrast to the Ukrainian approach, the Belarusian government, following the immediate months after independence, appeared entirely willing to renounce all claims to ownership of or control over the nuclear weapons on its territory—indeed, the only notable moment of difference with Russia over the issue occurred when Lukashenka apparently suspended the transfer of missiles to Russia on the grounds that integration of the two states' military policies would make such a transfer unnecessary. This willingness, even eagerness, to renounce an independent military policy during Lukashenka's presidency was still more evident in the Belarusian approach to the question of the Russian use of military facilities, which became subsumed into the wider issue of military integration and ultimately of the Russia-Belarus Union. In his approach to security relations with Russia, and in his contradictory attitude toward the union project more generally, Lukashenka appeared to be proceeding from a set of assumptions about Belarusian sovereignty that owed more to the Soviet than the Western approach.

Sovereignty: Retreat and Resurgence

By the end of the 1990s, all three security problems appeared to have been resolved—the last nuclear weapons left Ukraine and Belarus in 1996; a definitive agreement on the Black Sea Fleet had been signed in 1997; and a deal on the Russian bases in Georgia had finally been worked out in 1999. Midway through the next decade, however, the use of military facilities and the Black Sea Fleet had again become areas of dispute in Russia's relations with Georgia and Ukraine, with the Russian military presence in both states coming under various forms of pressure from new governments apparently keen to assert their independence from Russia on security matters. This marked a dramatic reversal from the situation immediately prior to the change of administrations in Georgia and Ukraine, when both states had been drawn into increasingly close relations with Russia. A key reason for the comparatively benign security environment for Russia in these states at the turn of the century was the domestic and external weakness of their governments; critical, related factors in the shift away from accommodating Russian security interests were the change of governments, and the growing engagement of powerful, extraregional states, undermining Russia's security and political dominance in the former Soviet Union. Paradoxically, then, the revival of attempts by Georgia and Ukraine to assert sovereignty in relation to one state, Russia, was triggered in part by the intervention of another, more powerful state in their domestic politics.

By the late 1990s, Ukraine had been effectively pulled back into Russia's orbit by the linked problems of poor economic performance, political scandal, and the increasing reluctance of the United States and members of the EU to provide any form of political support to the Kuchma administration. In particular, the perception of pervasive corruption at all levels of Ukrainian governmental structures, exemplified by the scandal surrounding Kuchma himself following the murder of journalist Heorhiy Gongadze in 2000, created an increasing unwillingness among the United States and Western European states either to provide financial assistance in the form of multilateral or bilateral loans or to encourage moves toward closer security cooperation within NATO structures. By mid-2001, both NATO and the EU were sending increasingly clear signals that not only had prospects for closer cooperation receded, but that existing relations with Ukraine were threatened by the Kuchma administration's failure to implement democratic and economic reforms, or to solve the Gongadze case.[1] Faced with both increasing domestic discontent and growing disapproval in the West, the Kuchma administration sought to establish a closer relationship with Russia on economic, political, and security matters. Kuchma and Putin met frequently in this period, even conducting a joint review of the Russian and Ukrainian Black Sea Fleets in Sevastopol in 2001—a symbolically significant action given the length and bitterness of the fleet dispute, and one that clearly indicated the extent of the change in the Ukrainian government's position toward Russia on security matters. Agreements on a wide range of issues were signed in 2001 and 2002, including a significant agreement on energy and a defense agreement on joint exercises and arms production.[2]

In the same period, Georgia was also continuing to be confronted with the necessity of accommodating Russian interests. Like Ukraine under Kuchma, Georgia under Shevardnadze appeared to be locked into structures of all-pervasive corruption and crippled by disastrous economic performance. The continued absence of effective control by the central government over much of the country and the unresolved, "frozen" separatist conflicts both contributed to these problems and were exacerbated by them. Both the general weakness of the Georgian state resulting from these problems and the various forms of Russian engagement in them—the Russian peacekeeping presence; the perception of Russian support for Abkhazia resulting from the opening of transport routes between Russia and Abkhazia and the issuing of visas to Abkhaz residents; and the economic, and especially energy, dependence of Georgia on Russia—prevented Georgia from establishing effective sovereignty over territory or policy within its borders, in relation to Russia. The absence of this authority was compounded by the comparatively weak interest shown by the United States, Western Europe, and key international institutions in Georgian security and economic problems during this period. Although security cooperation with the United States, in the form of training and financial assistance, had improved by the late 1990s, it was still limited in the context of overall Georgian security needs, and equally limited relative to the influence Russia was able to assert over Georgian security.[3] Despite statements by Shevardnadze that Georgia aspired to join NATO, the prospects for doing so appeared to be remote and the relationship with NATO proved to be more limited than Shevardnadze apparently wished.[4] Although more substantial than in the early 1990s, financial and other forms of support for the development of effective security structures, or indeed any other aspects of government activity, were modest compared with Georgian needs at the end of the 1990s—in part, a reflection of the concentration of extraregional interest specifically on Georgia as a site of transit for Caspian energy; in part, a reflection of the governance and other problems associated with what was sometimes, if contentiously, referred to as a "failed state." By the start of the twenty-first century, extraregional assistance in key areas such as the economy had declined once more, with international financial institutions expressing serious concerns about corruption and the weakness of economic structures.[5] As in Ukraine, this in turn pushed the Georgian government into closer cooperation with Russia.[6] Thus, by the end of the century, Georgia appeared to be locked into a vicious circle of corruption, economic weakness, the failure of internal authority, dependence on Russia, and limited relations with increasingly wary EU and NATO states. This left it without the political, economic, or military resources to mount any significant challenge to Russian security dominance within its borders.

In the same period, Belarus had moved firmly toward full political, economic, and military union with Russia, while becoming increasingly politically isolated in Europe and in relation to international political structures. Despite the serious problems with the proposed union and the growing implausibility of full economic or political integration between Belarus and Russia—especially after the election of Putin, who was clearly skeptical of the alleged merits of union—Belarusian governmental commitment to the project remained strong.[7] The desire for integration with Russia and the increasingly effective union of Russian and Belarusian defense structures indicated a voluntary dependence on and subordination to Russia on the part of the Belarusian government, which simultaneously maintained a commitment to Belarusian state sovereignty—as noted earlier, an abdication from the Western model of sovereignty, in favor of a return to the Soviet one.

Thus, by the start of the twenty-first century, for reasons of weakness, political preference, or dependence of political elites, and because of the increasing suspicion or continued indifference of Western European and North American states, all three states had been forced toward an increased reliance on Russia and an increased powerlessness in relation to it. Thus, despite the political and economic weakness of Russia itself in the late Yeltsin period, and despite the widely recognized deterioration of the Russian armed forces, each of these three states was radically compromised in its independence in relation to Russia. Whatever the rhetoric of Western-model sovereignty relating to these states, the reality in each case was a forced or a voluntary move away from sovereignty in relation to Russia.

In consequence, although these three states had achieved formally favorable outcomes in the negotiations over the military assets considered in earlier chapters—in the shape of the Trilateral Agreement, the 1997 Black Sea Fleet Agreement, and the 1995 and 1999 agreements on the Georgian bases—in practice, at the start of the twenty-first century, the Russian government had achieved key goals in each case, without significant losses in other areas. Russia had taken possession of most of the Black Sea Fleet; it continued to make use of bases and military facilities in all three states at little or no cost; and it was the sole nuclear successor state to the USSR. Although the other post-Soviet states had asserted their right, in principle, through international agreement, to recognition of independence, territorial integrity, and control over security policy and assets inside their territory, by the late 1990s the reality of relations with Russia for these states was one of dependence, weakness, penetration, and an absence of many of the most fundamental features of Western-model sovereign statehood.

By the middle of the first decade of the twenty-first century, however, the position of Georgia and Ukraine relative to Russia had changed dramatically. Changes of administration in both states, and the related increased US engagement in these states and the post-Soviet region as a whole, led to a shift away from political and security dependence on Russia and toward a more assertive position. In consequence, despite having apparently been formally resolved in the 1990s—with these resolutions consolidated in Russia's favor by the early twenty-first century—the status of the Black Sea Fleet and the Russian use of military facilities reemerged as key areas of tension in the Russia-Georgia and Russia-Ukraine relationships, with both Georgia and Ukraine attempting to force a new settlement of the problems—one more favorable to the consolidation of their state sovereignty.

The Black Sea Fleet

As discussed in Chapter 4, the future of the Russian Black Sea Fleet in Ukraine and the terms on which it continued to use Crimean bases reemerged as an issue immediately after the election of Yushchenko. During 2005, suggestions by Ukrainian politicians concerning revised terms of occupation and increased rent for the fleet's bases were accompanied by a renewal of demands for a complete inventory of the fleet's assets, which Ukraine had sought, but never obtained. The possibility of extending the Russian lease of naval facilities in Ukraine also emerged as an aspect of the revived disagreement, with Ukrainian government officials periodically asserting that no extension would be agreed.

Having deteriorated during 2005, Russian-Ukrainian relations over the fleet worsened in 2006, with two incidents turning a limited disagreement into a wider diplomatic dispute. In January, Ukrainian personnel seized the Yalta lighthouse, a facility that both states claimed had been awarded to them under the 1997 treaty dividing the fleet. This recalled the incident in 1994, at the height of the tensions over the status of the fleet, in which Ukrainian forces seized facilities in Odessa—a worrying development for the long-term survival of the fleet agreement, and a very concrete indication that some of those involved regarded the issue of the fleet as unfinished business. Russian-Ukrainian relations were damaged still more seriously in early June, when preparations for Ukraine's participation in joint military exercises in the Black Sea with NATO states, including the preparatory visit of a US vessel, led to protests in Crimea demanding the abandonment of the exercises and to the Crimean parliament voting to declare Crimea a NATO-free zone.[8] The perception on the part of the Ukrainian government that these protests were encouraged by some Russian politicians and journalists led to a Ukrainian presidential decree expelling non-Ukrainians involved in the protests and banning others, including the prominent Russian nationalist politician Vladimir Zhirinovsky, from entering Ukrainian territory. The Ukrainian governmental view of Russia's position in the dispute and the extent to which it was tied in to wider disagreements over the fleet was set out in a statement made by a Foreign Ministry spokesman at the height of the protests:

> The edifying tone of the commentaries in the context of cooperation of Ukraine with NATO used by the Russian side exceeds the limits of common international communication standards. We would propose the Russian side to focus on resolution of its own urgent issue of democratic reconstruction of the society. Ukraine is a sovereign democratic state and has an inherent right to determine the ways of its own national security independently, including the way of joining any international security structures. . . . It is astonishing that the Ministry of Foreign Affairs of the Russian Federation [claims that] the Russian Federation had not violated the agreements on temporary disposition of the Black Sea Navy of the Russian Federation in the territory of Ukraine. . . . Russia is not entitled to keep the units which were not given to it under the agreements of the Black Sea Navy; however, it continues unlawful and gratuitous use of them. At that, it blockades transparent and fair stock-taking of these units. . . . Finally, one should get used to the fact that international obligations should be fulfilled. This is a foundation of the contemporary system of international relations.[9]

The dispute, clearly the most serious since the signing of the 1997 treaty, was suspended, although not resolved, by the announcement that the exercises were to be postponed pending Ukrainian parliamentary approval for them to proceed. In late 2006 and early 2007, legal attempts to force the Russian fleet to hand over navigation facilities and the continuing debate over the proposed extension of the Russian lease beyond 2017 did nothing to reduce the tension over the current and future presence of the Russian fleet in Ukraine. A decade after the supposedly definitive agreement on the Black Sea Fleet, prospects for a final resolution of the issue appeared remote.

One explanation for the seemingly intractable nature of the disagreement is that the issue of the Black Sea Fleet was complicated by factors in the post–Orange Revolution period that tied it to domestic political divisions, to the wider problem of Russian-Ukrainian relations, and to the deteriorating relations between Russia and the NATO states. First, as noted in Chapter 4, Ukrainian perspectives varied sharply across the political spectrum. Expressions of Yushchenko's apparent wish to see the Russian fleet removed from Ukraine were notably more muted than those of some of his ministers and of nationalists in parliament; this could be seen in the varied responses to Putin's October 2006 proposal to extend the leasing agreement beyond 2017. Nevertheless, the clear tendency of the Yushchenko presidency has been to treat the Russian presence (both its future and the current activities of the Russian fleet) as a problem to be solved. In contrast, "blue" politicians including Prime Minister Yanukovych, identified with a more favorable approach to Russia, were, not surprisingly, more positive about the Russian naval presence, as Yanukovych's response to Putin's proposal also makes clear.[10] The division between "orange" and "blue" tendencies on the issue of the Black Sea Fleet complicated the Ukrainian governmental position, given the presence of both within the executive and the strengthening of the "blue" position following the 2006 parliamentary elections. By spring 2007, with president and parliament engaged in a constitutional struggle, the development of a unified Ukrainian approach to the issue appeared more uncertain than ever.

The second complicating factor in Russian-Ukrainian relations regarding the Black Sea Fleet has been the linkage to other aspects of relations between the two states. In particular, the scope of the dispute appeared to widen in late 2005, when the issue of the status of the Russian Black Sea Fleet in Ukraine was raised in the context of the Russia-Ukraine gas dispute—a linkage that was denied by the Ukrainian government but that was nevertheless circulated in media reports. The uneasy nature of energy relations between Russia and Ukraine, with Russia apparently using leverage over energy issues to encourage a more sympathetic Ukrainian approach on foreign and security issues (a strategy denied by Putin), was symptomatic of the third complicating factor—that Russian-Ukrainian relations during the Yushchenko presidency have become implicated in the deteriorating relations between Russia and the NATO states, particularly the United States.[11] The explicitly pro-Western orientation of the Yushchenko presidency, and in particular the desire to join NATO, was strongly opposed by the Russian government, which adopted an increasingly assertive approach to matters such as further NATO expansion and the proposed location of missile defense systems in Poland and the Czech Republic.[12] In this context, the continued presence of the Russian fleet on Ukrainian territory became a matter of heightened concern on all sides of the dispute, with one Russian analyst claiming, for example, that the primary Ukrainian objection to the continued presence of the Russian fleet was that it acted as an obstacle to NATO accession.[13]

Thus, activities such as joint naval exercises between Ukraine and NATO states appear to be regarded as evidence of movement toward the inclusion of Ukraine in a US sphere of influence and possibly toward NATO membership. In mid-2006, the Russian governmental protest at the actions and the language of the Ukrainian government in response to the involvement of some Russian journalists and politicians in the Crimean protests over proposed joint exercises was compounded by the implicit linkage made by both the Russian government and parliament of the planned exercises with possible Ukrainian accession to NATO. The Russian Duma passed a resolution in this period warning of the consequences to Russian-Ukrainian relations of Ukrainian

NATO membership, while the Russian ambassador to NATO asserted that Ukrainian accession would be counter to Russian interests and that Russia had the right to make use of diplomatic and economic leverage to oppose it.[14] The signing of an act supporting Ukrainian and Georgian NATO membership by President Bush in April 2007 further heightened tension over the issue, with one Russian analyst denouncing the act as part of a "comprehensive plan to remove Ukraine from Russia's geopolitical space" and "aimed at destroying the post-Soviet space and removing a number of states, including Ukraine, from the former geopolitical space of the commonwealth."[15] Once again, however, the future development of this issue is clouded by the fact that the Ukrainian political elite is divided in its external orientation. Whether Ukraine moves toward or away from NATO is uncertain given the deep divisions on the subject and the continuing political and constitutional conflict.

Thus, within eighteen months of the election of Yushchenko, the status of the Black Sea Fleet had moved from apparent resolution to diplomatic crisis and had become implicated in the Ukrainian domestic crisis. All aspects of the agreement were once again contested, including the inventory of assets, details of the division of assets, the length of the Russian lease for facilities in Ukraine, and the rent paid for them; in addition, issues around the Ukrainian and Russian navies in Crimea were now explicitly implicated in wider economic and political disputes, as well as the issue of the security orientation of Ukraine and Russian concerns about geopolitical threats to its security.

Bases

The Black Sea Fleet was not the only former Soviet military asset to emerge as a site of renewed dispute between Russia and it neighbors at the start of the twenty-first century. At the same time, and for closely related reasons, the issue of Russian bases in Georgia reemerged as a live issue between the two states. As discussed in Chapter 5, the 1999 agreement on the four Russian bases in Georgia led to the formal closure of the Vaziani and Gudauta bases in 2001, apparently resolving this particular aspect of the dispute. As late as March 2005, however, the Georgian parliament claimed that, although CFE Treaty–limited weapons had been removed from the Gudauta base, the base had not, in fact, been closed and that three hundred Russian personnel remained there; it also claimed that obstruction by the Russian armed forces was preventing verification of the extent of withdrawal from Gudauta.[16] In any case, even this limited Russian withdrawal from Georgian bases left the Akhalkalaki and Batumi facilities open, with complete Russian withdrawal not envisaged until the end of 2008, seventeen years after the Georgian parliament's first demand for immediate Russian withdrawal. In fact, the Russian position on the bases appears to have hardened over the course of eight sets of negotiations between the 1999 agreement and the end of the Shevardnadze presidency, with Russia demanding an increased withdrawal period and substantial compensation.[17]

This situation—the failure to fully close one base and the extension of the life of two others, despite the repeated assertions on the part of the host state's government and parliament that the bases must be closed—was, like the difficulties in resolving the issue in the 1990s, a product of Georgian weakness in relation to Russia. The failure to establish the basic aspects of Georgian state sovereignty in the 1990s meant that Georgia lacked the political, military, or economic capabilities required to enforce the desired Russian withdrawal.[18] The failure of internal and external sovereignty, as understood in the Western tradition, was exemplified by the problem of the Gudauta base—since it is located in Abkhazia, a region over which Tbilisi has no control, inspection of the base by the Georgian Ministry of Defense would have been difficult irrespective of the Russian attitude toward Georgian scrutiny; in fact, the effective absence of Georgian sovereignty in relation to Russia on security issues meant that the Russian armed forces were not required to be transparent about the extent of withdrawal from the base.

This changed dramatically, however, under the Saakashvili administration, following the "Rose Revolution" in late 2003. The new administration, like the Yushchenko administration in Ukraine, began to assert what it considered to be Georgian security interests in opposition to Russia, and to do so more effectively than the previous administration had been able to. This move toward a more assertive security policy in relation to Russia was supported by the parliament, which, in its resolution of 10 March 2005, stated that the failure to reach agreement by mid-May 2005 on the withdrawal of Russian troops from the two remaining bases, within a timeframe acceptable to Georgia, should result in the suspension of the issue of entry visas to Russian service personnel, restrictions on the movement of those Russian personnel inside Georgia, and the "rehabilitation" of Georgian citizens working for the bases.[19]

An agreement on the closure of the Akhalkalaki and Batumi bases was signed at the end of May 2005; it provided for the last Russian troops to leave Akhalkalaki by the end of 2007 and Batumi by the end of 2008.[20] A further agreement, signed in March 2006, revised the deadlines for Russian withdrawal, requiring pullout from both bases to be completed no later than the end of 2007; this demonstrated, once again, the shift in Russia-Georgia security relations that had occurred following the change of Georgian administration, since it was the first revision of a security agreement to bring Russian implementation deadlines forward, rather than to extend them. In the context of these agreements, the Georgian defense minister also demanded the inspection of the Gudauta base, to ensure that it had been vacated, as Russia claimed.[21] In addition, and also in contrast to other agreements, including the

1999 bases agreement, there appeared to be timely implementation on the part of Russia, with the Georgian Ministry of Defense reporting the withdrawal of equipment and the transfer of satellite bases proceeding on schedule during the first half of 2006.[22]

The far more assertive posture of the Georgian government under Saakashvili, and the apparent capability to demand Russian compliance with agreements signed, extended beyond the issue of Russian bases to the broader issue of Georgian security relations with Russia and with North American and European states—in other words, to Georgia's overall foreign and security policy orientation. This reorientation toward NATO states and away from Russia was signaled in the first year of the Saakashvili administration, when Georgia signed an Individual Partnership Action Plan with NATO—the first of the three South Caucasus states to do so.[23] In May 2006, a Georgian parliamentary resolution endorsed the Georgian government's goal of NATO accession and called on NATO to support it.[24]

This shift is clearly set out in the 2005 Georgian national security concept, a document that establishes the "fundamental national values of Georgia," Georgian "national interests," Georgia's main security threats, and the mechanisms for implementing national security policy. The coincidence of Georgian and US political ideology and security interests and the view that Russian policy toward Georgia has been one of the most serious threats to Georgian sovereignty throughout the post-Soviet period are both prominent features of the security concept. "Freedom," "democracy and the rule of law," and "prosperity" are all listed as fundamental national values, while strategic partnership with the United States—described as having "strongly supported [the] development and strengthening of Georgia's statehood, democracy, defense capabilities, and economy" and as being "instrumental to Georgia's pledge to become a full democracy with a viable market economy"—is the first point to be mentioned in the context of foreign relations.[25] Relations with post–Orange Revolution Ukraine are also given priority in the concept, with emphasis placed on the two states' "belief in common values of democracy and freedom."[26] In contrast, and using language that clearly marks an ideological divide between Georgia, Europe, and the United States on the one hand, and Russia on the other, the concept asserts that

> Georgia *aspires* [emphasis added] to build cooperation with Russia upon the principles of good neighborly relations, equality, and mutual respect. Georgia would welcome [the] transition of Russia into a stable democratic state with a functioning market economy and respect for European values.[27]

The Russian military presence and other aspects of Russian security engagement in Georgia are repeatedly described as threats. The bases are described as "no longer a direct threat to Georgia's sovereignty. However, until their final withdrawal, they remain a risk to national security, and still negatively affect the security environment in Georgia."[28]

The move on the part of the Georgian government to a more assertive policy in respect to the Russian military presence is evident in a series of governmental and parliamentary actions, of which the pressure on bases has been part. In July 2006, one of Georgia's deputy defense ministers announced that Georgia would only ratify the adapted CFE Treaty after Russia had withdrawn from all military bases; later the same month, the Georgian parliament passed a resolution calling for the withdrawal of all Russian peacekeeping troops from Georgia and their replacement with an international force.[29]

Russian withdrawal was thrown into question in late 2006, however, by the rapid and severe deterioration of Russian-Georgian relations. In September 2006, the arrest of Russian officers by Georgia on spying charges led to the withdrawal of the Russian ambassador to Georgia, the Russian imposition of sanctions on Georgia, including the suspension of transport links, and the expulsion of hundreds of Georgians from Russia. The decision of the Russian government to recognize the result of a November 2006 South Ossetian referendum in which voters backed independence from Georgia further worsened relations, as did the Russian Duma resolution in December supporting Abkhazia and South Ossetia's aspirations to independent statehood, producing a counter-resolution by the Georgian parliament describing Russian activity as making long-term cooperation between the states impossible.[30] At the height of the dispute, Russia announced that it was suspending the withdrawal from the remaining Georgian bases; although this decision was later reversed, and withdrawal continued into 2007, it suggested that the Russian government regarded military withdrawal as conditional on the status of relations with the Georgian government.

As suggested above, this shift in Georgia and Ukraine's security relations with Russia, and the impact on their attempts to consolidate internal sovereignty, needs to be located in the wider context of geopolitical changes and their impact on the ability of the Russian government to assert their security interests inside these states. These relate both to the response to the changes of administration in Georgia and Ukraine by other states and international organizations and to the apparently interdependent factors of administration change, the reorientation of security policy, and the impact of increased US engagement with the region as part of the twin strategies of democracy promotion and "war on terror."[31] As noted earlier, US engagement on defense issues has been particularly strong in Georgia during Saakashvili's presidency, with the US government making large increases in bilateral funding for the training and restructuring of the Georgian armed forces. Both explicit US engagement in Georgia and Ukraine, through funding and improved governmental relations, and the less overt engagement in the processes of political change during the "Color Revolutions" have strengthened the positions of these states in relation to Russia. This is a source of considerable concern for Russian politicians in and outside government, who view such activity as part of a wider attempt by the United States to

encroach on Russia's sphere of interest under the cover of the "war on terror" and the promotion of democracy.[32] As with Ukraine, the desire of Georgia to join NATO is strongly opposed by Russia, and US support for Georgian
membership, formalized in April 2007, seemed likely to exacerbate Russian
concerns about US motivations in the region. The strength of Russian feeling on this question was evident in February 2007 when the Russian foreign
minister, Sergei Lavrov, announced that Russia would not permit Georgia
to join NATO, an assertion that clearly indicated that he did not regard
Georgia as an equal and fully independent state—not, in other words, as a
sovereign state in the Western sense.[33] Paradoxically, it appears that the
opportunity to begin to (re)assert a Western model of sovereignty in relation
to Russia has occurred for Georgia and Ukraine as the result of increased
intervention in their internal affairs by another, more powerful state, the
United States; whether this can be sustained is likely to depend on the continued support of European states and the United States, and on the capability and willingness of these states to oppose Russian regional interests—a
much less likely prospect in Ukraine than in Georgia, given the divisions
within the Ukrainian political elite.

Conclusion

As is suggested by the case study findings, and as I have argued throughout, agreement (or lack of agreement) on the problem of what to do with
the former Soviet forces and how this related to the priorities and capabilities of the newly independent states needs to be understood in the context
of the concept of sovereignty. I argued in Chapter 2 that it is not useful to
think of sovereignty in relation to these or any other states as a universally
agreed upon term with a permanently fixed set of meanings. However, it is
clear that there are a number of points of commonality in different analysts'
understandings of the term that can allow us to broadly define the conceptual territory covered by the term *sovereignty*. I also argued that these understandings are fundamentally challenged within Soviet and post-Soviet discourses concerning security, which, I have indicated, display a set of different
and mutually contradictory assumptions about what sovereignty as a term
implies. Given this, I would argue that three distinct facets of the question of
sovereignty in the post-Soviet context informed the negotiations over the military issues considered earlier, two of which related to conceptions of sovereignty and one which was connected to the exercise of sovereignty.

First, as I have argued, two distinct models of sovereignty, Soviet and
Western, can be identified in the bilateral and multilateral interactions
between the states of the CIS. Key treaties and other agreements, both within
the CIS framework and bilaterally, reflect the prior, Soviet understanding of

the term, which does not necessarily imply independence, which formalizes the contradiction that sovereignty is illimitable, and which is, nevertheless, for actors other than the union (or in the post-Soviet environment, the CIS or Russian) center constrained to the point where it ceases to have any practical meaning. This use of the term, in which sovereignty is repeatedly asserted and yet simultaneously deprived of meaningful content, is evident in agreements and the way in which agreements are described both in the immediate period after the breakup of the USSR, in the CIS founding documents, and at the end of the period, in the agreements on the Russia-Belarus Union. There thus appears to be a continuum of understanding about the meaning of the term *sovereignty* on the part of some of the key actors involved in the discussions over the security issues considered earlier—most notably the CIS and Russian military elites and the Lukashenka administration.

In contrast, significant sections of the Ukrainian and Georgian political and military elites have, from the period immediately prior to independence, appeared in their language and their negotiation strategies to be proceeding from a Western understanding of the term *sovereignty,* one which implies factors such as territorial integrity, control over the legitimate means of force, and governmental control over key areas of state policymaking, including military and foreign policy.

In this sense, both the nature of the disputes over military issues (the way in which they are conducted) and the disputes themselves (both what is being disputed and the fact that any attempt is made to assert control in relation to the CIS or Russia over military assets) can be understood as a tension or contest between these two different understandings of what sovereignty means. The way that these states individually and collectively talk about and enact understandings of sovereignty in their dealings with one another needs, I have argued, to be understood in this context and an investigation of the presence of these two competing interpretations of the term clarifies both the nature of the debates around post-Soviet military issues and the structure of these debates. This does not mean, of course, that this tension between these two understandings of sovereignty can alone account for the behavior of the military and political actors involved; clearly, many other factors—including security priorities, states' economic constraints, and wider foreign policy approaches—were all critical to the resolution of the military problems considered. Rather, this investigation of the contested meaning of sovereignty has sought to clarify why these debates took the shape that they did and aims to describe structures of understanding that informed both the negotiations over these specific security problems and the dynamic of relations between post-Soviet states more generally.

In addition to the way in which these different understandings of the idea of sovereignty inflected the assumptions made by actors regarding the significance and nature of the discussions and disputes about these three military problems, the characteristics of the Soviet usage of the term *sovereignty* has, I have argued, shaped the structure of and understandings about the significance of agreements made between these states in the policy areas considered. As noted in the discussion of the Soviet ideas about sovereignty, the conceptual and practical meanings of the term were in some respects critically different. Republic sovereignty was constitutionally guaranteed but was not protected in reality even to the limited extent to which it was protected in theory. Thus, a disparity clearly existed, and was understood to exist, between theory as represented in official documents, such as the constitution, and practice. This, I would argue, established an expectation of unreality, of a similar gap between official theory and governmental practice, in the post-Soviet environment. This may help to explain why all parties appeared willing at various points to commit themselves to agreements that either had no clear connection to actual bilateral or multilateral relations or that were disregarded by one or all parties as soon as they were signed (the numerous Russian-Ukrainian agreements on the Black Sea Fleet were particularly clear examples of this practice). The meaning and function of such agreements thus appears to lie not in their literal content or the concrete actions that derive from them but in their declarative and performative value. If this is the case, then this necessarily has implications for any attempt at analysis of post-Soviet agreements and institutions. It may help to explain, for example, the persistence of the CIS and the Russia-Belarus Union despite the frequent reports of their imminent collapse through stagnation.

Finally, the negotiations over the three military issues considered earlier need to be understood in relation to the practice as well as the theory of sovereignty. Again, taking those core, generally agreed assumptions about sovereignty evident in the Western model, the differentiated outcomes of these three issues for these three states need to be understood in the light of both the willingness and the ability to exercise sovereignty in relation to Russia. Thus, Georgian failure to assert its position on both the issues of the Black Sea Fleet and the Russian use of bases in the 1990s needs to be understood in the context of failed Georgian sovereignty both within its borders and in relation to Russia. The stronger position of Ukraine on the commonly understood indicators of sovereignty noted above (territorial control, the monopoly on the legitimate use of force, control of state borders, and governmental control over key areas of state policymaking) helps to account for the Ukrainian government's greater success in negotiations with Russia on nuclear weapons and the Black Sea Fleet. In the case of Belarus, the comparative political disengagement on two issues with extremely significant implications for state security—the ownership and control of nuclear weapons on its territory, and the use of military facilities by another state's armed forces—needs to be understood in light of the weak commitment to Belarusian independence and national identity that ultimately led to moves toward union with Russia and the government's apparent reversion to Soviet understandings of what sovereignty entails. As demonstrated by the dramatic changes in Georgia's and Ukraine's policies in respect to the Black Sea Fleet and the bases issue, and by the continued attempts by the Belarusian government to move closer to Russia on security and other areas, the understanding of what sovereignty means and the ability to exercise it remain critical to the problem of security in the former Soviet Union.

Notes

1. Ahto Lobjakas, "Ukraine: European Union Expected to Keep Kyiv on Hold," *RFE/RL Newsline,* 13 February 2001; "NATO: Ukraine Must Respect Democratic Norms to Receive Aid," *RFE/RL Newsline,* 4 July 2001.
2. Askold Krushelnycky, "Ukraine: Kyiv Says Accord With Moscow Is Not Anti-NATO," *RFE/RL Newsline,* 24 January 2001. On Russian-Ukrainian rapprochement in the late Kuchma period, see Andrew Wilson and Clelia Rontoyanni, "Security or Prosperity? Belarusian and Ukrainian Choices," in Robert Legvold and Celeste A. Wallander, eds., *Swords and Sustenance: The Economics of Security in Belarus and Ukraine,* American Academy Studies in Global Security Series (Cambridge, MA: American Academy of Arts & Sciences, 2004), pp. 23–62; and J. L. Black, *Vladimir Putin and the New World Order: Looking East, Looking West?* (Lanham, MD: Rowman and Littlefield, 2004), pp. 247–266.
3. On US funding, see David Darchiashvili, "Georgia Courts NATO, Strives for Defence Overhaul," 26 July 2000, *Eurasia Insight,* available from www.eurasianet .org/departments/insight/articles/eav072600_pr.shtml.
4. On the desire for NATO membership, see, for example, Shevardnadze's statement at the NATO Euro-Atlantic Partnership Council Summit, 22 November 2002, available from www.nato.int/docu/speech/2002/s021122h.htm.
5. See, for instance the IMF's report of its Article IV consultations with Georgia for 2003, available from www.imf.org/ external/np/sec/pn/2003/pn03133.htm.
6. Damien Helly and Giorgi Gogia, "Georgian Security and the Role of the West," in Bruno Coppieters and Robert Legvold, eds., *Statehood and Security: Georgia After the Rose Revolution,* American Academy Studies in Global Security Series (Cambridge, MA: American Academy of Arts & Sciences, 2005), p. 296, note the mid-2003 twenty-five-year energy deal with Gazprom as an example of this; they also note "widespread donor fatigue" as a result of persistent failure to implement economic reform and stem corruption.
7. Ruth Deyermond, "The State of the Union: Military Success, Economic and Political Failure in the Russia-Belarus Union," *Europe-Asia Studies* 56, no. 8 (December 2004): 1191–1205.
8. "Parlament Kryma ob'yavil poluostrov 'territoriey bez NATO,'" 6 June 2006, *Moskovskie Novosti.*
9. "Commentary of the Spokesman of the Ministry of Foreign Affairs of Ukraine Relating to the Situation with Preparation for International Military Exercises in the Territory of the Autonomous Republic of Crimea," 6 June 2006, available from www.mfa.gov.ua/mfa/en/publication/print/6062.htm.
10. See, for example, Vladimir Socor, "Putin Testing Ukraine's Political System with His Black Sea Fleet Proposal," Jamestown Foundation *Eurasia Daily Monitor,* 1 November 2006.

11. "Russia Does Not Use Oil and Gas as a Political Weapon—Putin," RIA Novosti, 1 February 2007.

12. For one analysis, see Pavel Felgenhauer, "US Proposal to Base Missile Defence Systems in Poland, Czech Republic, Raises Alarm in Moscow," Jamestown Foundation *Eurasia Daily Monitor,* 24 January 2007.

13. Kryukov, "Evolution of Russian-Ukrainian Relations," p. 130.

14. "U NATO poyavilcya pobod ne prinimat' Ukrainu," 16 June 2006, *Moskovskie Novosti.*

15. "Bush podpisal zakon o podderzhke bstuplenniia Ukrainy i Gruzii b NATO," RIA Novosti, 10 April 2007; "US Seeks to Antagonise Post-Soviet State—Russian Expert," RIA Novosti, 11 April 2007.

16. "Resolution of the Parliament of Georgia on the Military Bases of the Russian Federation Located on the Territory of Georgia," available from www .parliament.ge/index.php?lang_id=ENG&sec_id=98&info_id=944.

17. Jaba Devdariani, "Georgia and Russia: The Troubled Road to Accommodation," in Coppieters and Legvold, *Statehood and Security,* p. 191.

18. For a detailed analysis of the problems surrounding Russian withdrawal from the Georgian bases, and the Russian reluctance to leave, see Robert L. Larsson, "The Enemy Within: Russia's Military Withdrawal from Georgia," *The Journal of Slavic Military Studies* 17, no. 3 (September 2004): 405–424.

19. Ibid.

20. Sovmestnoe Zayavlenie Ministerov Inostrannykh Del Rossiiskoi Federatsii i Gruzii, 30 May 2005.

21. Jean-Christophe Peuch, "Georgia: Russia Pledges to Complete Military Pullout on Schedule," 31 March 2006, *RFE/RL Newsline.*

22. Georgian Ministry of Defence News, available from www.mod.gov.ge/?l= E&m=13&sm=0&st=115&id=168.

23. Koba Liklikadze, "Georgia's NATO Test," Caucasus Reporting Service, Institute for War and Peace Reporting, 16 March 2006.

24. Resolution of the Parliament of Georgia on Integration of Georgia into NATO, available from www.parliament.ge/ index.php?lang_id=ENG&sec_id=98& info_id=11646.

25. National Security Concept of Georgia, Article 5.5.1, available from www .mod.gov.ge/?l=E&m=3&sm=1.

26. Ibid., Article 5.5.2.

27. Ibid., Article 5.5.5.

28. Ibid., Article 4.6.

29. "Georgia to Ratify Adapted CFE Only After Russia Closes Bases," RIA Novosti, 7 July 2006; "Georgian Parliament Votes to Expel Russian Peacekeepers," *RFE/RL Newsline,* 18 July 2006.

30. Georgian parliamentary appeal, 7 December 2006, available from www .parliament.ge/index.php?lang_id= ENG&sec_id=98&info_id=14195.

31. *The National Security Strategy of the United States of America,* especially chapters 3 and 7, available from www.whitehouse.gov/nsc/nss.html.

32. See, for example, Igor Torbakov, "Ivanov Restates Kremlin's Monroe Doctrine," *Eurasia Daily Monitor,* 13 January 2006, and Dov Lynch, *Why Georgia Matters,* Chaillot Paper 86 (Paris: European Union Institute for Security Studies, February 2006).

33. "Russian Foreign Minister Discusses Relations with Georgia," *RFE/RL Newsline,* 28 February 2007.

Abbreviations

ASSR	Autonomous Soviet Socialist Republic
BPF	Belarusian Popular Front
BSF	Black Sea Fleet
BSSR	Belarusian Soviet Socialist Republic
CDPSP	Current Digest of the Post-Soviet Press
CFE	Conventional Forces in Europe
CIS	Commonwealth of Independent States
CNDF	Congress of National Democratic Forces
CST	CIS Collective Security Treaty
EU	European Union
FBIS-SOV	Foreign Broadcast Information Service Daily Report (Central Eurasia)
GTEP	Georgia Train and Equip Program
ICBM	intercontinental ballistic missile
JAF	CIS Joint Armed Forces
NATO	North Atlantic Treaty Organization
NPT	Nuclear Non-Proliferation Treaty
OSCE	Organization for Security and Co-operation in Europe
PfP	Partnership for Peace
RFE/RL	Radio Free Europe/Radio Liberty
RGFT	Russian Group of Forces in the Transcaucasus
SSR	Soviet Socialist Republic
START	Strategic Arms Reduction Treaty
TASS	Telegraph Agency of the Soviet Union
USSR	Union of Soviet Socialist Republics

Bibliography

Abdulatipov, R. G. *Konstitutsiia SSSR i Natsional'nye Otnosheniia na Soveremen-nom Etape*. Moscow: Mysl', 1978.

Adams, Jan S. "Who Will Make Russia's Foreign Policy in 1994?" *RFE/RL Research Report* 3, no. 6 (11 February 1994): 36–40.

Adomeit, Hannes. "Russian National Security Interests." In Roy Allison and Christopher Bluth, eds. *Security Dilemmas in Russia and Eurasia*. London: Royal Institute of International Affairs, 1998, 33–49.

Allison, Roy. *Military Forces in the Soviet Successor States*. Adelphi Paper 280. London: International Institute for Strategic Studies, October 1993.

———. "The Network of New Security Policy Relations in Eurasia." In Roy Allison and Christopher Bluth, eds. *Security Dilemmas in Russia and Eurasia*. London: Royal Institute of International Affairs, 1998, 12–29.

Allison, Roy, ed. *Challenges for the Former Soviet South*. Washington, DC: Brookings Institution for the Royal Institute of International Affairs, 1996.

Allison, Roy, and Christopher Bluth, eds. *Security Dilemmas in Russia and Eurasia*. London: Royal Institute of International Affairs, 1998.

Anderson, Malcolm. *Frontiers, Territory and State Formation in the Modern World*. Cambridge: Polity, 1996.

Appatov, Semyen. "Problems and Prospects." *Politics and the Times: Ukraine in International Relations* 1 (1998): 38–42.

Arbatov, A. G. "Russian Nuclear Disarmament: Problems and Prospects." *Arms Control: Contemporary Security Policy* 14, no. 1 (January/February 1993): 103–115.

———. "Russian Security Interests and Dilemmas: An Agenda for the Future." In Alexei Arbatov et al., eds. *Managing Conflict in the Former Soviet Union: Russian and American Perspectives*. BCSIA Studies in International Security. Cambridge: MIT Press, 1997, 411–458.

Arbatov, A. G., ed. *Iadernye Vooruzheniia i Respublikanskiĭ Suverenitet*. Moscow: Mezhdunarodnye Otnosheniia, 1992.

Aspaturian, Vernon V. "The Theory and Practice of Soviet Federalism." *The Journal of Politics* 12, no. 1 (February 1950): 20–51.

———. "The Union Republics and Soviet Diplomacy: Concepts, Institutions, and Practices." *The American Political Science Review* 53, no. 2 (June 1959): 383–411.

Aves, Jonathan. *Post-Soviet Transcaucasia.* London: Royal Institute of International Affairs, 1993.

———. *Georgia: From Chaos to Stability?* London: Royal Institute of International Affairs, 1996.

———. "Independent Georgia." In Roy Allison, ed. *Challenges for the Former Soviet South.* Washington, DC: Brookings Institution for the Royal Institute of International Affairs, 1996, 167–185.

———. "The Caucasus States: The Regional Security Complex." In Roy Allison and Christopher Bluth, eds. *Security Dilemmas in Russia and Eurasia.* London: Royal Institute of International Affairs, 1998, 175–187.

Baev, Pavel K. *The Russian Army in a Time of Troubles.* London: Sage, 1996.

———. "Russia's Policies in the Southern Caucasus and the Caspian Area." *European Security* 10, no. 2 (Summer 2001): 95–110.

Baev, Pavel K., and Tor Bukkvoll. "Ukraine's Army Under Civilian Rule." *Jane's Intelligence Review* 8, no. 1 (January 1996): 8–10.

Ball, Deborah Yarsike. "Russia's Strategic View: Reduced Threats, Diminished Capabilities." *Jane's Intelligence Review* 10, no. 11 (November 1998): 8–10.

Balmaceda, Margarita M. "Myth and Reality in the Belarusian-Russian Relationship: What the West Should Know." *Problems of Post Communism* 46 (May/June 1999): 3–14.

Balmaceda, Margarita M., James I. Clem, and Lisbeth Tarlow, eds. *Independent Belarus: Domestic Determinants, Regional Dynamics, and Implications for the West.* Cambridge, MA: Ukrainian Research Institute and David Centre for Russian Studies, 2002. Distributed by Harvard University Press.

Barkin, J. Samuel, and Bruce Cronin. "The State and the Nation: Changing Norms and the Rules of Sovereignty in International Relations." *International Organization* 48, no. 1 (Winter 1994): 107–130.

Bartelson, Jens. *A Genealogy of Sovereignty.* Cambridge: Cambridge University Press, 1995.

Barylski, Robert V. *The Soldier in Russian Politics: Duty, Dictatorship and Democracy.* New Brunswick, NJ: Transaction, 1998.

Behnke, Andreas. "Grand Theory in an Age of Its Impossibility: Contemplations on Alexander Wendt." In Stefano Guzzini and Anna Leander, eds. *Constructivism and International Relations: Alexander Wendt and His Critics.* London and New York: Routledge, 2006, 48–56.

Belyaev, Sergei, Alexander Shabanov, Eduard Kovalev, et al. "Election 1995: Parties' Foreign Policy Views." *International Affairs* (Moscow) 40, no. 11–12 (1995): 3–27.

Bennett, Andrew. *Condemned to Repetition? The Rise, Fall, and Reprise of Soviet-Russian Military Interventionism, 1973–1996.* Cambridge, MA: MIT Press, 1999.

Bernier, Ivan. *International Legal Aspects of Federalism.* London: Longman, 1973.

Bertsch, Gary K., Cassady Craft, Scott A. Jones, and Michael Beck, eds. *Crossroads and Conflict: Security and Foreign Policy in the Caucasus and Central Asia.* London: Routledge, 2000.

Bhatty, Robin, and Rachel Bronson. "NATO's Mixed Signals in the Caucasus and Central Asia." *Survival* 42, no. 3 (Autumn 2000): 129–145.

Biersteker, Thomas J. "Critical Reflections on Post-Positivism in International Relations." *International Studies Quarterly* 33, no. 3 (September 1989): 263–267.

Biersteker, Thomas J., and Cynthia Weber, eds. *State Sovereignty as Social Construct.* Cambridge: Cambridge University Press, 1996.

Billingsley, Dodge. "Georgian-Abkhazian Security Issues." *Jane's Intelligence Review* 8, no. 2 (February 1996): 65–68.

———. "Truce Means Nothing in Western Georgia." *Jane's Intelligence Review* 10, no. 6 (June 1998): 13–17.

Black, J. L. *Vladimir Putin and the New World Order: Looking East, Looking West?* Lanham, MD: Rowman and Littlefield, 2004.

Blank, Stephen. "Russia's Draft Laws on Peacemaking and Defence—Part 1." *Jane's Intelligence Review* 7, no. 4 (April 1995): 156–157.

———. "Russia's Draft Laws on Peacemaking and Defence—Part 2." *Jane's Intelligence Review* 7, no. 5 (May 1995): 201–204.

———. "Russia's Real Drive to the South." *Orbis* 39, no. 3 (Summer 1995): 369–386.

———. "Yeltsin Fosters a Military Threat to Democracy." *Transition* 2, no. 15 (9 August 1996): 11–15.

Bluth, Christopher. *The Collapse of Soviet Military Power.* Aldershot, UK: Dartmouth, 1995.

———. "Russian Attitudes to START II." *Jane's Intelligence Review* 8, no. 3 (March 1996): 114–116.

———. "Russian Military Forces: Ambitions, Capabilities and Constraints." In Roy Allison and Christopher Bluth, eds. *Security Dilemmas in Russia and Eurasia.* London: Royal Institute of International Affairs, 1998, 67–93.

———. "Arms Control and Proliferation." In Roy Allison and Christopher Bluth, eds. *Security Dilemmas in Russia and Eurasia.* London: Royal Institute of International Affairs, 1998, 303–322.

Bodin, Jean. *On Sovereignty, Four Chapters from the Six Books of the Commonwealth.* Ed. and trans. by Julian H. Franklin. Cambridge: Cambridge University Press, 1992.

Bogaturov, Alexei. "Self-determination of Nations and Conflict Potential." *International Affairs* (Moscow) 38, no. 3 (1992): 5–14, 76.

Bogomolov, Vladimir, and Sergei Kortunov. "Russian Nuclear Strategy." *International Affairs* (Moscow) 44, no. 2 (1998): 23–37.

Bonesteel, Ronald M. "The CIS Security System: Stagnating, in Transition or on the Way Out?" *European Security* 2, no. 1 (Spring 1993): 115–138.

Bremmer, Ian, and Ray Taras, eds. *Nations and Politics in the Soviet Successor States.* Cambridge: Cambridge University Press, 1993.

Brzezinski, Zbigniew. "Ukraine's Critical Role in the Post-Soviet Space." In Lubomyr A. Hajda, ed. *Ukraine in the World: Studies in the International Relations and Security Structure of a Newly Independent State.* Cambridge, MA: Harvard University Press for the Ukrainian Research Institute, Harvard University, 1998, 3–8.

Bukkvoll, Tor. *Ukraine and European Security.* London: Royal Institute for International Affairs, 1997.

Burant, Stephen R. "Foreign Policy and National Identity: A Comparison of Ukraine and Belarus." *Europe-Asia Studies* 47, no. 7 (November 1995): 1125–1144.

Buzan, Barry, and Ole Wæver. *Regions and Powers: The Structure of International Security.* Cambridge: Cambridge University Press, 2003.

Calvez, Jean-Yves. *Droit International et Souverainete en U.R.S.S.* Paris: Armand Colin, 1953.

Caskie, Susan. "Military and Security Issues Around the Region." *Transition* 2, no. 5 (8 March 1996): 51.

Chakste, Mintauts. "Soviet Concepts of the State, International Law and Sovereignty." *The American Journal of International Law* 43, no. 1 (January 1949): 21–36.

Chervonnaya, Svetlana. *Conflict in the Caucasus: Georgia, Abkhazia and the Russian Shadow.* Glastonbury, UK: Gothic Image, 1994.

Cimbala, Stephen J. "From Deterrence to Denuclearization: US and Russian Nuclear Force Reduction Options." *The Journal of Slavic Military Studies* 7, no. 3 (September 1994): 421–442.

———. "Russian Nuclear Coercion: How Necessary? How Much?" *The Journal of Slavic Military Studies* 10, no. 3 (September 1997): 56–78.

Clarke, Douglas L. "Implementing the CFE Treaty." *RFE/RL Research Report* 1, no. 23 (5 June 1992): 50–55.

———. "Rusting Fleet Renews Debate on Navy's Mission." *RFE/RL Research Report* 2, no. 23 (18 June 1993): 25–32.

Clarke, Douglas L., ed. "Military and Security Notes." *RFE/RL Research Report* 1, no. 9 (28 February 1992): 48–53.

Collins, Brian J. "Russian Airpower—The First Year (Spring 1992–Spring 1993): Blueprint for the Future." *The Journal of Slavic Military Studies* 7, no. 2 (1994): 218–253.

Colton, Timothy J. "Belarusian Popular Opinion and the Union with Russia." In Margarita M. Balmaceda, James I. Clem, and Lisbeth Tarlow, eds. *Independent Belarus: Domestic Determinants, Regional Dynamics, and Implications for the West.* Cambridge, MA: Ukrainian Research Institute and David Centre for Russian Studies, 2002, 21–54.

Colton, Timothy J., and Robert C. Tucker, eds. *Patterns in Post-Soviet Leadership.* Boulder, CO: Westview, 1995.

Cooley, Alexander. "Imperial Wreckage: Property Rights, Sovereignty, and Security in the Post-Soviet Space." *International Security* 25, no. 3 (Winter 2000/01): 100–127.

Coppieters, Bruno, and Robert Legvold, eds. *Statehood and Security: Georgia After the Rose Revolution.* American Academy Studies in Global Security Series. Cambridge, MA: American Academy of Arts & Sciences, 2005.

Coppieters, Bruno, Alexei Zverev, and Dmitri Trenin, eds. *Commonwealth and Independence in Post-Soviet Eurasia.* London: Frank Cass, 1998.

Cornell, Svante E. "Autonomy as a Source of Conflict: Caucasian Conflicts in Theoretical Perspectives." *World Politics* 54, no. 1 (January 2002): 245–276.

Crawford, James. *The Creation of States in International Law.* Oxford: Clarendon Press, 1979.

Crow, Suzanne. "Russia's Relations with Members of the Commonwealth." *RFE/RL Research Report* 1, no. 19 (8 May 1992): 8–12.

———. "Russia Prepares to Take a Hard Line on 'Near Abroad.'" *RFE/RL Research Report* 1, no. 32 (14 August 1992): 21–24.

———. "The Theory and Practice of Peacekeeping in the Former USSR." *RFE/RL Research Report* 1, no. 37 (18 September 1992): 31–36.

———. "Russia Seeks Leadership in Regional Peacekeeping." *RFE/RL Research Report* 2, no. 15 (9 April 1993): 28–32.

———. "Russian Parliament Asserts Control over Sevastopol." *RFE/RL Research Report* 2, no. 31 (30 July 1993): 37–41.

———. "Russia Asserts Its Strategic Agenda." *RFE/RL Research Report* 2, no. 50 (17 December 1993): 1–8.

———. "Russia Promotes the CIS as an International Organization." *RFE/RL Research Report* 3, no. 11 (18 March 1994): 33–38.

———. "Why Has Russian Foreign Policy Changed?" *RFE/RL Research Report* 3, no. 18 (6 May 1994): 1–6.

Curtis, Glenn E., ed. *Armenia, Azerbaijan and Georgia Country Studies.* Federal Research Division, Library of Congress, 1995.

Daalder, Ivo H., and Terry Terriff. "Nuclear Arms Control: Finishing the Cold War Agenda." *Arms Control: Contemporary Security Policy* 14, no. 1 (April 1993): 5–37.

Danilovich, A. A. "On New Military Doctrines of the CIS and Russia." *The Journal of Slavic Military Studies* 5, no. 4 (December 1992): 517–538.

Danopoulos, Constantine P., and Daniel Zirker, eds. *Civil-Military Relations in the Soviet and Yugoslav Successor States.* Boulder, CO: Westview, 1996.

Darchiashvili, David. "The Russian Military Presence in Georgia: The Parties' Attitudes and Prospects." *Caucasian Regional Studies* 2, no. 1 (1997). Available from http://poli.vub.ac.be/ publi/crs/eng/0201-04.htm.

———. "Georgian Defence Policy and Military Reform." In Bruno Coppieters and Robert Legvold, eds. *Statehood and Security: Georgia After the Rose Revolution.* American Academy Studies in Global Security Series. Cambridge, MA: American Academy of Arts & Sciences, 2005, 117–151.

Dawisha, Karen, and Bruce Parrott. *Democratic Changes and Authoritarian Reactions in Russia, Ukraine, Belarus and Moldova.* Democratisation and Authoritarianism in Postcommunist Societies 3. New York: Cambridge University Press, 1997.

De Andreis, Marco, and Francesco Calogero. *The Soviet Nuclear Weapons Legacy.* SIPRI Research Report 10. Oxford: Oxford University Press, 1995.

De Haas, Marcel. "An Analysis of Soviet, CIS and Russian Military Doctrines 1990–2000." *The Journal of Slavic Military Studies* 14, no. 4 (December 2001): 1–34.

Devdariani, Jaba. "Georgia and Russia: The Troubled Road to Accommodation." In Bruno Coppieters and Robert Legvold, eds. *Statehood and Security: Georgia After the Rose Revolution.* American Academy Studies in Global Security Series. Cambridge, MA: American Academy of Arts & Sciences, 2005, 153–203.

Deyermond, Ruth. *Competing Sovereignties in the Former Soviet Union.* Essex Papers in Politics and Government 145. Colchester: University of Essex, June 2000.

———. "The State of the Union: Military Success, Economic and Political Failure in the Russia-Belarus Union." *Europe-Asia Studies* 56, no. 8 (December 2004): 1191–1205.

———. "Matrioshka Hegemony? Multi-levelled Hegemonic Competition and Security in Post-Soviet Central Asia." Paper, British International Studies Association Conference, 19–21 December 2005.

Dick, C. J. "Soviet Military Doctrine—Preparing for the Future." *Jane's Intelligence Review* 4, no. 1 (January 1992): 33–36.

———. "Crisis in the Soviet Military." *Jane's Intelligence Review* 4, no. 2 (February 1992): 72–75.

———. "Initial Thoughts on Russia's Draft Military Doctrine." *The Journal of Slavic Military Studies* 5, no. 4 (December 1992): 552–566.

———. "Counter-Blows in Russian Military Thinking." *The Journal of Slavic Military Studies* 6, no. 3 (September 1993): 397–425.

———. "The Military Doctrine of the Russian Federation." *The Journal of Slavic Military Studies* 7, no. 3 (September 1994): 481–506.

———. "The Military Doctrine of Ukraine." *The Journal of Slavic Military Studies* 7, no. 3 (September 1994): 507–522.

———. "A Bear Without Claws: The Russian Army in the 1990s." *The Journal of Slavic Military Studies* 10, no. 1 (March 1997): 1–10.

Drohobycky, Maria, ed. *Crimea: Dynamics, Challenges and Prospects.* Lanham, MD: Rowman and Littlefield; Washington, DC: American Association for the Advancement of Science, 1995.

Duncan, Andrew. "START Cuts Begin to Make Their Mark." *Jane's Intelligence Review* 11, no. 2 (February 1999): 15–19.

Dunn, John. "The Ukrainian Nuclear Weapons Debate." *Jane's Intelligence Review* 5, no. 8 (August 1993): 339–342.

Duursma, Jorri. *Fragmentation and the International Relations of Micro-States: Self-determination and Statehood.* Cambridge: Cambridge University Press, 1996.

Efimov, Mikhail. *APN Comments on the USSR Constitution.* Moscow: Novosti, 1979.

Eke, Steven M., and Taras Kuzio. "Sultanism in Eastern Europe: The Socio-Political Roots of Authoritarian Populism in Belarus." *Europe-Asia Studies* 52, no. 3 (May 2000): 523–547.

Fedor, Helen, ed. *Belarus and Moldova, Country Studies.* Washington, DC: Federal Research Division, Library of Congress, 1995.

Feldbrugge, F.J.M., ed. *The Constitutions of the USSR and the Union Republics: Analysis, Texts, Reports.* Alphen aan den Rijn, the Netherlands: Sijthoff and Noordhoff, 1979.

Fierke, Karin M., and Knud Erik Jørgensen, eds. *Constructing International Relations: The Next Generation.* Armonk, NY: M. E. Sharpe, 2001.

Fowler, Michael Ross, and Julie Marie Bunck. *Law, Power, and the Sovereign State: The Evolution and Application of the Concept of Sovereignty.* University Park, PA: Pennsylvania State University Press, 1995.

Foye, Stephen. "CIS: Kiev and Moscow Clash over Armed Forces." *RFE/RL Research Report* 1, no. 3 (17 January 1992): 1–3.

———. "Armed Forces Confront Legacy of Soviet Past." *RFE/RL Research Report* 1, no. 8 (21 February 1992): 9–13.

———. "Post-Soviet Russia: Politics and the New Russian Army." *RFE/RL Research Report* 1, no. 33 (21 August 1992): 5–12.

———. "The CIS Armed Forces." *RFE/RL Research Report* 2, no. 1 (1 January 1993): 41–45.

———. "Civilian-Military Tension in Ukraine." *RFE/RL Research Report* 2, no. 25 (18 June 1993): 60–66.

———. "End of CIS Command Heralds New Russian Defense Policy?" *RFE/RL Research Report* 2, no. 27 (2 July 1993): 45–49.

———. "The Armed Forces of the CIS: Legacies and Strategies." *RFE/RL Research Report* 3, no. 1 (7 January 1994): 18–21.

Fuller, Elizabeth. "Eduard Shevardnadze's Via Dolorosa." *RFE/RL Research Report* 2, no. 43 (29 October 1993): 17–23.

———. "Stopping the Shooting Is Only Half the Battle." *Transition* 2, no. 1 (12 January 1996): 22–24, 72.

———. "Georgia Stabilizes." *Transition* 3, no. 2 (7 February 1997): 64, 82–83.

Gachechiladze, Revaz. *The New Georgia: Space, Society, Politics.* London: UCL Press, 1995.

———. "Geographical and Historical Factors of State Building in Transcaucasia." *Caucasian Regional Studies* 1, no. 1 (1996). Available from http://poli.vub.ac .be/publi/ crs/eng/0101-03.htm.

———. "The Making of the New Georgia: Development Factors—Pluses and Minuses." *Caucasian Regional Studies* 3, no. 1 (1998). Available from http://poli .vub.ac.be/publi/ crs/eng/0301-03.htm.

Galeotti, Mark. "The Belarusian Army—An Example of Successful Reform?" *Jane's Intelligence Review* 7, no. 6 (June 1995): 258–260.

———. "Russia's National Security Concept." *Jane's Intelligence Review* 10, no. 5 (May 1998): 3–4.

Gareev, M. A. "On Military Doctrine and Military Reform in Russia." *The Journal of Slavic Military Studies* 5, no. 4 (December 1992): 539–552.

———. "Problem Areas in Military Doctrine and Russian-American Military Cooperation." *The Journal of Slavic Military Studies* 7, no. 1 (March 1994): 9–15.

Garnett, Sherman W. "The Sources and Conduct of Ukrainian Nuclear Policy: November 1992 to January 1994." In George Quester, ed. *The Nuclear Challenge in Russia and the New States of Eurasia.* Cambridge, MA: M. E. Sharpe, 1995, 125–151.

———. *Keystone in the Arch: Ukraine in the Emerging Security Environment.* Washington, DC: Carnegie Endowment for International Peace, 1997.

———. "U.S.-Ukrainian Relations: Past, Present, and Future." In Lubomyr A. Hajda, ed. *Ukraine in the World: Studies in the International Relations and Security Structure of a Newly Independent State.* Cambridge, MA: Harvard University Press for the Ukrainian Research Institute, Harvard University, 1998, 103–124.

Garnett, Sherman W., and Robert Legvold, eds. *Belarus at the Crossroads.* Washington, DC: Carnegie Endowment for International Peace, 1999.

Garrity, Patrick J., and Steven A. Maaranen. *Nuclear Weapons in the Changing World: Perspectives from Europe, Asia and North America.* New York: Plenum Press, 1992.

Garthoff, Raymond L. "Russian Military Doctrine and Deployments." In Bruce Parrott, ed. *State Building and Military Power in Russia and the New States of Eurasia.* The International Politics of Eurasia 5. Armonk, NY, and London: M. E. Sharpe, 1995, 44–63.

Gelber, Harry G. *Sovereignty Through Interdependence.* London: Kluwer Law International, 1997.

German, Tracey. *Faultline or Foothold? Georgia's Relations with Russia and the USA.* Conflict Studies Research Centre Papers P41. Camberley, UK: Conflict Studies Research Centre, January 2004.

Giragosian, Richard. "The US Military Engagement in Central Asia and the Southern Caucasus: An Overview." *The Journal of Slavic Military Studies* 17, no. 1 (March 2004): 43–77.

Glantz, Mary E. "The Origins and Development of Soviet and Russian Military Doctrine." *The Journal of Slavic Military Studies* 7, no. 3 (September 1994): 443–480.

Glebov, Viktor. "The Black Sea Region, European Security, and Ukraine." In David E. Albright and Semyen J. Appatov, *Ukraine and European Security.* Basingstoke, UK: Macmillan, 1999.

Goncharenko, Alexander. *Ukrainian-Russian Relations: An Unequal Partnership.* RUSI Whitehall Paper Series 32. London: Royal United Services Institute, 1995.

———. "Ukraine: National Interests Between the CIS and the West." In Roy Allison and Christopher Bluth, eds. *Security Dilemmas in Russia and Eurasia.* London: Royal Institute of International Affairs, 1998, 121–133.

Gousseinova, Manana. "Russian Interests in the Abkhazian Conflict and the Position of the USA." *The Journal of Slavic Military Studies* 8, no. 3 (September 1995): 470–475.

Gribincea, Mihai. *The Russian Policy on Military Bases: Georgia and Moldova.* Oradea, Romania: Cogito, 2001.

Gross, Natalie. "Reflections on Russia's New Military Doctrine." *Jane's Intelligence Review* 4, no. 8 (August 1992): 339–341.

Guzzini, Stefano. "A Reconstruction of Constructivism in International Relations." *European Journal of International Relations* 6, no. 2 (June 2000): 147–182.

Guzzini, Stefano, and Anna Leander. "Wendt's Constructivism: A Relentless Quest for Synthesis." In Stefano Guzzini and Anna Leander, eds. *Constructivism and International Relations: Alexander Wendt and His Critics.* London: Routledge, 2006, 73–92.

Guzzini, Stefano, and Anna Leander, eds. *Constructivism and International Relations: Alexander Wendt and His Critics.* London and New York: Routledge, 2006.

Hajda, Lubomyr A., ed. *Ukraine in the World: Studies in the International Relations and Security Structure of a Newly Independent State.* Cambridge, MA: Harvard University Press for the Ukrainian Research Institute, Harvard University, 1998.

Handler, Joshua. "The Future of Russian Strategic Forces." *Jane's Intelligence Review* 7, no. 4 (April 1995): 162–165.

Hannum, Hurst. *Autonomy, Sovereignty, and Self-determination: The Accommodation of Conflicting Rights.* Rev. ed. Philadelphia: University of Pennsylvania Press, 1996.

Hashmi, Sohail H., ed. *State Sovereignty: Change and Persistence in International Law.* University Park, PA: Pennsylvania State University Press, 1997.

Hazard, John N. "The Soviet Union and International Law." *Soviet Studies* 1, no. 3 (January 1950): 189–199.

———. "Renewed Emphasis upon a Socialist International Law." *The American Journal of International Law* 65, no. 1 (January 1971): 142–148.

Helly, Damien, and Giorgi Gogia. "Georgian Security and the Role of the West." In Bruno Coppieters and Robert Legvold, eds. *Statehood and Security: Georgia After the Rose Revolution.* American Academy Studies in Global Security Series. Cambridge, MA: American Academy of Arts & Sciences, 2005, 271–305.

Herzig, Edmund. *The New Caucasus: Armenia, Azerbaijan and Georgia.* Chatham House Papers. London: Royal Institute of International Affairs, 1999.

Hinsley, F. H. *Sovereignty.* London: C. A. Watts, 1966.

Hlushchenko, Anatoliy. "Ukraine and the Problem of Nuclear Weapons." *The Ukrainian Review* 40, no. 3 (Autumn 1993): 13–19.

Holcomb, James. "Russian Military Doctrine—Structuring for the Worst Case." *Jane's Intelligence Review* 4, no. 12 (December 1992): 531–534.

Holden, Gerard. *Russia After the Cold War: History and the Nation in Post-Soviet Security Politics.* Frankfurt: Campus Verlag; Boulder, CO: Westview, 1994.

Hrechaninov, Vadim. "Democratic Control over the Military Sector? A Truly Urgent Task." *Politics and the Times: Ukraine in International Relations* 2 (1998): 6–14.

Hrunkevych, Oleksandr, and Valeriy Kuzmenko. "Yet Another Step in the Proper Direction." *Politics and the Times: Ukraine in International Relations* 1 (1998): 24–37.

Hunter, Shireen T. *The Transcaucasus in Transition: Nation-Building and Conflict.* Washington, DC: Center for Strategic and International Studies, 1994.

Ioffe, Grigory. "Understanding Belarus: Belarusian Identity." *Europe-Asia Studies* 55, no. 8 (December 2003): 1241–1272.

———. "Understanding Belarus: Economy and Political Landscape." *Europe-Asia Studies* 56, no. 1 (January 2004): 85–118.

Ivanov, Igor S. *The New Russian Diplomacy.* Washington, DC: Nixon Center and Brookings Institution, 2002.

Jackson, Robert H. *Quasi-States: Sovereignty, International Relations, and the Third World.* Cambridge Studies in International Relations 12. Cambridge: Cambridge University Press, 1990.

James, Alan. "Sovereignty: Ground Rule or Gibberish?" *Review of International Studies* 10, no. 1 (January 1984): 1–18.

———. *Sovereign Statehood: The Basis of International Society.* London: Allen and Unwin, 1986.

———. "Comment on J. D. B. Miller." *Review of International Studies* 12 (1986): 91–93.

———. "The Equality of States: Contemporary Manifestations of an Ancient Doctrine." *Review of International Studies* 18, no. 4 (1992): 377–391.

Jaworsky, John. "Ukraine's Armed Forces and Military Policy." In Lubomyr A. Hajda, ed. *Ukraine in the World: Studies in the International Relations and Security Structure of a Newly Independent State.* Cambridge, MA: Harvard University Press for the Ukrainian Research Institute, Harvard University, 1998, 223–247.

Jones, Ellen, and James H. Brusstar. "Moscow's Emerging Security Decisionmaking System: The Role of the Security Council." *The Journal of Slavic Military Studies* 6, no. 3 (September1993): 345–374.

Jones, Robert A. *The Soviet Concept of "Limited Sovereignty" from Lenin to Gorbachev: The Brezhnev Doctrine.* Basingstoke, UK: Macmillan, 1990.

Jones, Stephen F. "Georgia's Power Structures." *RFE/RL Research Report* 2, no. 39 (1 October 1993): 5–9.

Jonson, Lena, and Clive Archer, eds. *Peacekeeping and the Role of Russia in Eurasia.* Boulder, CO: Westview, 1996.

Kanevsky, Boris, and Pyotr Shabardin. "Russia Needs a New Type of Army." *International Affairs* (Moscow) 40, no. 5 (1994): 117–120.

Karp, Marek J. "Escape from Freedom." *The Journal of Slavic Military Studies* 11, no. 4 (December 1998): 146–163.

Kaufman, Stuart. "Lessons from the 1991 Gulf War and Russian Military Doctrine." *The Journal of Slavic Military Studies* 6, no. 3 (September 1993): 375–396.

———. "Organizational Politics and Change in Soviet Military Policy." *World Politics* 46, no. 2 (April 1994): 355–382.

Kelebay, Yarema Gregory. "Aspects of Nation-Building in the Newly Independent Countries of the Former USSR." *The Ukrainian Review* 40, no. 2 (Summer 1993): 8–17.

Khasbulatov, Ruslan. "The Commonwealth of Independent States: Conflicts, Problems, Perspectives." In Teresa Pelton Johnson and Steven E. Miller, eds. *Russian Security After the Cold War: Seven Views from Moscow.* Washington, DC: Brassey's, 1994, 165–184.

Kiva, Alexei. "A Super-Power Which Ruined Itself." *International Affairs* (Moscow) 38, no. 2 (1992): 13–22.

Kortunov, S. "Russia's Way: National Identity and Foreign Policy." *International Affairs* (Moscow) 44, no. 4 (1998): 138–163.

Kozyrev, Andrei. "Russian Interests in the CIS." *International Affairs* (Moscow) 40, no. 11 (1994): 11–30.

Kramer, Mark. "Beyond the Brezhnev Doctrine: A New Era in Soviet–East European Relations?" *International Security* 14, no. 3 (Winter 1989/1990): 25–67.

Krasner, Stephen D. *Sovereignty, Organized Hypocrisy.* Princeton, NJ: Princeton University Press, 1999.

Kratochwil, Friedrich. "Constructing a New Orthodoxy? Wendt's *Social Theory of International Politics* and the Constructivist Challenge." In Stefano Guzzini and Anna Leander, eds. *Constructivism and International Relations: Alexander Wendt and His Critics.* London and New York: Routledge, 2006, 21–47.

Kryukov, N. A. "Evolution of Russian-Ukrainian Relations: The Legal Status of the Black Sea Fleet." *Military Thought* 15, no. 2 (April 2006): 120–132.

Kubalkova, Vendulka, Nicholas Onuf, and Paul Kowert, eds. *International Relations in a Constructed World.* Armonk, NY: M. E. Sharpe, 1998.

Kulagin, Vladimir. "The World Between Hobbes and Kant: A View from Russia." *Contemporary Security Policy* 20, no. 2 (August 1999): 116–126.

Kutovoi, Yevgeny. "The CIS: Not to Stop Halfway." *International Affairs* (Moscow) 38, no. 8 (1992): 101–108.

Kuzio, Taras. "Nuclear Weapons and Military Policy in Independent Ukraine." *The Harriman Institute Forum* 6, no. 9 (May 1993).

———. *Ukrainian Security Policy.* Westport, CT, and London: Praeger, 1995.

———. *Ukraine Under Kuchma: Political Reform, Economic Transformation and Security Policy in Independent Ukraine.* Basingstoke, UK: Macmillan, 1997.

———. *Ukraine: State and Nation Building.* London and New York: Routledge, 1998.

———. "Is Ukraine Part of Europe's Future?" *Washington Quarterly* 29, no. 3 (Summer 2006): 89–108.

Laba, Roman. "How Yeltsin's Exploitation of Ethnic Nationalism Brought Down an Empire." *Transition* 2, no. 1 (12 January 1996): 5–13.

Lapid, Yosef. "The Third Debate: On the Prospects of International Theory in a Post-Positivist Era." *International Studies Quarterly* 33, no. 3 (September 1989): 235–254.

Lapidus, Gail. "Contested Sovereignty: The Tragedy of Chechnya." *International Security* 23, no. 1 (Summer 1998): 5–49.

Lapidus, Gail, Viktor Zaslavsky, and Philip Goldman, eds. *From Union to Commonwealth: Nationalism and Separatism in the Soviet Republics.* Cambridge: Cambridge University Press, 1992.

Lapychak, Chrystyna. "Crackdown on Crimean Separatism." *Transition* 1, no. 8 (26 May 1995): 2–5.

Lapychak, Chrystyna, and Ustina Markus. "Ukraine's Continuing Evolution." *Transition* 3, no. 2 (7 February 1997): 29–32.

Larrabee, F. Stephen. "Ukraine's Place in European and Regional Security." In Lubomyr A. Hajda, ed. *Ukraine in the World: Studies in the International Relations and Security Structure of a Newly Independent State.* Cambridge, MA: Harvard University Press for the Ukrainian Research Institute, Harvard University, 1998, 249–270.

Larsson, Robert L. "The Enemy Within: Russia's Military Withdrawal from Georgia." *The Journal of Slavic Military Studies* 17, no. 3 (September 2004): 405–424.

Laski, Harold J. *Studies in the Problem of Sovereignty.* New Haven, CT: Yale University Press, 1917.

Legvold, Robert, and Celeste A. Wallander, eds. *Swords and Sustenance: The Economics of Security in Belarus and Ukraine.* American Academy Studies in Global Security Series. Cambridge, MA: American Academy of Arts & Sciences, 2004.

Lepingwell, John W. R. "Soviet Civil-Military Relations and the August Coup." *World Politics* 44, no. 4 (July 1992): 539–572.

———. "The Black Sea Fleet Agreement: Progress or Empty Promises?" *RFE/RL Research Report* 2, no. 28 (9 July 1993): 48–55.

———. "Negotiations over Nuclear Weapons: The Past as Prologue?" *RFE/RL Research Report* 3, no. 4 (28 January 1994): 1–11.

————. "The Trilateral Agreement on Nuclear Weapons." *RFE/RL Research Report* 3, no. 4 (28 January 1994): 12–20.

————. "Ukraine, Russia, and Nuclear Weapons: A Chronology." *RFE/RL Research Report* 3, no. 4 (28 January 1994): 21–25.

————. "Ukrainian Parliament Removes START-1 Conditions." *RFE/RL Research Report* 3, no. 8 (25 February 1994): 37–42.

Lievan, Anatol. "The Secret Policeman's Ball: The United States, Russia and the International Order After 11 September." *International Affairs* 78, no. 2 (April 2002): 261–276.

Light, Margot. *The Soviet Theory of International Relations*. Brighton, UK: Wheatsheaf, 1988.

Lindner, Rainer. "The Lukashenka Phenomenon." In Margarita M. Balmaceda, James I. Clem, and Lisbeth Tarlow, eds. *Independent Belarus: Domestic Determinants, Regional Dynamics, and Implications for the West*. Cambridge, MA: Ukrainian Research Institute and David Centre for Russian Studies, 2002, 77–108.

Lo, Bobo. *Russian Foreign Policy in the Post-Soviet Era: Reality, Illusion and Mythmaking*. Basingstoke, UK: Palgrave Macmillan, 2002.

————. *Vladimir Putin and the Evolution of Russian Foreign Policy*. Chatham House Papers. Malden, MA: Blackwell; London: Royal Institute of International Affairs, 2003.

Lobov, Oleg. "Russia's National Security Council and National Interests." *International Affairs* (Moscow) 41, no. 10 (1995): 11–16.

Lockwood, Dunbar. "New Data on the Strategic Arsenal of the Former Soviet Union." *Jane's Intelligence Review* 7, no. 6 (June 1995): 246–249.

Lombardi, Ben. "Ukrainian Armed Forces: Defence Expenditure and Military Reform." *The Journal of Slavic Military Studies* 14, no. 3 (September 2001): 31–68.

Lough, John. "The Place of the 'Near Abroad' in Russian Foreign Policy." *RFE/RL Research Report* 2, no. 11 (12 March 1993): 21–29.

Löwenhardt, John, Ronald J. Hill, and Margot Light. "A Wider Europe: The View from Minsk and Chisinau." *International Affairs* 77, no. 3 (July 2001): 605–620.

Lukashuk, Alexander. "Belarus: A Year on the Treadmill." *RFE/RL Research Report* 2, no. 1 (1 January 1993): 64–68.

Lukashuk, Igor. "Military Doctrine of a Law-Governed State." *International Affairs* (Moscow) 40, no. 5 (1994): 113–116.

Lukov, Vadim. "Russia's Security: The Foreign Policy Dimension." *International Affairs* (Moscow) 41, no. 8 (1995): 3–8.

Lynch, Allen C. "The Realism of Russia's Foreign Policy." *Europe-Asia Studies* 53, no. 1 (January 2001): 7–31.

Lynch, Dov. *Russian Peacekeeping Strategies in the CIS: The Cases of Moldova, Georgia and Tajikistan*. Basingstoke, UK: Macmillan, 2000.

————. *Why Georgia Matters*. Chaillot Paper 86. Paris: European Union Institute for Security Studies, February 2006.

Main, Stephen J., James Sherr, and Mark A. Smith. *The Pattern of Russian Policy in the Caucasus and Central Asia*. Conflict Studies Research Centre Occasional Brief 101 Camberley, UK: Conflict Studies Research Centre, December 2003.

Malcolm, Neil, Alex Pravda, Roy Allison, and Margot Light. *Internal Factors in Russian Foreign Policy*. Oxford: Oxford University Press, for Royal Institute of International Affairs, 1996.

Markus, Ustina. "Belarus Debates Security Pacts as a Cure for Military Woes." *RFE/RL Research Report* 2, no. 25 (18 June 1993): 67–73.

———. "Belarus a 'Weak Link' in Eastern Europe?" *RFE/RL Research Report* 2, no. 49 (10 December 1993): 21–27.

———. "Recent Defense Developments in Ukraine." *RFE/RL Research Report* 3, no. 4 (28 January 1994): 26–32.

———. "The Ukrainian Navy and the Black Sea Fleet." *RFE/RL Research Report* 3, no. 18 (6 May 1994): 32–40.

———. "Business as Usual with Lukashenka." *Transition* 1, no. 8 (26 May 1995): 57–61.

———. "Missed Opportunities in Foreign Policy." *Transition* 1, no. 15 (25 August 1995): 62–66.

———. "Financial Woes Lead to Halt in Disarmament." *Transition* 1, no. 20 (3 November 1995): 54–57.

———. "Toothless Treaty with Russia Sparks Controversy." *Transition* 2, no. 9 (3 May 1996): 46–47.

Marples, David. *Belarus: From Soviet Rule to Nuclear Catastrophe.* Basingstoke, UK: Macmillan, 1996.

———. *Belarus: A Denationalized Nation.* Amsterdam: Harwood Academic Publishers, 1999.

———. "Color Revolutions: The Belarus Case." *Communist and Post-Communist Studies* 39, no. 3 (September 2006): 351–364.

Martinsen, Kaare Dahl. "The Russian Takeover of Belarus." *Comparative Strategy* 21, no. 5 (October–December 2002): 401–416.

Mathers, Jennifer G. "*Déjà Vu:* Familiar Trends in Russian Strategic Thought." *Contemporary Security Policy* 16, no. 3 (December 1995): 380–395.

McKay, David. *American Politics and Society.* 6th ed. Oxford: Blackwell, 2005.

McSweeney, Bill. *Security, Identity and Interests: A Sociology of International Relations.* Cambridge: Cambridge University Press, 1999.

Mearsheimer, John J. "The Case for a Ukrainian Nuclear Deterrent." *Foreign Affairs* 72, no. 3 (Summer 1993): 50–66.

Menon, Rajan, Yuri E. Fedorov, and Ghia Nodia, eds. *Russia, the Caucasus, and Central Asia: The 21st Century Security Environment.* Eurasia in the 21st Century: The Total Security Environment 2. Armonk, NY, and London: M. E. Sharpe for EastWest Institute, 1999.

Mihailisko, Kathleen. "Belorussia: Setting Sail Without a Compass." *RFE/RL Research Report* 1, no. 1 (3 January 1992): 39–41.

———. "Belarus Moves to Assert Its Own Military Policy." *RFE/RL Research Report* 1, no. 11 (13 March 1992): 47–50.

———. "Belarus: Neutrality Gives Way to Collective Security." *RFE/RL Research Report* 2, no. 17 (23 April 1993): 24–31.

Mihalka, Michael. "Ukraine: Salvaging Nuclear Arms Control." *Transition* 1, no. 7 (12 May 1995): 30–35.

The Military Tradition in Ukrainian History: Its Role in the Construction of Ukraine's Armed Forces. Cambridge, MA: Ukrainian Research Institute, 1995. Distributed by Harvard University Press.

Miller, J. D. B. "Sovereignty as a Source of Vitality for the State." *Review of International Studies* 12 (1986): 79–89.

Molchanov, Mikhail A. "Ukraine Between Russia and NATO: Politics and Security." *The Ukrainian Review* 45, no. 3 (Autumn 1998): 3–16.

Moroney, Jennifer D. P. "The Lack of Determinacy in Ukraine's Foreign and Security Policy." *The Ukrainian Review* 45, no. 4 (Winter 1998): 3–14.

Morozov, Kostiantyn P. "Current Ukrainian Military Policy and Issues in Its Forma-tion." In *The Military Tradition in Ukrainian History: Its Role in the Construc-tion of Ukraine's Armed Forces.* Cambridge, MA: Ukrainian Research Institute, 1995, 25–38.

——. *Above and Beyond: From Soviet General to Ukrainian State Builder.* Cam-bridge, MA: Harvard University Press for the Ukrainian Research Institute, 2000.

Moshes, Arkady. "Conflict and Cooperation in Russo-Ukrainian Relations." In Bruno Coppeiters, Alexei Zverev, and Dmitri Trenin, eds. *Commonwealth and Independence in Post-Soviet Eurasia.* London: Frank Cass, 1998.

——. *Russia's Belarus Dilemma.* PONARS Policy Memo 182. Washington, DC: Center for Strategic and International Studies, December 2000.

Motyl, Alexander J. *Dilemmas of Independence: Ukraine After Totalitarianism.* New York: Council on Foreign Relations Press, 1993.

Musatov, V. "Russian-Ukrainian Treaty Ratified." *International Affairs* (Moscow) 45, no. 2 (1999): 154–161.

Nahaylo, Bohdan. "The Massandra Summit and Ukraine." *RFE/RL Research Report* 2, no. 17 (17 September 1993): 1–6.

Narochnitskaia, Natalia. "Russia in the New Geopolitical Context." *International Affairs* (Moscow) 50, no. 1 (2004): 60–73.

Naumkin, Vitaly. "Russia and Transcaucasia." *Caucasian Regional Studies* 3, no. 1 (1998). Available from http://poli.vub.ac.be/publi/crs/eng/0301-02.htm.

Nikonov, Vyacheslav. "The Place of Belarus on Russia's Foreign Policy Agenda." In Sherman W. Garnett and Robert Legvold, eds. *Belarus at the Crossroads.* Wash-ington, DC: Carnegie Endowment for International Peace, 1999, 105–129.

Nodia, Ghia. "Georgia: Dimensions of Insecurity." In Bruno Coppieters and Robert Legvold, eds. *Statehood and Security: Georgia After the Rose Revolution.* American Academy Studies in Global Security Series. Cambridge, MA: Amer-ican Academy of Arts & Sciences, 2005, 39–82.

Odom, William E. *The Collapse of the Soviet Military.* New Haven, CT: Yale Uni-versity Press, 1998.

Onuf, Nicholas G. *World of Our Making: Rules and Rule in Social Theory and Inter-national Relations.* Columbia, SC: University of South Carolina Press, 1989.

Österud, Öyvind. "The Narrow Gate: Entry to the Club of Sovereign States." *Review of International Studies* 23, no. 2 (April 1997): 167–184.

Parrott, Bruce, ed. *State Building and Military Power in Russia and the New States of Eurasia.* The International Politics of Eurasia 5. Armonk, NY: M. E. Sharpe, 1995.

——. "State-Building and Post-Soviet Affairs: From the Past to the Future." In Bruce Parrott, ed. *State Building and Military Power in Russia and the New States of Eurasia.* The International Politics of Eurasia 5. Armonk, NY: M. E. Sharpe, 1995, 276–306.

Pastukhova, Nadezhda. "The Union Between Russia and Belarus." *International Affairs* (Moscow) 46, no. 4 (April 2000): 126–131.

Paul, Darel E. "Sovereignty, Survival and the Westphalian Blind Alley in International Relations." *Review of International Studies* 25, no. 2 (April 1999): 217–231.

Payin, E. "Trends and Objectives of Russia's Principal Concepts." *International Affairs* (Moscow) 41, no. 2 (1995): 66–68.

Paznyak, Vyachaslau. "Belarusian Denuclearisation Policy and the Control of Nuclear Weapons." In George Quester, ed. *The Nuclear Challenge in Russia and the New States of Eurasia.* Cambridge, MA: M. E. Sharpe, 1995, 152–179.

———. "Belarus: In Search of a Security Identity." In Roy Allison and Christopher Bluth, eds. *Security Dilemmas in Russia and Eurasia*. London: The Royal Institute of International Affairs, 1998, 152–174.

Pelton Johnson, Teresa, and Steven E. Miller, eds. *Russian Security After the Cold War: Seven Views from Moscow*. Washington, DC: Brassey's, 1994.

Perepelitsa, Hrihory. "Belarusian-Russian Integration and Its Impact on the Security of Ukraine." In Sherman W. Garnett and Robert Legvold, eds. *Belarus at the Crossroads*. Washington, DC: Carnegie Endowment for International Peace, 1999, 81–103.

———. "The Belarus Factor in the European Policy of Ukraine." In Margarita M. Balmaceda, James I. Clem, and Lisbeth Tarlow, eds. *Independent Belarus: Domestic Determinants, Regional Dynamics, and Implications for the West*. Cambridge, MA: Ukrainian Research Institute and David Centre for Russian Studies, 2002, 302–319.

Petersen, Phillip A. "Control of Nuclear Weapons in the CIS." *Jane's Intelligence Review* 5, no. 7 (July 1993): 297–300.

Pikaev, A. A. "Respublikanskaia Bomba: Iadernye Illuziĭi Real'nosti." In A. G. Arbatov, ed. *Iadernye Vooruzheniia i Respublikanski Suverenitet*. Moscow: Mezhdunarodnye Otnosheniia, 1992.

Pikhovshek, Vyacheslav, and Christopher Pett. "Transformation of the Ukrainian Armed Forces." *NATO Review* 42, no. 5 (October 1994): 21–25.

Pleshakov, Konstantin. "Integration and Disintegration in the Modern World." *International Affairs* (Moscow) 38, no. 1 (1992): 41–50.

———. "The St. Andrew's Flag Flying over the Oceans." *International Affairs* (Moscow) 41, no. 12 (1995): 54–58.

Polokhalo, Volodymyr, ed. *The Political Analysis of Postcommunism: Understanding Post-Communist Ukraine*. College Station: Texas A&M University Press, 1997.

Prasad, Bhagirath. *The Post-Communist Dilemma: Sovereignty as Fulcrum of Change in Eastern Europe*. New Delhi: Har-Anand, 1997.

Primakov, Yevgeny. *Russian Crossroads: Towards the New Millennium*. New Haven, CT: Yale University Press, 2004.

Prizel, Ilya. *National Identity and Leadership in Poland, Russia and Ukraine*. Cambridge: Cambridge University Press, 1998.

Pustogarov, Vladimir. "What Erosion of the Union Spells Internationally." *International Affairs* (Moscow) 38, no. 1 (1992): 66–72.

———. "The Commonwealth in the Context of International Law." *International Affairs* (Moscow) 38, no. 10 (1992): 3–10.

———. "Trouble Spots in the CIS and International Law." *International Affairs* (Moscow) 40, no. 8 (1994): 52–60.

Pyskir, Bohdan. "The Silent Coup: The Building of the Ukrainian Military." *European Security* 2, no. 1 (Spring 1993): 140–161.

Quester, George. *The Politics of Nuclear Proliferation*. Baltimore and London: Johns Hopkins University Press, 1973.

Quester, George, ed. *The Nuclear Challenge in Russia and the New States of Eurasia*. Cambridge, MA: M. E. Sharpe, 1995.

Raevsky, Andrei. "Development of Russian National Security Policies: Military Reform." *The Journal of Slavic Military Studies* 6, no. 4 (December 1993): 529–561.

Reppert, John C. "The Security Dimension in the Future of Belarus." In Margarita M. Balmaceda, James I. Clem, and Lisbeth Tarlow, eds. *Independent Belarus: Domestic Determinants, Regional Dynamics, and Implications for the West*.

Cambridge, MA: Ukrainian Research Institute and David Centre for Russian Studies, 2002, 256–269.

Rondeli, Alexander. "Georgia in the Post-Soviet Space." *Caucasian Regional Studies* 1, no. 1 (1996). Available from http://poli.vub.ac.be/publi/crs/eng/0101-07.htm.

Rozanov, Anatolii. "Belarusian Perspectives on National Security and Belarusian Military Policy." In Bruce Parrott, ed. *State Building and Military Power in Russia and the New States of Eurasia.* The International Politics of Eurasia 5. Armonk, NY: M. E. Sharpe, 1995, 193–206.

————. "Belarus: Foreign Policy Priorities." In Sherman W. Garnett and Robert Legvold, eds. *Belarus at the Crossroads.* Washington, DC: Carnegie Endowment for International Peace, 1999, 19–35.

Rubin, Barnett, and Jack Snyder. *Post-Soviet Political Order: Conflict and State Building.* London: Routledge, 1998.

Rylach, Yuriy, and Volodymyr Sviatun. "The 'Zero Option.'" *Politics and the Times: Ukraine in International Relations* 2 (1998): 20–25.

Sagan, Scott D. "Why Do States Build Nuclear Weapons? Three Models in Search of a Bomb." *International Security* 21, no. 3 (Winter 1996–1997): 54–86.

Sakwa, Richard. *Russian Politics and Society.* 3rd ed. London: Routledge, 2002.

Sakwa, Richard, and Mark Webber. "The Commonwealth of Independent States, 1991–1998: Stagnation and Survival." *Europe-Asia Studies* 51, no. 3 (May 1999): 379–415.

Sanders, Deborah. *Security Cooperation Between Russia and Ukraine in the Post-Soviet Era.* Basingstoke, UK: Palgrave, 2001.

Sanford, George. "Nation, State and Independence in Belarus." *Contemporary Politics* 3, no. 3 (September 1997): 225–245.

Sannikov, Andrei. "Russia's Varied Roles in Belarus." In Margarita M. Balmaceda, James I. Clem, and Lisbeth Tarlow, eds. *Independent Belarus: Domestic Determinants, Regional Dynamics, and Implications for the West.* Cambridge, MA: Ukrainian Research Institute and David Centre for Russian Studies, 2002, 197–231.

Schadlow, Nadia. "The Denuclearisation of Ukraine: Consolidating Ukrainian Security." In Lubomyr A. Hajda, ed. *Ukraine in the World: Studies in the International Relations and Security Structure of a Newly Independent State.* Cambridge, MA: Harvard University Press for the Ukrainian Research Institute, Harvard University, 1998, 271–283.

Schwebel, Stephen M. "The Brezhnev Doctrine Repealed and Peaceful Co-Existence Enacted." *The American Journal of International Law* 66, no. 4 (October 1972): 816–819.

Sezer, Duygu Bazoğlu. "Russia and the South: Central Asia and the Southern Caucasus." *European Security* 5, no. 2 (Summer 1996): 303–323.

Shaposhnikov, Evgenii. "The Armed Forces: To a New Quality." In Teresa Pelton Johnson and Steven E. Miller, eds. *Russian Security After the Cold War: Seven Views from Moscow.* Washington, DC: Brassey's, 1994, 185–208.

Shcherbak, Yuri. *The Strategic Role of Ukraine: Diplomatic Addresses and Lectures (1994–1997).* Cambridge, MA: Ukrainian Research Institute, 1998.

Sheehy, Ann. "The CIS: A Progress Report." *RFE/RL Research Report* 1, no. 38 (25 September 1992): 1–6.

————. "The CIS: A Shaky Edifice." *RFE/RL Research Report* 2, no. 1 (1 January 1993): 37–40.

————. "The CIS Charter." *RFE/RL Research Report* 2, no. 12 (19 March 1993): 23–27.

Sherr, James. *A New Storm over the Black Sea Fleet.* Conflict Studies Research Centre Occasional Brief 51. Camberley, UK: Conflict Studies Research Centre, November 1996.

———. "Russia-Ukraine Rapprochement? The Black Sea Fleet Accords." *Survival* 39, no. 3 (Autumn 1997): 33–50.

———. "Challenges After the May, 1997 Accords." *Politics and the Times: Ukraine in International Relations* 1 (1998): 43–47.

———. "Ukraine's New Crisis." Conflict Studies Research Centre Central and Eastern Europe Series 06/32. Camberley, UK: Conflict Studies Research Centre, October 2006.

———. "Ukraine: Prospects and Risks." Conflict Studies Research Centre Central and Eastern Europe Series 06/52. Camberley, UK: Conflict Studies Research Centre, October 2006.

Shevardnadze, Eduard. *Foreign Policy and Perestroika.* Moscow: Novosti Press Agency Publishing House, 1989.

Shevtsov, Anatoliy. "A Relic of the Cold War." *Politics and the Times: Ukraine in International Relations* 2 (1998): 60–64.

Shevtsov, V. S. *National Sovereignty and the Soviet State.* Moscow: Progress Publishers, 1974.

———. *The State and Nations in the USSR.* Moscow: Progress Publishers, 1982.

Shinoda, Hideaki, *Re-examining Sovereignty: From Classical Theory to the Global Age.* Basingstoke, UK: Macmillan; London and New York: St. Martin's, 2000.

Shtromas, A. "The Legal Position of Soviet Nationalities and Their Territorial Units According to the 1977 Constitution of the USSR." *Russian Review* 37, no. 3 (July 1978): 265–272.

Sikorski, Kazimierz. "The Role of Regional Organizations in the International Security Environment." *The Journal of Slavic Military Studies* 7, no. 4 (December 1994): 673–681.

Simpson, John. "Achieving Nuclear Weapon Non-proliferation and Non-possession: Problems and Prospects." In Robert G. Patman, ed. *Security in a Post–Cold War World.* Basingstoke: Macmillan, 1999, 130–156.

Smirnov, P. "When Mars Is Stronger Than Venus—U.S. Revises Its Allied Priorities." *International Affairs* (Moscow) 49, no. 4 (2003): 53–63.

Smith, Graham, Vivien Law, Andrew Wilson, Annette Bohr, and Edward Allworth. *Nation-Building in the Post-Soviet Borderlands: The Politics of National Identities.* Cambridge: Cambridge University Press, 1998.

Smith, Graham, ed. *The Nationalities Question in the Soviet Union.* London: Longman, 1990.

Sokov, Nikolai. "Crises and Breakthroughs: Notes Toward the History of Soviet Decision-Making on START Talks." *The Journal of Slavic Military Studies* 9, no. 2 (June 1996): 261–282.

———. *The Withdrawal of Russian Military Bases from Georgia: Not Solving Anything.* PONARS Policy Memo 363. Washington, DC: Center for Strategic and International Studies, June 2005.

Solchanyk, Roman. "Ukraine and the CIS: A Troubled Relationship." *RFE/RL Research Report* 2, no. 7 (12 February 1993): 23–27.

———. "The Ukrainian-Russian Summit: Problems and Prospects." *RFE/RL Research Report* 2, no. 27 (2 July 1993): 27–30.

———. "Crimea's Presidential Election." *RFE/RL Research Report* 3, no. 11 (18 March 1994): 1–4.

———. "Ukraine, Russia and the CIS." In Lubomyr A. Hajda, ed. *Ukraine in the World: Studies in the International Relations and Security Structure of a Newly*

Independent State. Cambridge, MA: Harvard University Press for Ukrainian Research Institute, Harvard University, 1998, 19–43.

Sørensen, Georg. *Changes in Statehood: The Transformation of International Relations.* Basingstoke, UK: Palgrave, 2001.

The Soviet Constitution: A Dictionary. Moscow: Progress Publishers, 1986.

Suganami, Hidemi. "Wendt, IR, and Philosophy: A Critique." In Stefano Guzzini and Anna Leander, eds. *Constructivism and International Relations: Alexander Wendt and His Critics.* London and New York: Routledge, 2006, 57–72.

Suny, Ronald Grigor. "Provisional Stabilities: The Politics of Identities in Post-Soviet Eurasia." *International Security* 24, no. 3 (Winter 1999/2000): 139–178.

Sushko, Oleksandr. *Ukraine's Search for a Regional Foreign Policy: One Year After the Orange Revolution.* PONARS Policy Memo 377. Washington, DC: Center for Strategic and International Studies, December 2005.

Sussen, Saskia. *Losing Control? Sovereignty in an Age of Globalisation.* New York: Columbia University Press, 1996.

Svetova, Svetlana, and Roman Solchanyk. "Chronology of Events in Crimea." *RFE/RL Research Report* 3, no. 19 (13 May 1994): 27–33.

Tarakanov, Andrei. "The Rise of Russia's 'Military Opposition.'" *Transition* 2, no. 16 (9 August 1996): 6–10.

Tarasyuk, Boris. "Ukraine in the World." In Lubomyr A. Hajda, ed. *Ukraine in the World: Studies in the International Relations and Security Structure of a Newly Independent State.* Cambridge, MA: Harvard University Press for Ukrainian Research Institute, Harvard University, 1998, 9–15.

Taylor, Brian D. *Politics and the Russian Army, Civil-Military Relations, 1689–2000.* Cambridge: Cambridge University Press, 2003.

Teague, Elizabeth. "The CIS: An Unpredictable Future." *RFE/RL Research Report* 3, no. 1 (7 January 1994): 9–12.

Tolz, Vera. "Conflicting 'Homeland Myths' and Nation-State Building in Post-Communist Russia." *Slavic Review* 57, no. 2 (Summer 1998): 267–294.

Tolz, Vera, and Iain Elliot. *The Demise of the USSR.* Basingstoke, UK: Macmillan, 1995.

Towster, Julian. *Political Power in the USSR 1917–1947.* New York: Oxford University Press, 1948.

Trubnikov, V. I. "Tenth Anniversary of the Commonwealth of Independent States." Interview with V. I. Trubnikov. *International Affairs* (Moscow) 48, no. 1 (2002): 17–31.

Tserteli, Irakli. "Seeking Stability Under Shevardnadze." *Transition* 2, no. 15 (26 July 1996): 42–45.

Umbach, Frank. "Who Controls the Nuclear Arsenal of the CIS?" *Jane's Intelligence Review* 4, no. 8 (August 1992): 353–356.

———. "Back to the Future?—The Security Policy of Belarus." *Jane's Intelligence Review* 5, no. 9 (September 1993): 410–414.

———. "The Role and Influence of the Military Establishment in Russia's Foreign and Security Policies in the Yeltsin Era." *The Journal of Slavic Military Studies* 9, no. 3 (September 1996): 467–500.

Urban, Michael, Vyacheslav Igrunov, and Sergei Mitrokhin. *The Rebirth of Politics in Russia.* Cambridge: Cambridge University Press, 1997.

Utkin, Yevgeny. "The CIS in Moscow's Strategic Course." *International Affairs* (Moscow) 41, no. 11–12 (1995).

Vadimov, V. *Mezhdunarodnoe Znachenie Konstitutsii SSSR.* Moscow: Mezhdunarodnye Otnosheniia, 1977.

Varyvoda, Borys. "Ukraine's Dynamic Place in the System of International Security (Political and Economic Dimensions)." *The Ukrainian Quarterly* 57, no. 3–4 (Autumn–Winter 2001): 181–188.

Vasilenko, Vladimir. "START-2: Benefits Outweigh Costs." *International Affairs* (Moscow) 44, no. 4 (1998): 22–28.

Vishniak, Mark. "Sovereignty in Soviet Law." *Russian Review* 8, no. 1 (January 1949): 34–45.

Walker, R. B. J., and Saul H. Mendlovitz, eds. *Contending Sovereignties: Redefining Political Community.* Boulder, CO: Lynne Rienner, 1990.

Wallander, Celeste A. *The Sources of Russian Foreign Policy After the Cold War.* Boulder, CO: Westview, 1996.

Warshaw, Matt. "Reintegration with Russia, Soviet Style." *Transition* 1, no. 20 (3 November 1995): 58–62.

Waters, Trevor. "The New Russian Army One Year On—Hopes and Fears." *Jane's Intelligence Review* 5, no. 7 (July 1993): 305–306.

Webber, Mark. *The International Politics of Russia and the Soviet Successor States.* Manchester, UK: Manchester University Press, 1996.

Weber, Cynthia. *Simulating Sovereignty: Intervention, the State and Symbolic Exchange.* Cambridge: Cambridge University Press, 1995.

Wendt, Alexander. "Anarchy Is What States Make of It: The Social Construction of Power Politics." *International Organization* 46, no. 2 (Spring 1992): 391–425.

———. *Social Theory of International Politics.* Cambridge: Cambridge University Press, 1999.

———. "On the Via Media: A Response to the Critics." *Review of International Studies* 26, no. 1 (January 2000): 165–180.

Wheatley, Jonathan. *Georgia from National Awakening to Rose Revolution: Delayed Transition in the Former Soviet Union.* Aldershot, UK: Ashgate, 2005.

White, Stephen, Ian McAllister, Margot Light, and John Löwenhardt. "A European or a Slavic Choice? Foreign Policy and Public Attitudes in Post-Soviet Europe." *Europe-Asia Studies* 54, no. 2 (March 2002): 181–202.

Whitlock, Erik. "The CIS Economy." *RFE/RL Research Report* 2, no. 1 (1 January 1993): 46–49.

Wilson, Andrew. *Ukraine's Orange Revolution.* New Haven, CT: Yale University Press, 2005.

Wilson, Andrew, and Clelia Rontoyanni. "Security or Prosperity? Belarusian and Ukrainian Choices." In Robert Legvold and Celeste A. Wallander, eds. *Swords and Sustenance: The Economics of Security in Belarus and Ukraine.* American Academy Studies in Global Security Series. Cambridge, MA: American Academy of Arts & Sciences, 2004, 23–62.

Woff, Richard. "The High Command of the CIS—Putting the Pieces Together Again." *Jane's Intelligence Review* 4, no. 4 (April 1992): 174–177.

———. "A Russian Army." *Jane's Intelligence Review* 4, no. 5 (May 1992): 198–200.

———. "The Black Sea Fleet." *Jane's Intelligence Review* 4, no. 11 (November 1992): 492–495.

———. "The Armed Forces of Georgia." *Jane's Intelligence Review* 5, no. 7 (July 1993): 307–310.

———. "The Armed Forces of Belarus." *Jane's Intelligence Review* 7, no. 1 (January 1995): 19–22.

———. "The Border Troops of the Russian Federation." *Jane's Intelligence Review* 7, no. 2 (February 1995): 70–73.

———. "The Armed Forces of Georgia—An Update." *Jane's Intelligence Review* 8, no. 2 (February 1996): 69–70.

———. "Minsk: Making Limited Progress with Reform." *Jane's Intelligence Review* 8, no. 6 (June 1996): 248.

Wolczuk, Roman. "The Evolution of Ukrainian Foreign and Security Policy, 1990–1994." *The Journal of Slavic Military Studies* 12, no. 3 (September 1999): 18–37.

Zagorski, Andrei. "The Commonwealth: One Year On." *International Affairs* (Moscow) 39, no. 2 (1993): 65–72.

———. "Russia, the CIS and the West." *International Affairs* (Moscow) 40, no. 12 (1994): 65–72.

———. "CIS Regional Policy Structures." In Roy Allison and Christopher Bluth, eds. *Security Dilemmas in Russia and Eurasia.* London: Royal Institute of International Affairs, 1998, 281–300.

Zagorski, Andrei, Anatoli Zlobin, Sergei Solodovnik, and Mark Khrustalev. "Russia in a New World." *International Affairs* (Moscow) 38, no. 7 (1992): 3–11.

Zaloga, Steven J. "Armed Forces in Ukraine." *Jane's Intelligence Review* 4, no. 3 (March 1992): 131–136.

Zaprudnik, Jan. *Belarus: At a Crossroads in History.* Boulder, CO: Westview, 1993.

Zehfuss, Maja. *Constructivism in International Relations: The Politics of Reality.* Cambridge: Cambridge University Press, 2002.

———. "Constructivism and Identity: A Dangerous Liaison." In Stefano Guzzini and Anna Leander, eds. *Constructivism and International Relations: Alexander Wendt and His Critics.* London and New York: Routledge, 2006, 93–117.

Zemskii, V. "Collective Security in the CIS." *International Affairs* (Moscow) 45, no. 1 (1999): 97–104.

Zlenko, Anatoly. "The Ukraine, the UN and World Diplomacy." Interview with Anatoly Zlenko. *International Affairs* (Moscow) 39, no. 12 (1992): 3–14.

———. "Ukrainian Security and the Nuclear Dilemma." *NATO Review* 41, no. 4 (August 1993): 11–14.

———. "The Foreign Policy of Ukraine: Principles of Shaping and Problems of Implementing." *International Affairs* (Moscow) 40, no. 1–2 (1994): 12–18.

Index

About the Book

Among the contentious issues that come into play in relations between Russia and the other post-Soviet states, security concerns are arguably at the top of the list. Ruth Deyermond explores the linkage between post-Soviet security politics and the development of state sovereignty in the region, focusing on Russia's interactions with Ukraine, Georgia, and Belarus.

Deyermond's discussion ranges from ownership of nuclear weapons, to the use of military bases, to control of the Black Sea Fleet to show how competing understandings of sovereignty and the willingness of the smaller states to assert their independence from Russia have shaped both the nature and the outcome of disputes about military assets. Her analysis of the complex interconnections involved highlight a critical aspect of the post-Soviet security environment.

Ruth Deyermond is lecturer in the Department of War Studies at King's College London.